ROSA RAISA

ROSA RAISA

*A Biography of a Diva
with Selections
from Her Memoirs*

CHARLES MINTZER

Northeastern University Press
BOSTON

Northeastern University Press

Copyright 2001 by Charles Mintzer

Frontispiece: Aida, 1914 Covent Garden debut. The photo is dedicated to Barbara Marchisio: "Alla mia Grande Maestra con affeto e devozione dalla Sua Raisa, 22.7.914." Dover Street Studio, London.

Library of Congress Cataloging-in-Publication Data
Mintzer, Charles.
Rosa Raisa : a biography of a diva with selections from her memoirs / Charles Mintzer.
p. cm.
Includes discography, bibliographical references, and index.
ISBN 1-55553-504-6 (cloth : alk. paper)
1. Raisa, Rosa, 1893–1963.   2. Singers—United States—Biography.   I. Raisa, Rosa, 1893–1963.   II. Title.

ML420.R275 M56   2001
782.1'092—dc21
[B]   2001040198

Designed by Dean Bornstein

Composed in Aldus by G&S Typesetters, Austin, Texas. Printed and bound by Thomson-Shore, Inc., Dexter, Michigan. The paper is Supple Opaque Recycled, an acid-free stock.

MANUFACTURED IN THE UNITED STATES OF AMERICA
05   04   03   02   01   5   4   3   2   1

*For my brother William Mintzer, and my
friends Arthur Naftal, Ronald Klein,
and Anthony Arturi, all of whom exited
this world much too soon.*

Contents

Illustrations

Preface

WITH the release in 1998 of the Marston "Rosa Raisa, The Complete Recordings" on CD and the worldwide interest it created, I was asked by Larry Lustig, editor of *Record Collector*, to write a feature article about her. I gladly accepted this assignment, but once I started writing, it became clear to me that I was in reality producing the Raisa book I had been talking about for almost a third of a century. I had done most of the research and I had so much information I wanted to share that even a feature article was not going to do justice to what I thought I had to offer the opera-loving and record-collecting communities. A few years ago I was so keen about the new Internet technology that I planned to create a Raisa Web site where I could publish my essay, evaluation, and career chronology. Luckily I found in Larry Lustig an enthusiast, and a supporter in Murray Goldenberg, Raisa's nephew, who promised to underwrite this effort. Even with all the wonders of the Internet it is still every writer's fondest dream to see his book in hard cover. I was fortunate that Northeastern University Press found the manuscript of merit and set in motion the process that has produced this book on a significant but somewhat forgotten artist.

Acknowledgments

NO work this ambitious could have been written without the help and encouragement of many good people over the years. My interest in Rosa Raisa was stimulated almost fifty years ago when as a young opera lover and standee at the old Metropolitan Opera House I met older operagoers who waxed ecstatic about the great singers they had heard in their youths. In 1952, when our operatic gods were Zinka Milanov, Mario Del Monaco, Leonard Warren, and Cesare Siepi, I was being regaled by comparisons, usually unfavorable, with Rosa Ponselle, Elisabeth Rethberg, Giovanni Martinelli, Giuseppe De Luca, and Ezio Pinza from still relatively young people. And men in their fifties were still enthusiastic about Enrico Caruso, Titta Ruffo, and Rosa Raisa. I knew most of these names even then, but who was Rosa Raisa? I started spending long hours in the nearby New York Public Library Music Division at Fifth Avenue and West 42nd Street. I pored over the music magazines and clipping files while copying by hand in those pre-photocopy days the articles I read about this soprano who had been so praised in her time. Even then her story resonated with me; this Jewish woman who came from the same part of eastern Europe from which my ancestors had come had fled persecution and had a glorious and important but now largely forgotten career. I thought her story fascinating, and started asking questions about her of opera lovers who remembered her. Another standee, the late Ronald Klein, played for me many of her records, and although I didn't "get" them at first, I was intrigued. My journey was starting.

I wrote to people who valued Raisa for additional impressions to supplement their published tributes: people such as Claudia Cassidy, Paul Hume, and Vincent Sheean. Their appraisals were so generous and glowing that I continued searching the written record for more and more information to complete the portrait. In February 1962, after hearing her on a Met *Turandot* intermission feature, I wrote to Raisa and received a beautiful written response, and one of my first autographed photos. I was on my way!

If one focuses on a particular artist, one has to read the period literature for context and historical "flavor." In the process I learned a great deal about the Chicago Opera, its internal politics, and its fabulous national tours. I also educated myself about the history of the Metropolitan Opera and its worldwide impact, and about the rich concert life in America in Raisa's time. Not only was I becoming acquainted with the written record of her career, I was acquiring the additional information about the late teens, twenties, and thirties of the twentieth century that gave my research the proper background.

An important contact was the late Charles Jahant. I had seen his name in the acknowledgments of many opera biographies and wanted to know if he had any Raisa information to supplement that which I had already amassed. People from the record-collecting community who knew him told me he probably would not even answer. However, I did write to him in 1978 and that contact proved most fortunate. He adored Raisa; he had heard her often in the twenties and thirties in opera and concert in his native Akron, Ohio, and in Chicago, and information just poured out of his incredible memory and research notes. It was he who suggested I contact Carol Longone, Raisa's accompanist, who he thought might be interested in talking to me. Mme. Longone and I spent many hours in her Central Park South apartment talking about that rich period in American musical life. Although almost ninety years old, she had very clear and definite memories and opinions she wanted to share. Pat Palmer, the executor of Carol Longone's estate, has been a good friend and has encouraged me in my work. It was Carol who suggested, and then helped me establish, contact with Raisa's sister Frieda Goldenberg, who lived in the Washington Heights area of Manhattan. That proved to be a very deep well of interest and support, indeed. Frieda and her husband, Irving, had very specific and delightful family memories of Raisa, as well as rare photographs and unique memorabilia.

Perhaps just as important was Jahant's suggestion that I contact Robert Tuggle for help with photo research. Not only was this a good suggestion in terms of photos; it was also the genesis of a very close friendship that has continued without interruption for more than twenty years. When I first met Bob he was at work on his *Golden Age of Opera* book with the great Mishkin photos as its theme, and my interests seemed to mesh with many of his. Bob has not only helped me with my project; he has initiated me into the world of the Metropolitan Opera Archives, the richness of whose collection cannot but fascinate a person such as myself, whose interest in operatic performing history is now almost limitless.

In 1977 I began corresponding with Raisa's daughter, the late Giulietta Segala of Santa Monica, California. Jolly, as she was known, was at first reserved, but when she warmed to me she helped me as much as she could. Our mail and telephone relationship was capped in October 1983, when for two days she graciously allowed me into her beautiful home so that I might go through what remained of Raisa's clippings, scrapbooks, photos, and memorabilia. We talked practically nonstop during these two days. As Jolly spent much of her time in Italy, it was not possible to sustain the relationship at this intense level. Beset with health problems, she passed away in 1990 — much too soon. Her daughter, Suzanne Homme of Rancho Mirage, has been a wonderful source of support and help over the past twenty years. Both Jolly and Suzy gave me copies of the different drafts of the autobiography Raisa was still working on at the time of her death. Suzy has given me permission to quote liberally from the drafts and to use Raisa's correspondence in this work. She has told me several times how important the autobiography was to her grandmother, and assures me that my book, which incorporates some of the best parts of her story, would have made her very happy. She views Raisa's story as her family's history and is pleased that this book will offer her children a greater opportunity to know that history. If I seem to emphasize Raisa's strong Jewish attachment, it is partly to complete this aspect of her story for the family. Giorgio Segala, Raisa's grandson, and his dynamic wife, Karen, were most generous in allowing me access to his mother's remaining papers, which included many items pertaining to Raisa that helped clarify some points.

Over the years I have met and talked with many people who knew Raisa and who willingly shared their knowledge and interest. The late Beatrice Balter of Pittsburgh, the daughter of Mrs. Julius Stone, Raisa's surrogate mother, shared her memories and photos with me; she also referred me to Mrs. Theodore Cornbleet of Chicago, with whom I carried on a fifteen-year correspondence. Mrs. Cornbleet, better known as Dea, first met Raisa in the early twenties in Milwaukee after a Chicago Opera performance. She was an aspiring young singer whom Raisa befriended; Dea relocated to Chicago to serve as her secretary. She handled correspondence and the many chores that attend a prima donna. In the late twenties Dea went to Italy to study for the operatic stage, but her own career never materialized. In 1987 I was her guest for a week. Dea filled in some of the more personal and domestic aspects of Raisa's character. Dea asked her niece Jeannie Grossman to contact me. Jeannie, on Dea's behalf, had befriended Raisa during her last years in Los Angeles. She particularly remembered taking Rosa for long drives, after which they dined on corned-beef sandwiches and "undone" pickles. One of Jeannie's most delightful stories was of the time her husband, Arthur, notified the press in Los Angeles that Rosa Raisa was to be in the audience for a 1957 *Turandot* performance with Leonie Rysanek and Licia Albanese. The press made a big thing of this and had cameras set up for photos and interviews. And when members of the audience realized that Raisa was among them, many approached her to get autographs and to tell her how much she had meant to them many years earlier. She loved the limelight, even though she protested that she didn't.

Dea also introduced me to the late Sonia Sharnova, a Chicago Opera contralto who was a family friend. It was fascinating to enter Sharnova's living room and to see a poster on the wall from her 1925 debut in Livorno in *La Favorita*. This American pupil of Jean de Reszke was at least ninety years old and could still boom out her "reverenzas" from *Falstaff*, to my delight. The wall leading to her living room held only four autographed portraits, those of Johanna Gadski, Claudia Muzio, Kirsten Flagstad, and Raisa. She was a leading singer with Gadski's German Grand Opera Company in the late twenties; she sang Brangäne to Flagstad's Isolde in Chicago; and she appeared with Muzio and Raisa in many Chicago Opera performances.

I also had the privilege of knowing and befriending the late Coe Glade, the popular American mezzo-soprano who sang with Raisa in the famous New Year's Eve revival of *Norma* that celebrated Raisa's return to the stage after a life-threatening illness. Coe had very warm memories of the many *Normas* they performed together. She especially recalled a *Norma* on the 1929 tour in Detroit where the audience clearly wanted to give Coe a singular ovation, and Raisa gently pushed her to the forefront and stepped back so Coe could have her moment of glory. Coe first heard Raisa at Ravinia in 1925 and was so inspired by her highly emotional performances that she decided then and there to rededicate herself to serious study for the operatic stage. Coe also shared her still vivid and loving memories of Muzio, Frida Leider, Eva Turner, and—most memorable for me—José Mojica, with whom she had a very special relationship. In 1983 I had the honor of interviewing Glade at the New York Vocal Record Collector's Society, for a well-received program produced by Eli Solis and the late Arthur Naftal. I had known Arthur since 1958; he had a fine collection of 78-rpm recordings, including most of Raisa's, and what was, for that time, the proper equipment on which to play them. Dan Hladik, the well-known recording conservationist, and Larry Holdridge, the premier dealer in the world of 78-rpm recordings, have at various times been extremely helpful to me in my work. Larry has a special interest in Charles Hackett, and he kindly allowed me to see some of Hackett's home movies from the late 1920s, some made during the Chicago Opera tours and others made in Europe. Several of these filmed snippets include Raisa and Giacomo Rimini.

I also interviewed Dame Eva Turner in 1985; she was still able (at the age of ninety-three) to recall with great specificity her three seasons at the Chicago Opera. Although she heard Raisa only a few times, she was particularly enthusiastic about her Rachel in *La Juive*.

The late Elsa Alsen, a consequential though somewhat forgotten Wagnerian soprano, shared with me her memories of Raisa at the Chicago Opera in the mid-twenties. Vivian Della Chiesa was most charming when I interviewed her for a whole afternoon in 1990; she had vivid recollections of her early career at the Chicago Opera and her own distinguished career as a television and radio talk-show hostess, pioneering a format that has since become very popular, perhaps too much so. James Drake and Mary Jane Phillips-Matz, who were working on their biographies of Rosa Ponselle, consulted me to check out their Ponselle-Raisa information. Ponselle has deservedly enjoyed three major books, and it was my honor to contribute in a small way to our knowledge of a very important professional friendship between these two remarkable stars.

My friend of more than forty years, Richard Miller of New York City, has served as a sounding board and helper on my project. Richard has acquired a vast knowledge of operatic and concert performing history and it is my hope that one day he will publish some of this important work. Over the years I have shared with him my research and discoveries. He has been both a friend and a staunch supporter through all my efforts. Last summer, Richard and I spent a delightful afternoon with Professor Louis Stein and his wife, Edith. Lou is Raisa's nephew, the son of her older sister, Sonya. Lou recounted his vivid memories of growing up in New York and attending Passover Seders with his Aunt Raisa, Rimini, and assorted celebrities from the Metropolitan Opera. He remembered Cantor Rosenblatt participating in the funeral service of his grandfather Herschel. He so appreciated that Raisa helped support his family during the Depression, even though she herself was financially strapped. He also let me copy rare family photographs. Years earlier, Lou's sister, the late Roslyn Meyerson, shared some family memorabilia and acquainted me with Mrs. Stone's biography, *My Caravan of Years*, with its extensive chapter on Rosa Raisa about which I otherwise would never have known. Jules Burton (né Burchstein), Raisa's nephew from her brother Aron, sent me rare family photographs.

Murray Goldenberg, Raisa's nephew from her younger sister,

Frieda, has been incredibly supportive. He helped with the 1986 limited edition Rosa Raisa boxed LP set (RS312), published by Rubini Records. He put up the financial resources to make that project a worthy tribute to both his aunt and mother. He has enthusiastically supported this effort to publish my work both in book form and as a future Web site. He has done this without demanding any editorial control. I know he thinks his aunt must have been the greatest, but he has not asked me to filter out any of the less than glowing quotes I have used to round out the picture. It is interesting that Murray and Jolly barely knew each other, as they each represented different and conflicting aspects of Raisa's family, with contrasting religious and cultural traditions. Raisa rarely, if ever, brought her two families together. In a way, my work has reestablished some family contact, as I was on honest terms with both her Jewish and her Italian families.

In 1997, Ward Marston asked me to write liner notes for the new recording label that would bear his name, then in the planning stages. He was thinking of singers who had not yet had quality CD issues. I felt honored to be sought out by someone so highly regarded and universally praised as one of the best restoration artists of singers of the past. He told me that both my friend Andrew Karzas of Chicago and Gregor Benko of New York had mentioned my name as a possible resource if he decided to issue CDs of Rosa Raisa's recordings. I accepted the offer, and this has, in its own way, led to my book. Marston's "Rosa Raisa—The Complete Recordings," a three-CD set, received a very positive response from the collecting community and critics. This led me to review my research and to rethink my decision not to pursue my dream of producing this book. I had begun to think there was little or no interest (or market) in yet another opera star's biography, that the genre had begun to play itself out, at least for a successful artist whose career was relatively free of controversy. Would a Raisa biography be just another recitation of dates and casts coupled with a plea for her place in history? I determined that Raisa's is both the story of a very successful singer and an interesting bit of social history with a slightly different angle. Here was a woman who came out of a Polish ghetto, who endured the horrors of the 1906 pogroms, who used Italy rather than America as her escape route, and who embraced Italian opera and culture yet eventually became an American. And do not forget that she was the first to sing the role of Turandot, in an opera that is more popular today than ever before. It seemed to me that her story of bestriding three cultures, her solution to unique identity problems, and her newfound celebrity justified the publication of her fascinating story. I hope the public will agree.

Since from the start I had grave doubts that this work would see the light of day, I did not keep a formal list of persons who should be noted in the acknowledgments. I will do my best to name and describe these contributions, with the caveat that inevitably some that should be mentioned will not be; this is accidental, not deliberate. I have tried at every step, in the book proper, the recordings section, and the chronology, to be extremely careful and as accurate as possible in setting forth Raisa's story and to let the reader decide what is the truth about her life and career. I have tried to balance the often purple praise with other valid opinions; I have put out the facts of her life with my own interpretation of the more controversial parts, with room left for others to evaluate these facts in their own way and possibly arrive at different conclusions. The four situations that may be open to interpretation are the unusual announcement of her marriage to Rimini, the rupture with Lazar Samoiloff over whether he could legitimately advertise himself as one of her "teachers," the Berlin *Tosca* in 1933, and Raisa's puzzling burial arrangements (and their possible implications).

Giorgio Tozzi spoke with me in 1991 and 2000 and painted a warm portrait of his teachers. Norman Ross of Chicago sketched for me a loving memory; he had interviewed Raisa on a Chicago television show. Byron Belt shared his memories of Raisa, whom he escorted to some of the very earliest performances at the Lyric Theater of Chicago in the 1950s. Anna Hamlin shared with me memories of her days with the Chicago Opera. Max de Schauensee promised to help but died before he could give me anything substantial. Lanfranco Rasponi was going to help, but he too died before he could retrieve Raisa information from his files. Giulio Crimi's daughter, Francesca, was enthusias-

tic about this project and sent interesting clippings. Edith Pri-
lik Sania, Rosa Ponselle's friend and secretary, was eager to help. My
questions addressed to Orson Welles, one of Raisa's great admirers
who was raised in the milieu of the Chicago Opera, went unanswered
shortly before his death. The staff of the Chicago Historical Society
copied all pertinent materials they had in their files, including photos.
Lia Pierotti, the daughter of the conductor Gino Marinuzzi, shared
some of her special memories of her father's connection to Raisa,
whom he esteemed highly. She even remembered giving Raisa a bou-
quet of blue roses in Buenos Aires, possibly as early as 1915. Mildred
Kipnis related some of her husband Alexander's special memories of
Raisa's "ringing voice." The cultural attachés of the embassies of Brazil, Mexico, France, and Italy provided leads for me to follow and some
specific dates, later confirmed in books about the opera houses in their
respective countries. The curatorial staff of Chicago's Newberry Library was especially helpful in granting me access to relevant nonca-
talogued items in their collections. Rosemary Runciman of the Covent Garden archives, Carlos Saravia of the Teatro Colón Buenos Aires
archives, and the late Harold Rosenthal of Opera magazine all supplied relevant information. Eduardo Arnosi of Buenos Aires was helpful in the early stages of this project and located the rare Panizza
biography. Lim Lai of San Francisco showed some of his fabulous collection of photos and memorabilia, some of it relating to my work.
Vivian Liff was generous with photos and shared in several long letters the information he had acquired, especially Geraldine Farrar's
keen memories of Raisa and the story of how the historically important recordings of the Turandot premiere were inadvertently lost.
Bart Swindle, the curator of the Auditorium Theater in Chicago, gave
a special guided tour of the historic building and allowed me to copy
some rare photos in their collection. John Pennino and John Yoha-
lem of the Metropolitan Opera Archives have helped in many ways.
Scholars in Poland and Israel shared Raisa information with me—the
Polish because of her having been born in Poland, and the Israeli for
the Jewish connection. Rudi van den Bulck of Antwerp, who is com-
piling a comprehensive book on singers of Jewish heritage, has been

extremely generous with his vast knowledge of opera history and the European phases of Raisa's career. Rudi also reviewed the manuscript in an early stage, made many valuable suggestions, and even translated some of the Hebrew and Yiddish documents. Bernard and Ellen Lebow, of the original Club 99 record label, were early supporters of my work, as was the late and lamented William Violi of Brooklyn, the record collector and dealer who helped so many of us over the years. The late Eddie J. Smith related some Raisa stories, most of them unlikely and unverifiable. By his own account he seemed to have been at the center of all the important operatic activities and to have known everyone of importance at a very young and tender age! James Camner of La Scala Autographs has supplied me over the years with numerous Raisa and Rimini photos and autographs as well as those of other celebrities of the Chicago Opera. Bill Ecker, an up-and-coming collector of all things operatic and historic, has been extremely resourceful. He located and photographed Raisa's grave in Los Angeles. He has shown great interest in Raisa's story. Andrew Farkas of Amadeus Press looked at the manuscript and made many valuable suggestions. George Parous of Pittsburgh has been a staunch supporter and brought a second set of eyes to the manuscript, helping me express my ideas more clearly. George is working on an ambitious work about the great German soprano Johanna Gadski, and it is my hope that I can help him as much with Gadski as he has helped me with Raisa.

Tom Kaufman, first of Boonton, New Jersey, and more recently of Baltimore, Maryland, has been a major source of information about Raisa and Rimini in South America and Mexico. While working on my project I helped Tom with some of his chronologies of major singers, sharing what relevant information I had. Tom has been absolutely selfless in sharing his vast archive of historic data, and in the process Tom and his wife, Marion, became treasured personal friends. Through Tom I was put in contact with Carlo Marinelli-Roscioni, that scholar and archivist of the leading Italian theaters and opera houses throughout the world that staged Italian opera seasons. His unimpeachable day-by-day information was used in the Raisa chronology wherever there were discrepancies with existing official chronologies, as Marinelli-Roscioni's information always seemed more reliable. Tom also helped put me in contact with Gaspare Nello Vetro of Parma, who has authored a three-volume study of the brothers Campanini, Italo and Cleofonte, and Arturo Toscanini, all from Parma; and he referred me to Suzanna Salgado, who is producing an authoritative book on opera at the Teatro Solis in Montevideo, the venue of many of Raisa's performances. Bob Rideout, relatively new to the field of chronologies, has been extremely helpful in bringing a fresh set of eyes to my work and has shown great interest and made many valuable suggestions. David Stein of Boonton, New Jersey, helped in translating Spanish and Italian documents. David's linguistic abilities and his vast knowledge of opera made his translations nuanced and accurate. The late Anthony Arturi, an extremely wise and erudite opera lover, always showed interest and support in this project; he will be very much missed. César Dillon of Buenos Aires, who has authored important books of chronologies of opera theaters in Buenos Aires, was very helpful in reconciling discrepancies among some sources I used. His information appears both well-researched and unimpeachable. Jim McPherson of Rexdale, Ontario, reviewed the chronology and made many valuable suggestions, as well as additions and deletions, that were incorporated into the final draft. Jim's knowledge of opera history is truly formidable. Edwin McArthur, so well known for his connection with Flagstad, was eager to reminisce with me about his love of Raisa, which dated back to his youth in Denver when he first heard her in opera and concert. Graziella Polacco, daughter of Maestro Giorgio and Edith Mason, shared memories of growing up in Chicago surrounded by the opera community. The brilliant Michael Scott recommended that I contact Professor L. J. Wathen of Houston, Texas. The good professor cherished Raisa and shared very specific memories of her powerful performances on tour in the 1920s. José (Pepé) Domenesch of Valencia, Spain, was helpful in locating information regarding Raisa's 1935 performance in Madrid. Steven Smolian, the recording engineer, explained to me some of the reasons why her voice was so difficult to record; his explanations of the particular problems of Vocalion and Brunswick methods seemed to make sense to this technical novice. Brother Matthew Shanley was a particularly devoted fan and we spent several hours together going over information and speculating about Raisa's life and career. An especially informative contact was the late Olga Trevisan, the daughter of the Chicago Opera basso buffo Vittorio. Olga knew Raisa and Rimini as personal friends and had spent hours chatting with them about the often taboo subjects of politics, finances, and religion. Julian Morton Moses spoke to me at length about the world of acoustic recordings. Ross Laird of Australia helped with dating the Brunswick recordings.

Silvia Ascarelli, Richard Bebb, Michael Bott, Robert Baxter, David Benesty, Harold Bruder, George Burr, Harold Byrnes, Patrick Casali, Luciano di Cave, Stephen Herx, the late Vincent Alfano, Rhoda Jongsma, Charlotte Bernhardt, Alfred Moritz, Claudia Boynton, Oscar Bramson, Harold Barnes, Arbe Bareis, Aida Favia-Artsay, Syd Gray, Bill Park, Roger Gross, Don Jackson, Albert Arrujo, George Bergman, Don Levine, Michael Bavar, Bill Seward, André Tubeuf, and Richard Tomback all helped me in some way with information, recordings, or just plain encouragement at different stages of my work.

This first-time writer has had the incredible good fortune to have the close support of the staff of Northeastern University Press, who walked me through the process of a professionally produced book. Not only were they very helpful, but they at all times seemed to be on top of the various steps that go into the process and kept me informed in a timely manner of all developments. Bill Frohlich, my editor, and his assistant, Sara Rowley, at the early stages were very considerate. Ann Twombly, my production editor, and Evan Young, the copyeditor, made valuable suggestions. Dean Bornstein is responsible for the attractive design. Jill Bahcall has been extremely resourceful in the promotion of the book. My thanks to all.

Even when they didn't understand what I was doing, my family and friends were always supportive. They seemed to know instinctively that I was involved in a labor of love and that eventually my work would be published. I thank them all, and all those whose names I fear I have left out, more than they can ever know. If in the future I create a Raisa Web site it will be possible to add information, make called-for corrections, and display the photos in an attractive "state-of-the-art" presentation. If when all this is accomplished I have added in some small way to opera history, I will feel that this was all worth the effort.

ROSA RAISA

· *Chapter One* ·

BEGINNINGS

THE scene: Milan's La Scala, April 25, 1926. An opera house packed to capacity to witness the first performance of Puccini's new and last opera, *Turandot*. Luminaries from all over the music world, celebrities from many walks of life, and just ordinary opera lovers crowd the famous theater, the scene of so many historic premieres. Would Puccini, with this opera, posthumously take the world by storm? Rome had already planned its premiere for the following week; Vienna, Berlin, Dresden, Buenos Aires, Rio de Janeiro, Brussels, and New York had planned theirs for the coming months. The casts of sopranos and tenors scheduled to perform the various local premieres read like a "who's who" of the international opera world. And who were the soprano and tenor awarded these most coveted assignments at this momentous world premiere? Rosa Raisa and Miguel Fleta.

Just who was this soprano whom composers and conductors—in this case, Puccini and Toscanini—thought a rare phenomenon? Why did journalists and critics grope for new superlatives to describe the thrill of hearing her voice? Why can't we hear this "force of nature" voice on her all too few recordings? Who was Rosa Raisa? Why is her story capturing our attention now, after all these years? Why has this soprano who came from an East European ghetto to make her mark on the international opera world as a "name among names" finally caught the imagination of opera historians?[1] Could the new-found popularity of Puccini's *Turandot* and, by extension, curiosity about its creators be the answer? Possibly, but the very popular tenor aria "Nessun Dorma" was first sung by Miguel Fleta, and his legend has not enjoyed a similar rediscovery—at least outside the Spanish-

[3]

speaking world, where he was always an icon. Raisa has never been completely forgotten, but as so little has been written about her in recent years, and as her recordings are so few, her reputation had descended from the very top echelon of historic dramatic sopranos to a notch just below her true worth. In most books and articles about operatic history she had been relegated to an interesting footnote, not a major entry. Yet she enjoyed one of the most stellar careers in all of opera, and in her day and in the venues in which she sang she was a star of the first magnitude.

Raisa was born May 30, 1893, in Bialystok, near the Russian border in what is now Poland.[2] Bialystok, under Russian Imperial rule at the time, was a major city in the "Pale of Settlement," that designated part of Eastern Europe in which, since the reign of Catherine the Great, Jews were "allowed" to live. In 1893 two-thirds of the residents of Bialystok embraced the Jewish faith.[3] Her actual first name was Raitza (the Yiddish equivalent of the Russian "Raisa"). Her parents were Herschel Burchstein and Frieda Leah Krasnatawsky.[4] Frieda was the daughter of Rabbi Israel Halevei Krasnatawsky. It is not clear whether he was an ordained rabbi, or whether he carried the title "rabbi" on his tombstone as a mark of respect and a recognition of his piety, as was often the case in this society. Raisa had an older sister named Sonya, and a younger brother named Morris (Moishe). Her mother died from pneumonia at twenty-six, before Raisa was six years old; her father remarried, and he and her stepmother, Chaya, had two more children, Frieda and Aron.

The Burchsteins were solid, middle-class citizens. Yiddish was the language spoken at home; the children attended Russian-language schools. The family was traditional in its values, dress, politics, and religion. Raisa's mother Frieda wore the traditional *sheitel* (wig) of orthodox Jewish women and her father often wore a black caftan. There is no evidence that Raisa knew much, if any, Polish. Most Jews of Bialystok gravitated toward the Russian culture. One never finds Polish-language material on her concert programs; yet they almost always included Russian folk and art songs, and Yiddish songs were frequent encores. Raisa's languages included Yiddish, Hebrew (for

[4]

Raisa's parents, Frieda and Herschel Burchstein. Raisa carried these photos with her everywhere. (Collection of Suzanne Homme.)

prayer), Russian, Italian, French, English, and probably Spanish and some Portuguese from her extensive stays in South America. One suspects her German skill was rudimentary and probably derived from words common to German and Yiddish. These points are made because many reference works identify Raisa as Polish, while others refer to her as Russian. Hers is a case where nationality and ethnicity, as well as cultural factors, converge to create definitional problems. Considering that she eventually became a naturalized U.S. citizen, probably the best definition of her ethnicity and unique persona is as an Italian-trained Russian Jew who ultimately lived the American dream of success as an internationally acclaimed opera singer.

From her unpublished autobiography and other interviews over the years there are descriptions and accounts of everyday life in Bialystok. Raisa tutored students in Russian and Yiddish to earn extra money. A cantor Berman who supervised the choir of the great synagogue in Bialystok was very impressed with her natural voice, but he was unable to interest any of the wealthy Jews of Bialystok in underwriting her musical studies. It is likely that in this very conservative and traditional orthodox Jewish milieu a talented young girl was not considered as good a career prospect as would be a similarly talented young boy. Singing at school and at weddings, singing in the forests outside Bialystok in order for friends to hear her already powerful voice echoing, imitating the music heard while following organ-grinders, and attending opera performances given by itinerant companies—these activities were her introduction to the world of singing and performing. Her best friend, Bertha Levin, who immigrated to America in 1905, gave Raisa an anthology of classical European songs, and this introduction excited her imagination and fanned her desire to become a singer. The very first song she tried from the Western musical literature was Massenet's "Elégie."

(I should interject here a word about Raisa's unpublished autobiography, which will be quoted extensively so as to cast important events in her life in the first person. At the urging of many friends, including ninety-year-old Margherita Clausetti, her "guardian angel," Raisa started writing her life story in 1962. The work has a great deal of interesting information, most of it consistent with the public record, as her memory was remarkably good. Her writing style picked up some of her well-known speech patterns and therefore has an authentic ring. Professional assistance was needed to help integrate what is essentially a collection of anecdotes about her life and career, many of which she told over and over through the years, into a coherent narrative. Raisa was still working on her book at the time of her death in late September 1963. Months earlier, Francis Robinson of the Metropolitan Opera had promised to help her organize her book, but he later begged off, citing the pressure of his professional responsibilities.)[5]

In early June 1906 there were major upheavals and pogroms in Bialystok, and Raisa's experiences scarred her for life. Fifty-seven years later, in her memoir, Raisa specifically remembered those frightening days.

🙞 As I carried Frieda [cousin Pavel's daughter] in my arms, running as fast as I could, I heard people shouting at me to go home, that there was a big pogrom in town, that stores were being ransacked and people killed. I arrived at my destination and for three days and nights we all remained hidden in the cellar. The child cried constantly from hunger, and I often had to hold my hand over her mouth to keep her sobs from being heard. During the night I would crawl up the stairs to the apartment to find some food. On the third day, when the pogrom halted, I left Frieda in the care of the doctor's parents [Raisa's aunt and uncle] for a few hours and returned to the home of my family. On my way I passed a hospital where hundreds of dead people lay scattered on the ground of the courtyard, victims of the enraged, savage mobs. I joined the crowds there who were searching for their dead, fearfully looking for mine. I cannot describe the horror I experienced at the sight of women with their breasts cut off and abdomens slit from which their unborn babies had been removed; people whose feet had been amputated from the ankles, people nailed against the walls through their eye sockets; hundreds of burned bodies—adults and children; a brother and sister who had been shot in front of their window while the mother was forced to witness it. I saw all these horrors with my own eyes while uncovering the bodies in my frantic search for my father. Not finding him among the dead I rushed home where, to my great joy, he too had been hiding for three days. We were all reunited, but grieved for the unfortunates who had lost their lives so uselessly. I shudder at the cruelty and injustice of man to fellow man. 🙟

The 1906 Bialystok pogrom was considered "the most violent of the mob outbreaks against Russian Jewry that year."[6] What seemed to the thirteen-year-old Raisa like hundreds of corpses were actually seventy-five dead and hundreds severely injured. In response to international public outcry and in an attempt to allay concerns about how

[7]

Early 1907 family group. From left: younger sister Frieda, Raisa, brother Aron, and older sister Sonya. (Collection of Jules Burton.)

they treated their Jews, the Russian government ordered a commission to report to the Duma on the Bialystok pogrom. The commission found that the violence was actually instigated by the authorities.[7] Years later Raisa again vividly described these events to a friend: "Do you know what it is to see a drunken peasant take a Jewish baby by its legs and crush its skull against the wall of a house, by swinging it as though it were a club? I wondered if a song could live after that, but human beings must be made of iron."[8] In mature reflection she felt that the horrors she had witnessed gave her a profound understanding of the injustices of life. She was convinced that these events had an effect on her ability to express the deepest human emotions. She remembered feeling as a thirteen-year-old that it was her destiny to go on the stage, that she was pushed by a desire to express these emotions growing within her.

Jews were emigrating from Poland in great numbers and Rosa's sister Sonya and brother Morris were poised to leave for America. A cousin on her father's side, Pavel Vigdorchick, a dentist, sent to Siberia and subsequently exiled for his activities in socialist politics, was at this time living on Capri with hundreds of other political refugees from the Russias, including the novelist Maxim Gorky.[9] Raisa recounted years later:

⚘ After the doctor had become established in Italy, he sent for his wife and two children, Sasha and Frieda. Once more I saw the bottom dropping out of my world. Desperate, I approached my dear cousin Fanny, with bitter tears, begging her to take me with her, pleading that I would help her with the children and the housework. I don't know what saint interceded for me, but a miracle took place.[10] I persuaded her to take me with her. All I needed to do was to convince my father. When he heard my intentions he was speechless for a few moments. But he finally agreed to give me fifty rubles, all he had. Jubilant, I immediately rushed to Fanny's and asked her to go with me to a cheap section of town to buy the necessary "wardrobe" for my trip: a pleated skirt, a jacket, a straw hat, and the first pair of shoes that I tried on. With what was left we bought a fourth-class railroad ticket.

My good stepmother prepared dinner for us that night, dazed at the suddenness of my decision to leave for Italy. She wrapped my few belongings in a small bundle, together with another bundle containing pumpernickel bread and a herring, without which she felt I dared not to leave. I can still see my father leaning against the pole at the station sobbing and heartbroken. But as much as I adored him I left without a tear in my eye, so sure I was that I was doing the right thing, and that this was my destiny. I carried Frieda in my arms, who was a year and a half, and Fanny carried the little boy. The pumpernickel and herring served us in good stead on the trip. My shoes, which I had bought so hurriedly proved less useful; they were so tight that, once having removed them, I could not get them on again. And they were the only pair I had. When Fanny had decided to take me with her she had already made out her passport for herself and the maid who was supposed to have gone with her to Italy. Now, I was

[9]

that maid! I therefore had to memorize her name indelibly in my mind if I were to assume her identity. I remember that it was an unusually difficult one to memorize! Xenia Vasielevna Stanislawskaia! During the night, the border police would awaken me with their little lanterns in order to ask me my name and see if it agreed with the one on the passport. How I could ever remember that most unusual name and repeat it to the police is beyond me. God knows I have repeated it to myself a thousand times since. But once across the border I was Raisa Burchstein again.

We arrived in Italy where my cousin was waiting for us at the station. I held my little cousin in my arms, my one remaining bundle under my arm, and my shoes in my hand. Capri looked like a dream to me. I lived with my cousins, who took care of me, as though I was one of their own children. We were all very happy on that divine island, in that balmy climate. We had wonderful food and swam in the beautiful sea of the Piccolo Marina, which was a thrilling experience for me who had never seen the ocean before. In a few months I blossomed under the Italian sun and life became a day by day and even an hour by hour delight. At night, when my cousins went out to the Café Morgano, the only entertainment at that time, I would remain at home with the children. When they were sound asleep, I would open the windows to look at the white houses bathed in the moonlight and felt compelled to sing from a sense of joy! Of course the whole island could hear me, and the next day everyone knew it was the dentist's cousin who had been singing. The priest asked my cousin if he would allow me to sing in his church, which I did gladly. I sang the "Ave Maria"[11] by ear, naturally, as I had not had any musical training in reading. ❧

Not long after her arrival on Capri, the young Raisa was invited along with her cousins on a Sunday outing. She was asked to show off the rumored "echo effect" of her voice. Among the attendees at this gathering were Dario and Ester Ascarelli of Naples, wealthy and cultured citizens, who were impressed by the teenager's personality and vocal potential. She sang Massenet's "Elégie" and some Russian songs. They promised to help her, and soon they had arranged for their friend Maestro Vincenzo Lombardi of Naples (a teacher of Enrico Caruso and Fernando De Lucia) to hear her. Raisa remembered the day of her audition:

My cousin Pavel and I left for Naples. At Ricordi's [a branch of the famous music publishing house] we found the manager Mr. Carlo Clausetti, Maestro Lombardi, Dario Ascarelli, and his cousin, Mr. Foá. I sang the only few things I knew, that is, the "Elégie," and some Russian songs, and then Maestro Lombardi made me vocalize. His enthusiasm I could see in his beaming face as he predicted a great career for me. He advised me to study at the Conservatory of Naples (San Pietro a Majella), where I could study voice, music, piano, languages, and all that is important to a singing career. We went back to Capri elated and looking forward to the fall session at the Conservatory. . . . I could hardly wait for the day when I would go there and audition for them. This time it was to be for Mme. Marchisio, a phenomenal singer who had been a contemporary of Adelina Patti. The supervisor took me to Barbara Marchisio's class which was filled with her many pupils. She protested that she would not have time to take on yet another pupil. But noticing how sad I looked at her refusal, and perhaps taking into account my extreme youth—I was only fourteen—she decided to give me a chance. I vocalized and again sang the "Elégie," after which she said to the supervisor: "This girl's voice is an exceptional organ! Although I have no room in my class, I will still accept her, and I will come to the Conservatory earlier in the morning to give her lessons." After finishing her teaching that day she talked to the Director, Maestro Giuseppe Martucci, the great composer, and I was accepted on a scholarship to the Conservatory of Naples, at that time the finest in Italy.

The Ascarellis subsidized her tuition, room, and board, and provided her a small allowance. While attending the Conservatory Raisa lived in Naples with a Miss Pavia, a spinster dressmaker.

Mr. and Mrs. Ascarelli, those angels who had made all this possible for me, would send Miss Pavia a check every month for my board. Forty-five liras a month was all she asked. [Raisa recalled that the exchange rate at that time was six lire to the dollar.] For this sum I had a room in which, during the day, she received her customers and where, at night, I would use the couch for a bed. In the morning I would get café latte, bread and butter. At eight in the morning I would be on my way to the Conservatory where Mme. Marchisio would wait for me at the main door and lead me to the big studio where she would give me a singing lesson before classes started for the others. At one in the afternoon there was a recess, and I would receive a little sandwich with ricotta cheese or two slices of salami. Then I would have my piano lesson, *solfeggio*, Italian and French. At four o'clock I would leave for home, practice the piano on a small upright . . . until eight o'clock in the evening when Miss Pavia would finish her work and we would have our dinner which consisted of soup or pasta, meat, and a vegetable or fruit. My appetite was enormous; I could have eaten twice as much. But I would compensate for it on Sundays when I was invited to my teacher's house for a big lunch. During the holiday season when Miss Pavia was busiest, I would often help her with her sewing and she, in turn, would make me a present of a dress when I needed one. When the Ascarellis felt I should have a larger allowance to afford myself a little more comfort I steadfastly refused, explaining to them that to become an artist one had to suffer in order to develop a soul, so necessary in an artistic career, a credo which I probably inherited from my Russian forebears.

Barbara Marchisio's own biography is a fascinating story. Born in Turin in 1833, she and her younger sister, Carlotta, the soprano, were a famous soprano-contralto sister combination from 1856 to 1872, singing throughout Italy, Iberia, Germany, Poland, England, and Russia in the great bel canto operas, especially *Semiramide* and *Norma*. They were always booked to appear together in the same seasons; in some operas Barbara sang with Adelina Patti. Verdi and Rossini were among their acquaintances. Rossini wrote his *Petite Messe Solennelle*

Barbara and Carlotta Marchisio. Raisa annotated this 1860s photo from Norma,
planning to use it in her autobiography. (Collection of the late Giulietta Segala.)

for Carlotta and Barbara. In her memoir Raisa gives the Marchisio
family history she had learned firsthand:

🖎 Barbara and Carlotta had two brothers, Giuseppe and Antonio.
Giuseppe was the one who taught the two sisters singing and he was

also the piano teacher of Queen Margarita of Savoia in Torino. Later, Antonio became a piano teacher and together they founded a great piano establishment where they gave concerts which the aristocracy of Torino would attend. Giuseppe took the two sisters on their first trip to Spain where Barbara made her debut in concert at the Royal Court Theater and received a gift from Queen Isabella herself, a parure of beautiful emeralds which I sometimes saw her wear at important functions and occasions. Carlotta's husband, Eugenio Kuh, a Viennese, was also a singer who adopted the name of Cosselli, a great baritone who had died many years earlier. This name he kept after he became an Italian citizen. Eugenio's voice was not a beautiful one and Carlotta persuaded him to give up his career. After a glorious career of her own, Carlotta died in childbirth when little Margherita was born on 29 June, 1872. . . . Eugenio Kuh and his little girl Margherita lived with Barbara at her villa. There was also a little Gioacchino; he got his name from Rossini who had baptized him. Unfortunately the little boy when on tour with his mother and his aunt contracted a deadly disease of which he died at the age of four, to the great despair of both Carlotta and Barbara.

It was this which was really the cause of Carlotta's death since, desiring, above all other things to have another child, she died while giving birth to little Margherita. As for Barbara, she was engaged to marry a Spanish lawyer, but while singing *I Capuleti e I Montecchi* by Bellini she received a cable that her fiancé Juan Tressera had died of an infection in the Canary Islands. In the midst of her portrayal of the part of Romeo, the news stunned her, but she continued to sing her role with great emotion. The audience, noticing her realistic portrayal of the suffering Romeo, attributed this to her great artistry in interpreting the despair of Romeo, unaware of the tragedy that had come to her.

Barbara, left alone without a companion, refused to sing with anyone else, deprived as she was of the incomparable Carlotta, who had been with her throughout her entire life and career. She was forty years old when Carlotta died, and decided to devote the rest of her life to little Margherita. She refused all contracts saying "I cannot see myself on the stage with any other person than my sister Carlotta." And when they attempted to offer her roles that did not need a partner she refused these too. "The theatrical life holds no fascination for me anymore" she said. "I will retire to my villa and dedicate myself to my niece." It was Giuseppe Martucci, the great conductor and composer, the first to introduce Wagner to Italy, who persuaded her finally to accept the post at the vocal department of the Conservatory in Naples, San Pietro a Majella. "When you leave the stage there is a new mission ahead of you—to teach and transmit your knowledge and experience to others." Barbara Marchisio then resolved to accept that mission. ॐ

Margherita, who knew Raisa from the latter's study with her aunt Barbara, was to become one of Raisa's lifelong friends, as well as an advisor and mentor. Margherita was married to Carlo Clausetti, the general manager of the House of Ricordi, and this connection was to provide Raisa with her introduction to the upper echelons of the Italian operatic establishment.

About her lessons with Marchisio Raisa remembered the thrice-weekly sessions at the Conservatory and daily lessons during the summer at Marchisio's villa at Mira, Veneto. Raisa recalled that Marchisio forced her to learn the bel canto operas *Lucia di Lammermoor*, *Il Barbiere di Siviglia*, *La Sonnambula*, and even *Rigoletto*, in order to develop her florid skills. Marchisio assured her that although she was definitely not a lyric soprano, Lucia, Rosina, Adina, and Gilda constituted the proper foundation for the roles she would inevitably sing: Norma and the *Trovatore* Leonora. Raisa recalled that at Marchisio's beautiful villa at Mira, between Padua and Venice, she enjoyed some of her happiest times.

ॐ There I had an hour lesson every day, and what an inspiration this great artist was for me it would be difficult to describe. I learned so much from her! . . . She was a great lady. During these summer vacations I improved tremendously. For two years I did nothing but vocalizing and solfeggios. In the third year I studied Italian classical songs, and Schubert, Schumann, and Brahms. In the fourth year I worked on operatic arias—*Semiramide, Hamlet, Aida, Masked Ball,* and *Vespri Siciliani.* ⮜

Raisa lovingly remembered that Marchisio not only took a teacher's interest in her voice, but also gave motherly counsel about organizing and maintaining a career, as well as strict rules regarding smoking and partying, proper sleep, good nutrition, and other nonmusical career essentials. In autumn 1924, just back from Italy and about to leave for Chicago, Raisa gave an interview to the periodical *Musical America.*

Do you know who is going to be there? Toti Dal Monte. We were together when we were little more than children. We studied with the same teacher, Barbara Marchisio, in Italy. She was a teacher of the old school and a wonderful woman. Toti is so adorable. Everyone loves her, but she is not spoiled. She has no prima donna airs. That is what Mme. Marchisio taught us. She was not only our singing teacher. We lived with her and she planned our lives like a mother. She taught us not to act like proverbial opera stars, to be simple and natural above everything. And she taught us to save money. She used to point out singers of another day who passed their last years in terrible poverty because they had spent all their money recklessly in their youth. She made us realize that the number of years you can sing is limited and that when you are through you should be able to live comfortably and happily, not keep on singing after your voice is gone because you need the money.[12]

Raisa graduated from San Pietro a Majella on June 31, 1911; she performed "Bel raggio" from *Semiramide* with orchestra at her graduation ceremony.[13] Her diploma reads: examination of literature—7.6; pianoforte skills—7.5; scenic art—10*; execution of two pieces prepared by the candidate—the first selection from the most important works of the old Italian school up to and including Bellini, the second from accepted modern operas—8.8; execution of a specialized vocal piece chosen at random from the six pieces prepared by the candidate—8.8; interpretation and accompaniment of a piece selected by the Examination Commissioner, after three hours behind closed doors—10; sight reading and transposition of a piece for voice and piano selected by the Examination Commissioner—8; interrogation on the methods, on the technique of voices, and on the physiology and hygiene of the vocal organs—7.6; tested to give proof of knowing the works of the best composers and authors—7.6; conduct—10*.

On April 12, 1912, Raisa made her public debut in a concert in Rome at the Accadèmia di Santa Cecilia. The program, repeated April 16 at the Augusteo, included music by Monteverdi, De'Cavalieri, and Cavalli; Raisa performed with the aging baritone Giuseppe Kaschmann. The Sistine Chapel Choir sang the choral parts at these concerts. Raisa continued studying with Marchisio after graduation and the Rome concerts, preparing the repertoire needed for future auditions. Marchisio, who had been enthusiastic about Raisa and had told important people in the profession about her, promised Cleofonte Campanini that when she thought Raisa ready he would be the first to evaluate her. She took Raisa to Milan in early autumn 1912 for this important audition.[14] Eva Tetrazzini went to this tryout with her conductor husband. Raisa sang Aida's "O patria mia," Norma's "Casta Diva," and "Ecco l'orrido campo" from *Un Ballo in Maschera*. Campanini was so impressed that he immediately engaged her for his September 1913 Verdi Centenary Festival in Parma; if she proved successful, and it was assumed she would be, he said, he would launch her American career at his Chicago-Philadelphia Opera. She was only nineteen years old and could not legally sign the contract; the understanding was sealed with a handshake. For Parma she was to prepare Leonora in Verdi's first opera, *Oberto, Conte di San Bonifacio*, and *Un Ballo in Maschera*. On June 1, 1913, Marchisio wrote to Campanini:

Raisa left for Capri for some sea bathing with her cousins and at the same time prepare for her going to America. I told her to study *Don Giovanni*, *Linda* [*di Chamonix*], [*Cristoforo*] *Colombo*, *Werther*, and *Rigoletto* for all of which I did some basic preparation and later we can go over them together when she returns here in August. *Ballo* we already went over together at the conservatory, but then we had to give

·CENTENARIO · VERDIANO · PARMA·1913·

E.PESCI   PARMA

DOMENICHETTI   FOSSETTA   MASINI   BASSI   CRISTALLI   BENASSO
DE CISNEROS   BURSTEIN   TITTA RUFFO   CAMPANINI   BONCI   FRASCANI   RUSS

Parma Verdi Centenary group photo, September 1913. Raisa, to the left of Titta Ruffo, is still Burstein. E. Pesci Studio, Parma. (Archives, Teatro Regio.)

it up to study other operas, especially those you have announced for the Centenary. I am convinced that Amelia would rather be more suited to her temperament than the page. All the more since she has always rebelled against soprano leggero parts and won't study them even though she has precise agility. I would be in favor of the Amelia and I believe she would be not only good, but also even a worthy partner of the Divo [Alessandro Bonci]. I believe there would be time to go over it seriously, first with me and then with you. Only have the courtesy to let me know when you have made your decision [on repertory] so that I'll be able to work with her. Barbara Marchisio.[15]

Raisa made her operatic debut at Parma's Teatro Regio, under the name Raisa Burstein, on September 6, 1913. She sang the role of Leonora in *Oberto* with Nini Frascani, Italo Cristalli, and Angelo Masini-

Pieralli; Campanini conducted. The Teatro Regio is a notoriously difficult theater whose very knowledgeable public is unwilling to accept any but the very best artists. Over the years many established performers had been heckled off its stage. In reviewing the festival, *Orfeo* magazine wrote:

> To make her debut at the Teatro Regio, and moreover on such an occasion, was considered risky but Raisa Burstein won a triumphant success. She possesses a magnificent voice, rich in sonorous and powerful notes of beautiful timbre; she is very successful in impetuous and accented passages, eminently dramatic and her phrasing is also correct. She cannot yet show off her dramatic talent, for she is still awkward, and her singing is not animated by that artistic fire which makes the greatest singers of the lyric theater live in our memory; but she will be splendidly successful.[16]

Of her Parma *Oberto* debut, Raisa often told this story to illustrate her youthful lack of professionalism. The opera was scheduled to start at 9 P.M. Before going to the theater she prepared zabaglione (eggs, sugar, and Marsala wine); she had been told that this treat was good for the voice. Almost in a trance, she lost all sense of time. When Eva Campanini went to her dressing room at the opera house and did not find her there, she rushed to Raisa's apartment. Eva got her young charge to the theater with just enough time for her to apply her makeup and don her costume before taking the stage.

In the same festival she also sang one performance of *Un Ballo in Maschera* with Bonci. Raisa remembered some of the critics commenting that she was good enough to go to America, suggesting, as she had been told at the time, that only the very best voices and artists were exportable. In the fewer than seven years between her leaving Russian Poland in early 1907 and her operatic debut in September 1913, Raisa at age twenty became one of the emerging luminaries of the opera world.

· *Chapter Two* ·

AMERICA

WHEN Cleofonte Campanini took Raisa to America, a very important decision was made. Campanini thought the name Burchstein (spelled Burstein in Parma) too ethnic and lacking glamour; he prevailed upon Raisa to take a stage name. His only motive was to eliminate any element that might prevent her from achieving the acclaim he was so positive she deserved. They settled on Rosa Raisa, which they found euphonious and even a bit exotic. This name change and its implications caused Raisa anguish, because to her it implied there was something wrong with who she really was. In interviews later in life one hears great emotion in her voice as she recounts the story of her name change, although she treats it with good humor. Campanini told her that Raisa Burchstein was too long a name for American tastes, but did he have the same problem with Amelita Galli-Curci's name three years later? It is noteworthy that Campanini believed there was significant anti-Semitism in both the opera world and the general public at that time, especially in the United States, and that one could not make a successful career in opera with an obviously Jewish-sounding name. This certainly was not always true in the other classical musical arts, as it was never a handicap to Heifetz, Horowitz, or Rubinstein.

Raisa's North American debut was with the Chicago-Philadelphia Company, not in either of those cities, but at the Lyric Theater in Baltimore, on November 14 in *La Bohème* with Giovanni Martinelli, in his first North American season on loan from the Metropolitan Opera. "Her tone at times inclined to stridency, but during the less intense moments it appeared youthfully vibrant and of a very appealing character" (*Musical America*). In Philadelphia she sang Queen Isabella

Raisa as Aida, 1913. Raisa is only twenty years old here. Matzene Studio, Chicago.

in the North American premiere of Franchetti's *Cristoforo Colombo* with Titta Ruffo and Amedeo Bassi. "Rosa Raisa is young, still girlish in appearance, with an attractive personality, and her vocal equipment promises glowing results in the future. Her voice is a soprano of pure lyric quality, a trifle shrill at times and noticeably reedy, but of crystalline clearness and sweetness, and capable of dramatic expression"

(*Musical America*). Her Chicago operatic debut (she had sung at a Monday Morning Musicale earlier in the week at the Blackstone Hotel) was in *Aida*, during a Saturday matinee on November 29 with Cyrena Van Gordon, Bassi, Giovanni Polese, and Gustave Huberdeau; Campanini conducted. "Raisa has a clear soprano voice of fine range and brilliant in the upper register, although a trifle cold. She was an appealing Aida and an actress of merit" (*Musical Leader*). Edward Moore, in his history, *Forty Years of Opera in Chicago*, thought that the most notable revelation "was a voice the like of whose power had never been heard on that stage."[1] A month later Clarence Eddy reported of a repeat *Aida*:

> She has a dramatic soprano voice of unusual brilliancy and luster, which has been well trained. She sings in admirable tune and makes most excellent use of some remarkably effective low chest tones which she joins to the middle register with the utmost skill. Although not particularly sympathetic in quality, her voice is very expressive, large and musically assertive, and without the slightest forcing it is always a dominant feature in the powerful climaxes of the chorus and orchestra ensembles.[2]

This was a red-letter day for the Chicago Opera, the first performance of two singers—Van Gordon and Raisa—who would go on to be headliners of the company until its collapse in 1932. Campanini used Raisa in some of his Sunday afternoon concerts at the Auditorium. In press conferences Campanini proudly proclaimed Raisa's one of the greatest voices he had ever heard in his long career, but he cautioned that as she was so young there were naturally going to be occasional "diamond in the rough" moments.

It was at this time that Raisa met and was befriended by the woman who would become a sort of surrogate mother and an important anchor in her life: Goldie (Mrs. Julius) Stone. Twenty-year-old Raisa was very nervous about her name change and its larger implications. Campanini was aware of her unease and asked Mr. and Mrs. Julius Rosenwald, board members of the Chicago Opera, to intervene. Through their charitable work the Rosenwalds knew Mrs. Stone, a Russian and a "bridge" figure in the Chicago Jewish community. Mrs. Stone worked with the older German families of fortune and with the more newly arrived poorer immigrants from eastern Europe. In her memoir, *My Caravan of Years*, Mrs. Stone recounts her first meeting with Raisa, at the Congress Hotel in early 1914, and how Raisa poured out her heart: "I have been very troubled for a long time. Maestro Campanini has been so dear a friend. I am a Jewess and I wanted the public to know; yet Maestro said, 'No Raisa, not yet. Wait till the public has truly received you. Wait till you are assured of your success.' But I could not be silent. I am a Jewess and all the fire of my people burns in my heart. I could not sleep; I could not go on. I told Maestro Campanini that they must receive me as a Jewess or not at all—that art has not room for prejudice or hate. . . . Forgive me, but all my life I have hungered for mother love. I lost my own mother when I was just six. Many women have been kind to me and I have loved them, but always there is some restraint and I cannot pour out the affection I crave to give. You are the one I used to dream about."[3] This mother-daughter relationship was to last more than forty years. In a 1950 photograph inscription Raisa wrote, "To the most wonderful woman in the world."

Mimì, Queen Isabella, and the First Flower Maiden in *Parsifal* were the other Chicago roles Raisa sang in this first season. The *Parsifal* Flower Maiden was the only secondary role Raisa ever performed. There is a longstanding tradition in major opera houses of casting the lesser roles in the Wagner operas with young, healthy voices, some of them belonging to stars of the future. In the past, and even today, in some major theaters well-established leading singers are cast in these secondary roles; such was and still is the prestige that attends the Wagner operas. When the company returned to Philadelphia she added Donna Anna in *Don Giovanni* and Klytemnestra in the North American premiere of Vittorio Gnecci's *Cassandra*. In the subsequent tour to California and back to the northern Midwest she added Santuzza in *Cavalleria Rusticana* in Dallas and Elsa in *Lohengrin* in

Seattle. In Seattle Campanini alerted the press that he had a wonderful surprise awaiting them in *Lohengrin*. The *Seattle Times* noted:

> The mighty impressive fact was that a brand new divinity among the stellar people in the Campanini list of great artists was heard for the first time in her life in a part in which she gave a physical and vocal interpretation of ethereal beauty and of such sympathy and girlish charm. . . . The voice of Elsa was of a perfection and purity to fit the part, but of such honeyed sweetness, of such luscious coloring in the middle register and of such pellucid and lovely quality in the upper register as to cause all who had expected something really wonderful to believe that more was provided than had been promised. . . . the best of it all lay in the fact . . . that in Miss Raisa's voice was that quality alone found in young singers—the youthful and untarnished beauty of the voice that gradually is lost by constant singing and which at best can endure but for a few years.

The next-to-last stop on the winter/spring national tour was Saint Paul, Minnesota. A critic there wrote of Raisa's Mimì:

> There is nothing fragile about Rosa Raisa. The radiant hue of her cheeks is too pronouncedly healthy to suggest the hectic flush of an incipient decline, and the glow in her dark eyes is clearly the evidence of youth and vigor, and not to be confused with the fitful light of fever. Rosa Raisa can sing, however, and she can also act. The seasoned opera-goer who has been forced to associate Mimì with prima donnas "fat, fair, and more than forty [Nellie Melba?]," can readily condone the slight incongruity of a maiden abundantly endowed with strength and health, especially when she brings to the part the beauty of voice and the dramatic art of this Russian girl. There is an emotional element about Rosa Raisa's voice, and a refinement and finish about both her singing and acting which bore their full share in making "La Bohème" one of the notable presentations of the season.[4]

A note about the Philadelphia *Don Giovanni*: in the original plan, Raisa was to sing Zerlina in a cast that included Ruffo and Aristodemo

Giorgini. The story gets a bit complicated with the three female leads, but it is best recounted by Campanini himself in this excerpt from a report by the journalist Byron Hegel. "Alice Zeppilli, cast for Donna Elvira, wanted to sing Zerlina. I did not object if Raisa would consent to change parts. Raisa did and learned the role of Donna Elvira. Mme. [Martha] Dorda, who was to have sung Donna Anna, fell ill. Carolina White knew Donna Elvira but not Donna Anna. I asked Raisa if she could learn Donna Anna in four days. She did so."[5] Raisa had learned, if not totally mastered, all three roles. Campanini obviously did not feel that there was anything unusual in casting a dramatic voice as Zerlina, a part often sung by much lighter voices. Performance practices at that time, even with major companies, often saw casting decisions made at the last minute, owing either to a lack of long-range planning or to unforeseen emergencies.

The tenor of the critiques at the very beginning of Raisa's career reveals an awareness of her youth but also of her obvious talent. Regarding her voice, the critics were undecided as to whether she was merely a loud lyric or a dramatic soprano; her upper register, generally thought to be the glory of her voice, was heard as either brilliant, strident, shrill, easy, or forced, depending on the critic consulted and the performance being reviewed.

Harry Higgins of London's Covent Garden auditioned Raisa in Chicago and engaged her for the 1914 international season. In one month Raisa sang three Aidas, three Elenas in *Mefistofele*, and two Countesses in *Le Nozze di Figaro*, interspersing these with performances in Paris with the touring Boston Opera Company in a joint venture with Covent Garden. With this company she sang the only Nedda in *Pagliacci* of her career, as well as Amelia; at a Paris Opéra gala she sang the second act of *Otello* with Edoardo Ferrari-Fontana and Jean-Emile Vanni-Marcoux. Plans were being made for her to perform in a run of *Aida* at the Opéra, but this never materialized.

The confusion over Raisa's name continued in London. A typographical error in the *Aida* program was picked up by the reviewers, and suddenly, errors having a way of taking a life of their own, she was known in London as Rosina Raisa. The error was finally corrected at

Stellar cast of the Covent Garden Mefistofele, *1914.*

the end of her London engagement. The reviews of her Covent Garden debut with Caruso as Radamès were mixed but on the whole favorable to the newcomer: "Rosina Raisa has a clear and telling voice, even if at times penetrating in timbre" (*Standard*). At the repeat with Martinelli *The Telegram* reported: "Rosina Raisa seemed to be better at her ease than at her previous appearance in this opera, for her Aida had much more force and dignity, while her singing was often really brilliant."

The *Mefistofele* Elena with Adamo Didur, John McCormack, and Claudia Muzio was barely commented upon, but her Countess (as a last-minute replacement for Claire Dux) revealed that she was "decidedly more at home in modern Italian music than in Mozart" (*Star*). Cast with some of the foremost singers of the time in one of Europe's most important opera houses, Raitza Burchstein of Bialystok had arrived!

· *Chapter Three* ·

THE BIG CAREER

WITH the outbreak of the Great War and the cancellation of the 1914–1915 Chicago season (due as much to bankruptcy and reorganization as to the war) Raisa found herself stranded in Italy. Campanini advised her to contact the prestigious agent Giuseppe Lusardi for new engagements. Lusardi set up an audition with Maestro Gino Marinuzzi at his home in Milan. The audition went so well that Marinuzzi wanted to hear her on La Scala's stage. Raisa recounts that, inexplicably, the stage audition went so poorly that she was told they wouldn't consider her even for the chorus. Margherita Clausetti had accompanied Raisa to the Scala audition, and the two went to meet Clausetti's husband, Carlo, and Tito Ricordi shortly afterward near the Galleria. After Raisa tearfully recounted her dismal showing on the Scala stage, Tito invited her to sing for him at his salon in the House of Ricordi. As can happen in the unpredictable world of auditions, this time Raisa performed her best and Ricordi assured her that she need not worry. In her memoirs Raisa recalled,

ക I don't know where I got my courage but I made a fine impression on Tito Ricordi. [For him Raisa sang "O patria mia" from *Aida* and "Ma dell'arido stelo" from *Un Ballo in Maschera*] After I finished, he went to his book to write down his observations, as was his habit with every auditioning artist. Then he walked out. Signora Clausetti, out of curiosity, went over to the book and read out what he had to say. She summoned me to read it too, and there it was: "Extraordinarily beautiful voice, very musical, beautiful girl with fine personality; great possibilities." ക

The manager of the Modena opera was in the market for a soprano to sing Francesca da Rimini in Zandonai's new opera, and Ricordi promised to recommend Raisa for this engagement. Raisa later remembered,

*§ Tito himself taught me the role of Francesca. He was very severe but he knew what he wanted. [Tito Ricordi was the librettist of this opera.] After I had learned the score, he asked me to sing excerpts from *Francesca* for his mother, whom he adored and [who] was the only person who could influence him. I felt very flattered and encouraged to sing for Mme. Giuditta Ricordi since I knew from Margherita Clausetti that rarely was an artist invited to sing in her salon. A little later, a party was arranged and I sang for the chosen few of Milan. They received me with warm enthusiasm. Tito Ricordi himself patted me on the shoulder, saying, and these were his exact words: "Brava, vada sicura che farà un gran successo!" (Bravo, rest assured you will be a great success!) §*

In her memoir Raisa remembered with great specificity singing Francesca in Modena nineteen times; performance density of this kind was not rare in this period—a successful new opera being given in a moderate-size theater (one thousand seats) four to five times a week for a month. In Modena the *Francesca* cast included tenor Remo Andreini and Enrico Roggio, who later made a specialty of the baritone role of Giovanni. At the end of the run Raisa was awarded a night in her honor (*Serata d'onore*), at which the aristocracy of Modena gave her gifts of precious jewelry. After her successful Francesca performances in Rome a month later Zandonai inscribed a score, "To Miss Rosa Raisa, immortal Francesca, who gave utterance to its beauties. Riccardo Zandonai."[1]

The Modena engagement opened the door to two whirlwind years in Raisa's early career. It led to a great success in Rome and a truly international showcase in South America; Raisa then returned to Italy, revisiting Rome and successfully debuting at La Scala, and then went back again to South America, this time as an acknowledged star. In this period she made the acquaintance of Emma Carelli, Walter

Raisa as Francesca da Rimini, Modena, 1914. Zandonai told Raisa that "divinity is within you." P. Orlandini e Figlie Studio, Modena.

Mocchi, Arturo Toscanini, Giacomo Puccini, Gabriele d'Annunzio, and most important, Giacomo Rimini.

At the Costanzi in Rome, under the management of Emma Carelli, Raisa sang the local premiere of *Francesca*, the world premiere of Romano Romani's prizewinning opera *Fedra*[2] (with Hipólito Lázaro and Cesare Formichi), and the Brazilian composer Alberto Nepomuceno's *Abul* (with Aureliano Pertile), as well as *Aida* (with Flora Perini, Bernardo De Muro/Pertile, and Giuseppe Danise). *Musical Courier's* Roman correspondent wired:

> It was her first appearance in Rome in one of the "standard" roles and she strengthened and bettered the excellent impression she had made the week before in *Francesca da Rimini*. In fact it was a great personal triumph for her and well deserved, for, taken all in all, it was the best performance of the part which I have ever heard. She is bound to become one of the very great artists of the Italian stage within the next few years, for both voice, singing and acting belong to the first class; in fact to the most exceptional class.

The 1915 season in South America, under the management of Walter Mocchi, at that time the husband of Emma Carelli, was important on many counts: it marked the return of Caruso, last heard there in 1903, and boasted Ruffo and the relatively unknown Amelita Galli-Curci. Raisa debuted in *Francesca* (with debutante Hina Spani, Lázaro, and Danise), and followed that with *Aida* (with Frascani, Caruso/De Muro, and Danise). Legend has it that Caruso was not in top form at the start of the opera and needed a few acts to warm up, while Raisa was at her best from the outset and captured the audience's affection. In his *Voci Parallele* Giacomo Lauri-Volpi embellishes this story.[3] In its summary of the season the magazine *Arte y Artistas* reported:

> If the triumph of Caruso was complete, no less was that of the soprano Rosa Raisa, a singer who in the same score has placed herself among the best and most brilliant interpreters of the role of Aida, winning out in comparisons with the most celebrated that we have heard in the last ten years. In order to find anything comparable to la Raisa, one would

The hopeful twenty-two-year-old singer aboard ship on her way to South America, 1915. (Collection of the late Giulietta Segala.)

have to resort to the remembrance of singers of days of yore, the mold of whom appears today to have been lost. The performance of the soprano was on Thursday night a true revelation for our public who could not have suspected that this singer would be such an authentic treasure, and even if one had appreciated her in *Francesca da Rimini*, her stock rose considerably in *Aida*. Voice, diction, scenic art are a union of beautiful qualities which adorn la Raisa and her interpretation of the role of Aida has placed her on a pedestal from which she will be dislodged with difficulty by other sopranos.

An examination of the rich operatic history of Buenos Aires Aidas since 1905 reveals among them Matilda De Lerma, Eugenia Burzio, Giannina Russ, Lucia Crestani, Juanita Capella, Celestina Boninsegna, Elena Rakowska (Mrs. Tullio Serafin), Emma Carelli, Cecilia Gagliardi, Salomea Kruszelnicka, and Elena Zboinska-Ruszkowska.[4]

On the steamer *Tomasso di Savoia* on which Caruso also traveled, I could hear him practicing *Samson et Dalila* every morning in the music room with his accompanist, Mr. Barthélemy, preparing this part for his next season at the Metropolitan Opera House. In Buenos Aires I lived at the Plaza Hotel on the same floor with Caruso, and I used to hear him practicing in the bathtub while his accompanist from the adjoining room would play the score that he was to sing that same night—which proves that great artists never cease to study! Caruso was a truly fine colleague, kind, generous, and good. Several times he invited me to have tea with him on the mezzanine floor, while the orchestra played the Argentine tangos that he and I loved to listen to. One day, after another of his triumphs in Puccini's *Manon Lescaut*, while sipping tea with him, I remarked: "You should consider yourself the happiest man in the world. Everyone worships you." His answer was that happiness was not possible for him because the woman he adored, the mother of his two sons, had deserted him. How sad to think that this man who so deserved all the joys of life should have been deprived of so much!

L'Africana (*L'Africaine*), with Spani, De Muro, and Ruffo, and *Il Cavaliere della Rosa* (*Der Rosenkavalier*), with Gilda Dalla Rizza, Galli-Curci, and Giulio Cirino, were her other showcase operas this season; *Cavalleria Rusticana* and *La Bohème* rounded out her assignments.

[34]

Gran Compañía **Teatro Colón** Maestro Concertador y
Lírica Italiana Director de Orquesta:
Comm. Gino Marinuzzi

TEMPORADA OFICIAL. — AÑO 1915 ◉ EMPRESA: DA ROSA, MOCCHI Y CÍA.

45.ª FUNCIÓN **Jueves 29 de Julio de 1915** A las 8.45 p. m.
DE ABONO EN PUNTO

La comedia lírica en 3 actos. música del maestro Ricardo Strauss:

Il Cavaliere della Rosa

REPARTO

La Marescialla......................	Rosa Raisa	Il maestro di casa del Sig. de Fanival	L. Nardi	
Il Barone Ocha di Lerchenau........	G. Cirino		⎧ A. Remba	
Ottavio Detto Quin-quin	G. Dalla Rizza	Le tre orfani d'un nobile..........	⎨ M. Caleffi	
Signor di Fanival..........	E. Caronna		⎩ J. Mannarini	
Sofia, sua figlia......................	A. Galli-Curci	Una modista..........................	L. Toreili	
Mariana Leitmetzerin, gobernante....	A. Giacomucci	Un venditore d'uccelli...	L. Nardi	
Rys-Galla............................	Paltrinieri		⎧ S. Menni	
Zephyra..............................	Flora Perini		⎪ Gasperini	
Un commisario......................	T. Dentale	Cuatro Lacche della Marescialla...⎨ Depetris	
Il maestro di casa delle Marescialla..	N. Fanelli		⎩ Ziori	

Un notaio, Un oste, Un cantante, Un scienzcato, Un flautista, Un parrucchiere, Un garzone, Un nobile
vedora, Camerieri, Un piccolo negro, Lacché, Corridori, Annunciadori, Guardia Ungarica, Personnale
di cucina, Ospite, Musicanti, Guardie, Bambini, ecc.
L'azione a Viena durante i primi anni del Regno María di Teresa.

Program of the Italian-language Rosenkavalier, Buenos Aires, 1915, with the
three young sopranos on the eve of their great careers.

One wonders what this Italian-language *Rosenkavalier* was like, as the
three young and gifted sopranos were destined to have huge careers in
their respective voice categories. On paper at least this has to be one of
the most fascinating and curious vocal combinations ever. Dalla Rizza's
stellar career as a verismo soprano included many successful engagements as Octavian on the Italian and South American stages, and the
following year Galli-Curci would take the North American musical
world by storm, in the process becoming famous around the globe. But
what about the twenty-two-year-old Raisa? Leaving aside issues of interpretation, the Marschallin's music is mostly middle-voice declamation and word-pointing with occasional arching phrases; she gets to
really open up her voice only in the final trio, and even there ideally
there should be transparent vocal balance. Marinuzzi, in preparing this

[35]

opera for its South American premiere, must have worked mightily to blend his three sopranos in this mostly ensemble opera. Rosario, Montevideo, Rio de Janeiro, and São Paulo were the other destinations on this tour. In all, Raisa sang fifty-two times in operas and concerts this first season in South America; she returned to the opera-loving South American continent four more times during her career, in 1916, 1918, 1921, and 1929.

Returning to Italy, Raisa, now strongly identified as Zandonai's Francesca, sang eight performances at the Corso in Bologna with Pertile and Eduardo Faticanti, Tullio Serafin conducting. While preparing for her Scala debut as Aida Raisa attended a performance of *Falstaff* at Milan's Teatro Dal Verme, where Toscanini was giving an elaborate season of opera that included among other things Caruso singing *Pagliacci* in his very last appearances in his native land, indeed his last in all of Europe.[5] Margherita Clausetti had told her about the new and wonderful Falstaff, Giacomo Rimini, who was making a big name for himself in the title part. Born in Verona on March 22, 1888, Rimini had studied with the nineteenth-century soprano Amelia Conti-Feroni. He made his debut as Albert in *Werther* in Desenzano in 1910. He sang mostly in less prestigious companies in South America, Italy, Sweden, and France until his breakthrough year with Toscanini at the Dal Verme.

Raisa was introduced to Rimini backstage, and they were smitten with each other. Raisa and Rimini went on from this meeting to become friends, then lovers, and then husband and wife in 1920. Their relationship was complicated by the fact that Rimini was at the time a married man, the husband of Delizia and father of Rafaella; even though he was not living with his wife and daughter, he supported them financially. Opera history shows that husband-and-wife couples were far from rare, but the inseparable Raisa-Rimini combination was unique in many ways; their relationship was much written about and noted. From the time they met until their retirement Raisa and Rimini enjoyed virtually a joint career.[6]

At La Scala Raisa sang her first of nine *Aida*s on January 5, 1916. Her Aida reminded some oldtimers of Teresa Stolz, Verdi's friend and the first Scala *Aida* in 1872. Raisa sang Lida in a revival of Verdi's *La Battaglia di Legnano* on January 19, an opera last given there in 1861. On February 26 she presented her Francesca (with Dal Monte [making her operatic debut in the small role of Biancofiore], Pertile, and Danise, Marinuzzi conducting), sharing the role with Linda Canetti, who had sung the world premiere two years before in Turin.

*S At the first rehearsal of *Francesca* at La Scala an interesting episode occurred: Tito Ricordi, Maestro Marinuzzi, Zandonai, and Carlo Clausetti were present. I started to sing my first phrase, on the bridge, with my head leaning backward, enraptured at the thought of meeting Paolo il bello, as my sister, Samaritana, held me at the hips while the ladies in waiting sang. At this point, as I comment "amor le fa cantare," Tito Ricordi called me, saying that when I say "ah tu mi svegli" to Samaritana, he wanted me to be on the first step. Somehow this seemed a very unreasonable demand, which irritated me greatly at that moment. I answered that I was a spontaneous artist, that I sang with sincerity, not according to rules or directions, and I never know what step I will finish what phrase, since I am always prompted by a natural instinct to express the intention of the composer and the music. With that I walked off, stopping long enough to add that I had made a great success in this role to the delight of audiences at the Costanzi, Rome and the Colon, Buenos Aires, and that I would only sing it just as I felt it demands at each moment. And to my dressing room I went, like a real, incensed prima donna—something which I had never done before, nor have I ever done since! All four men came rushing after me, pleading that I continue just as I wished and thought proper.[7] ᘓ

At almost twenty-three, Raisa was now the toast of Milan. Puccini visited her backstage, and when she asked him which of all his operas she should sing, he replied, "There is no opera I have written to which your voice is not suited; they are all the same for you."[8] He then invited her to create his next opera, *La Rondine*, scheduled for the next season in Monte Carlo. Puccini was offering her the creation of one of his lightest and most lyric parts at about the same time Toscanini was hailing her as the "Tamagno of dramatic sopranos." Francesco Tamagno, the creator of Verdi's Otello, was famous for his huge dramatic tenor voice with its ringing top notes.[9] Perhaps Puccini was so taken with her youth and charm that he did not take pure vocal suitability into account. Eight years later Puccini was true to his original estimate of her wide-ranging vocal capabilities when he offered her Turandot, surely his most vocally heavy and challenging heroine, literally a role for a female Tamagno.

Back in Rome at the Costanzi, Raisa reprised her Aida and Francesca before returning to South America for another long tour. In Buenos Aires she added Loreley, Valentina in *Gli Ugonotti (Les Huguenots)*, and Alice Ford in *Falstaff* to her growing list of roles. She also sang Aida, Amelia, and Lida in this stagione. Unlike her debut year, this time her name was in bold letters in the Colón's program artist list. In her 1916 Colón *Falstaffs*, Titta Ruffo was Sir John; for the remainder of her career she sang Alice Ford many times, but only with Rimini. In São Paolo she sang her only Margherita in *Mefistofele*, with Giulio Crimi and Marcel Journet. On the voyage from Italy to South America the young couple was befriended by the composer Saint-Saëns, who was to conduct his opera *Samson et Dalila*. The composer was aware that Raisa and Rimini were very much in love, and he dedicated a photo of himself to Raisa with the inscription "Printemps qui commence."

· *Chapter Four* ·

CHICAGO

THE autumn of 1916 marks the real beginning of Raisa's great career at the Chicago Opera. True, she had debuted in 1913 and
made some impact both in Chicago and on the national tour; but when
she returned in 1916 with extensive European and South American
experience she was viewed not as merely a very young and promis-
ing artist, but as an established performer. Along with Mary Garden,
she should have dominated the 1916 season except for one matter:
the overwhelming impact of Amelita Galli-Curci's spectacular United
States debut. Raisa had given Campanini a very favorable evaluation
of the Italian coloratura Galli-Curci based on having sung with her
in *Der Rosenkavalier* in Italian and having heard her in her other
starring roles in South America. Caruso, on the other hand, for whatever reason, had in 1915 given Gatti-Casazza of the Metropolitan
a less favorable estimate of Galli-Curci, and this had some impact on the Met's decision not to audition and possibly engage her
at that time.[1] Campanini told Raisa that Galli-Curci's voice was the
only one that strongly reminded him of Adelina Patti.[2] It must have
been the "entrancing," mellifluous quality of her voice that brought
about this considered comparison, as Campanini had heard Patti often
in her prime years. Galli-Curci made a few recordings for Victor in
Camden before she went west to Chicago, and these were released
shortly after the full impact of her sensational debut became national
and world news. One can only wonder whether Victor had made test
recordings of Raisa at that time, as there was much "buzz" about her
and Muzio being the two most important new Italian singers on the
horizon.

Raisa opened the 1916 Chicago season as Aida, a role she would repeat on opening night in 1922 and 1929. For the 1916 season she added Maddalena in *Andrea Chénier*, Alice Ford in *Falstaff*, Valentina in *Gli Ugonotti*, and Zina in Gunsbourg's *Le Vieil Aigle* to her Chicago repertoire, and also offered Chicago the Francesca she had sung to such acclaim in Italy and South America. Her good friend (and probably, by this time, more than friend) Giacomo Rimini was now on the roster of the Chicago company, and his appearances with Raisa had an air of inevitability about them. He sang Amonasro in the opening night *Aida*, Gérard in *Chénier*, and Giovanni in *Francesca da Rimini*. The two presented the first of their many Chicago *Falstaffs* in the 1916–1917 season, and as he was the year's featured Italian baritone, Rimini was the Rigoletto in the Galli-Curci "headline-making" debut at the end of the first week. His other Chicago roles this season were Tonio, Germont, Marcello, Scarpia, and Figaro.

Nellie Melba heard Raisa in *Aida* and, impressed, invited her to tea the next day. Of that particular *Aida* Raisa later recalled,

Maestro Campanini made me repeat "Patria mia." The great Melba lauded my pianissimos in the third act saying "Always use them. Luckily your repetition of the aria came out even better, if that can be possible, than in the first rendition. It is best to avoid such repetitions . . . too difficult an aria to take any chances with. However, in the duet with Radamès you sang pianissimos that sounded like a Stradivarius. You should use them as often as you can." [Apropos her meeting with Melba, Raisa recalled that two nights later she heard Melba in *La Bohème*, and] I still remember her exit on the high C with McCormack, when their singing glittered like beautiful gems. In the third act, when she sings "Addio senza rancor," that last F was so beautiful it still rings in my ears.

(In her memoir Raisa places the Melba meeting in the 1916–1917 season, but Melba did not sing with the Chicago Opera that season. Melba could very well have heard Raisa's Aida in 1913–1914 or 1917–1918, seasons in which Melba was a member of the company.)[3]

Reviews often noted Raisa's youth as a positive and not an excuse for artistic immaturity. Karleton Hackett in the *Post* wrote after the *Aida* opening,

> She has a resonance when she sends forth the full power of her tone that is absolutely dominating in the biggest ensembles which makes her upper tones so brilliant . . . the Latins like theirs very brilliant, with a quality almost like a silver clarion, so I can understand how she is an ideal singer for the Italian stage. We in this country are apt to prefer a somewhat darker and richer quality in the tone. . . . When it comes to Miss Raisa's control of her voice from her high C away down to the chest register and with every degree of power from fortissimo to pianissimo there is no question. She can do with it as she likes, sustaining the phrase to any length, with the great variety of tone colors, and with a certainty that is marvelous.

Frederick Donaghey in the *Tribune* noted: "I have heard since Calvé no other Santuzza so good as Miss Raisa." Felix Borowski in the *Herald* added, "Clearly an actress of more than ordinary intelligence, she offered a moving impersonation of a character which is frequently overcooled. Nor did her brilliant voice fail to reflect the emotion of her soul." Herman Devries of the *Evening American*, reviewing *Andrea Chénier*, wrote: "She was all grace and charm and girlish naïveté in the first act, and sounded the note of passion and heart anguish in the last grim scenes. Vocally everything she did was timbered with silvery purity and varied expression. Her art has a hundred brilliant facets."

In Chicago Raisa spent much of her time with Maestro Campanini and his wife, Eva Tetrazzini. Raisa lived with the Campaninis in 1913 and 1914, and they treated her as though she were their own daughter. She sat in Eva's box most nights she was not on the stage herself. Eva had an enormous influence on her, and Raisa remembered:

≈ She was a great dramatic soprano. Her sisters Luisa Tetrazzini, a phenomenal coloratura, and Elvira, a concert singer, together with a

Cleofonte and Eva Tetrazzini Campanini on vacation in Maine, circa 1906. Raisa was forever grateful to the Campaninis for their early recognition of her talent and support of her career. (Robert Tuggle Collection.)

brother who was a concert pianist, made up this most unusual family of extremely talented musicians. Equal to the phenomenal Luisa was Eva in her own field. She taught me phrases from the great operas, and when she illustrated passages such as "Ora soave" from *Andrea Chenier*, "O patria mia" and the duet with Amonasro as well as "Là, tra foreste vergini" from *Aida*, and "Vo' farmi più gaia" in the duet with Barnaba from the last act of *La Gioconda*, she would rise to her full stature and at these moments she would become like a lioness, completely transformed by the part she was singing. She could penetrate and touch your heart and achieve the most thrilling effects inspired by the music and the drama of the score. In addition to this priceless relationship with her, musically, she was like a mother to me in advising and guiding me with much affection. She was of invaluable assistance in making her own wise observations on life gained through wide experience my own. Whenever I go back to those days I realize once more how lucky I was to have found such wonderful human beings as Madam and Maestro Campanini to instruct and guide me. ༂

Over the years Raisa often told the story of when the composer Ildebrando Pizzetti told her that one of the three greatest moments in his long operagoing life was hearing Eva Tetrazzini Campanini sing the second-act duet from *Andrea Chénier* and phrasing "Ora soave" in a magical way never since duplicated.[4] Eva coached Raisa in this opera. (Raisa did not recount whether Pizzetti described his other two greatest moments in the opera house.)

The revival of *Gli Ugonotti* suffered when Galli-Curci, the announced Margherita, canceled because of illness. Jesse Christian, an Iowa-born soprano who had been trained in France, replaced her. The *Musical Courier* offered the opinion that "Rosa Raisa was the star of the evening and her delineation and singing of Valentina will long be remembered as one of the best portrayals given this season by this gifted singer, whose transcendent success has reached unlimited bounds, and has placed her among the brightest and most popular

As Valentina in Gli Ugonotti, *1916. Victor Georg Studio, New York.*

stars that have ever graced the stage of the Auditorium. She sang gloriously and was a picture."

Chicago's love affair with Raisa, just beginning in 1916, was to last
almost a quarter century. Many have wondered why the Metropolitan
Opera in New York did not add Raisa to its ranks. Surely news of her
Italian, South American, and Chicago successes traveled even in those

days. In interviews over the years, Raisa claimed that the Metropolitan was interested in her and possible contracts were discussed at various times, but nothing ever materialized. Early in her career she indicated that her gratitude to Campanini, for believing in her and for first giving her opportunities to perform, was such that she wouldn't even consider leaving his Chicago Opera. Her condition that Rimini also be taken might also have been a problem. By the early 1920s Chicago and the Metropolitan had reached an "understanding" that neither would raid the other's roster. No unsigned contracts for Raisa have been found in the Metropolitan Opera Archives.[5] It is also true that even had the Metropolitan been interested in adding Raisa to its ranks, they could not have offered her the kind of primary ranking she would enjoy in Chicago. The Met already had great singers on their roster singing her repertoire. It is true that the absence of the Metropolitan Opera from her résumé is the one major gap of her great career. For many in the United States, at least, the Met is the summit. Raisa could become defensive when asked about this; the explanation that being a major star and the leading dramatic soprano of the prestigious Chicago Opera was an enormous accomplishment never seemed to satisfy her.

After the successful 1916 Chicago season Raisa was scheduled to go to Monte Carlo for the creation of Magda in *La Rondine*, but increased submarine activity in the Atlantic made travel to Europe dangerous. Her name was in the prospectus given to the press in January for the 1917 Monte Carlo season. (*Musical America*, in its February 10, 1917, issue, ran an article with a Paris dateline titled "Brilliant Season for Monte Carlo, New Puccini Opera and other Novelties Promised—A Stellar Array of Singers" in which, in the elaboration of the plans, it announced that "Rosa Raisa will create the leading role in the new opera of Puccini.") Instead of Europe, Raisa and Rimini took a needed vacation on the New Jersey shore. The Riccardo Stracciaris, the Giovanni Zenatellos, and the Campaninis all stayed in the same Asbury Park resort community. In April 1917 in New York Raisa and Rimini made their first recordings for the Pathé Frères Company. (The recordings were not particularly successful and were not heavily promoted by Pathé.) Then in late August they traveled to Mexico City for a two-month season under Giorgio Polacco at the Teatro Arabu, with some outdoor performances presented in the huge Plaza del Toreo. Raisa sang eleven *Aidas*, her first *Trovatores* seven times, and *L'Africana* twice. In his autobiography *I, a Sinner*, José Mojica recalled that on the train ride to Mexico the very curious Raisa and Rimini peppered him with questions about the Mexican revolution.[6] On the way back to Chicago they learned more about the turbulent Mexican scene than they ever wanted to know. Gunshots rang out, and their train braked to a halt. Pancho Villa, the revolutionary, politician, and sometime bandit, boarded the train with his confederates, apparently intending to rob the passengers. Raisa explained that they were merely opera singers, and proved this by rendering in operatic fashion the Mexican song "El Guitarrico." Villa was delighted; instead of robbing the singers he treated them to glasses of liquor and granted them safe passage. It is not clear whether the Pancho Villa incident, a staple of Raisa's publicity, took place in 1917 or 1919.

The preparation for Raisa's Mexico debut was not without incident. The company opened the season on August 31 with *Otello*, starring Zenatello in the title part with Anna Fitziu as Desdemona and Rimini as Iago, and *La Bohème* the next night with Maggie Teyte and Giuseppe Taccani as the lovers. The first two operas were not successful at the box office. In her memoir Raisa reports on this sorry beginning of their season:

᛭ Mr. Sigaldi, the impresario, was not happy about this, to say the least. So everyone looked forward to *Aida*, the well-known opera, beloved by the Mexicans and therefore, it was hoped, a moneymaker to pull them out of the red. The general rehearsal came, and right after "Ritorna vincitor," Mr. Sigaldi came with beaming face, already assured that the performance would be a great success. Then came the second act and everything went fine until my cadenza. When I took the B-flat pianissimo, swelled the tone and then back again to pianissimo, continuing on one breath until the next phrase "Ma-tu-o-re, tu-signore possente," Maestro Polacco stopped me, saying: "You made the cadenza too long." He wanted me to sing it without stopping on the B-flat. I was very upset about this and answered: "This is the way I always sang it at La Scala, the Costanzi in Rome, and the Colón, Buenos Aires." And here it was Mr. Rimini, the Amonasro, who stepped in to make an eloquent plea on my behalf. "Who are you anyway?" asked Maestro Polacco. "I only know you as Amonasro." "Let Miss Raisa do it her way," said Rimini, "the way in which she has been a great success. This *Aida* must be the triumph of the season. Let us all cooperate Maestro." And so the rehearsal finished quietly. The next evening it was just as we expected! The audience gave me a tremendous ovation right there, and on the cadenza with the B-flat, and when I sang the high C the applause was so thunderous I thought the house was on fire! And, after the "Patria mia," the public gave me a demonstration as is rarely given anywhere and that stopped the show! Maestro Polacco and the impresario came to my dressing room beaming with joy, and with a bottle of champagne, toasting and embracing me for rescuing the season out of its critical situation. ✒

This unpleasant rehearsal confrontation and later post-performance reconciliation was the beginning of what was to become a very close personal friendship between Polacco and Raisa and Rimini, a relationship that would continue throughout their stage careers and beyond, through the rest of their lives. (Although Raisa had sung *Aida* and *Mefistofele* under Polacco at Covent Garden in 1914, the 1917 Mexico season was their first serious collaboration in working on an opera from the ground up. In London she was in the second cast of *Aida*, following Destinn, and in the *Mefistofele* she sang Elena, the second soprano role.)

The 1917–1918 Chicago season was again one of consolidation, featuring repeats of operas that had been successful in past seasons. Mascagni's *Isabeau* was presented on opening night, November 12 (it was preceded by a "ringing rendition of the national anthem with stunning B-flats"). The season also included what was to be a Raisa-Rimini vehicle for the remainder of their careers, Wolf-Ferrari's *I Gioielli della Madonna (Jewels of the Madonna)*. This melodrama was always

Writing to her father in Poland. A set of Berlitz dictionaries can be seen on the desk to her left. Daguerre Studio, Chicago.

advertised in Chicago by its English title, although it was performed in Italian.

The *Isabeau* presentation was part of Campanini's policy of staging significant new works from the Italian stage. Press comment in Chicago and later in New York was not favorable to this opera, but Raisa's impersonation of Isabeau (based on the Lady Godiva legend) was generally well received. Regarding her Isabeau, Hackett in the *Post* opined,

Miss Raisa sang magnificently all the evening, and in the final scene reached the greatest height of dramatic intensity and tonal beauty she has ever attained. During the past summer the voice has matured in most gratifying fashion, so that the acidity which was apt to creep into the tone has mellowed into the lusciousness of ripe fruit. Her power seemed unlimited and the tones soared out over the orchestra as the dominating note, no matter what the thunderous volumes surged about her. The score was very rich and colorful and Mr. Campanini brought it all out with masterly command as if his heart was in his work. Also he knew just how much Miss. Raisa could stand, and let his men go with full confidence.

Regarding her Maliella in *I Gioielli della Madonna* there was no equivocation; this was to be "her" role and she played it to the hilt. The *Tribune* reviewed her interpretation:

Miss Raisa yesterday confirmed the suspicion that she would be a first rate reason for restoring "The Jewels of the Madonna" to the active repertoire of the Chicago Opera. The least praise that may be uttered for Raisa and Crimi is that they were better than their predecessors. She hung her Maliella on the line with the best achievements of the women in dramatic opera. The role submitted no musical task to the best singer of Santuzza, of Aida, and Mrs. Ford the stage has known. Her facile gift for good acting was again made clear with an imper-sonation of the sex-conscious foundling that may be described as vivid, live, in exact relation to the drama, and, in terms of opera, credible. Her acting had reason, detail, color, feeling, and the reticence which is this season's addition to her inventory of admirable attributes.

In this season Campanini took a big risk in taking his company to both New York and Boston for extended visits. This bold move placed him in direct competition with the Metropolitan Opera and held his company up to the closest possible critical scrutiny. He felt strongly that his forces were equal to the challenge. After all, he had Mary Garden, already a New York favorite from her Manhattan Opera days; Galli-Curci, whose recordings were already being issued by Victor

The young Giacomo Rimini, Mexico, 1917.

and who was the subject of a big publicity campaign; matinee idol Lucien Muratore; Nellie Melba, who returned to the Chicago company this season; and his new dramatic soprano, Raisa. The Chicago forces took up residence at the Lexington Opera House on East 51st Street. They opened January 23 with *Monna Vanna*, starring Garden, Muratore, Georges Baklanoff, and Huberdeau; the second night was *I Gioielli della Madonna*, with Raisa and Rimini. Excitement and anticipation were in the air, as some of the opera public had heard about

Raisa through the grapevine, but there was not a full house. The *New York Times* reported:

> Rosa Raisa has a voice of uncommon richness, power, warmth, and natural beauty, and she displayed the heedless prodigality of youth in her use of it. She seized in extraordinary fashion an opportunity to make the theater ring with that voice as she climbed the stairs in the Naples hovel in Act 2, while pouring down top notes, plaintive, passionate, hateful, hysterical, less to Gennaro's edification than to the delight of the house, and to its frankly invited ovation, which was a hearty one. Maliella is not a sympathetic character, the second act ending as the girl sinks into one lover's arms, while murmuring another's name, is a damper to most audiences. Nevertheless Miss Raisa received a dozen curtain calls, three of them alone after that episode, and her singing in other operas will be awaited with much interest.

William J. Henderson in the *Sun* noted, "Miss Raisa proved to be a singer of excellent qualities. Her voice is full and rich and of large power. It is not perfectly equalized—few voices are—and the upper register is prone to openness. But it is so fresh and so genuinely beautiful that it cannot fail to give pleasure to the hearer. Miss Raisa sang the music of Maliella with temperament and dramatic skill. Her impersonation as a whole had direct force and intelligence. And withal she is good to see." The *Tribune* said, "New York has made the acquaintance of an extraordinary voice, if not yet a perfect artist. Mme. Raisa's voice is one of tremendous power and great sensuous beauty. In her singing, even in fortissimo passages, she produces her tones without effort, yet she is able to carry the pianissimo into the furthest corners of the house. . . . Emotion is not properly expressed by frenzied rolling of the eyeballs." The public's desire to see her in other operas was satisfied a week later in *Aida*. The *Brooklyn Eagle's* reporter wrote:

> It was apparent when she sang in the *Jewels of the Madonna* that this Polish soprano was the possessor of a thrillingly beautiful dramatic voice, but it remained for last evening for her to disclose its full value.

Throughout she sang with wondrous opulence of tone, but in addition she tempered her singing with fine nuance and shading. In it is a full sensuousness which no other dramatic soprano of recent years has attained. The high point of her vocal achievement came in the Nile scene when she sang the "Patria mia" so well that the applause following held up the opera for many minutes. There was an urgent demand for a repetition, but the singer insisted upon continuing with the action. Raisa's characterization is not conceived along the lines of high tragedy, and accordingly is not the ideal performance. But it is so vital, so intense, so sweeping in its tragic power that it must rank with the great Aidas of all time. This Aida is a beautiful savage, rich in temperament and in emotional force, almost a young animal in its unrestricted action and singing, but it is one to stir the blood of even the most sluggish listener.

Henderson attended the *Isabeau* given on February 14 and evaluated the new work. "The opera will probably not make a deep scar upon the public memory. It was very kind of Mr. Campanini to let us hear it. We should always be ready to welcome new art works, to give them our attention and to bid them a kindly adieu if they turn out not to be to our taste." About the vocal performance Henderson wrote, "The best thing about *Isabeau*, as far as could be seen last evening, was the performance of Rosa Raisa, a young singer who was also commended in that uplifting opera *The Jewels of the Madonna*. She is a lyric soprano whose voice has abundant power and excellent quality. It has been fairly well trained, and is generally produced naturally and without forcing." He was less impressed with her embodiment of the title role: "Her impersonation was not of striking theatrical importance, but it had grace and modesty to commend it. Much fuss was made about her by auditors who had apparently gone to the theater purposely to make just that fuss." After the company left New York for a two-week stand in Boston, Henderson in one of his overview essays about the just-concluded Chicago Opera visit thought, "Miss Raisa turned out to be a good Italian dramatic soprano, quite worthy of attention and capable of giving general pleasure. That she was not the combination of Pasta, Malibran, and Giulia Grisi described by the 'passionate press agent' was not her fault. It is a pity that any one had been persuaded to expect so much of her." Is it possible that the aggressive press agentry employed by the Chicago company to boost their new star set up a somewhat negative reaction on the part of very knowledgeable critics and predisposed them to search out negatives, if only to disprove exaggerated claims?

When the company moved on to Boston critics as severe as those in New York, notably Philip Hale, Olin Downes (then the critic at the *Boston Post*), and Henry T. Parker evaluated Raisa. Hale opined:

> Miss Raisa took the part of Santuzza for the first time in this city and her impersonation will not soon be forgotten. Strikingly handsome, her face was as a tragic masque. She sang with a passionate intensity that swept all before it and the sensuous opulence of her beautiful and expressive voice was fully revealed. Her acting rivaled her singing in poignant emotional expression. Not for a moment did the character seem a creation of the librettist but a woman of flesh and blood tortured with loving, crazed by fear and shame, mad with jealousy. Miss Raisa has already shown herself to be an accomplished and versatile artist in roles of less flaming intensity. Last evening she was seen as a tragic actress of the first rank.

The "Bertha story," one of Raisa's choice anecdotes, recounted often over the years, dates from this first season in Boston. Raisa's Bialystok friend Bertha Levin challenged her in 1905 that she probably would not deign to recognize her childhood companion when she became a great opera star. Bertha had read about this Bialystok-born opera singer in a Yiddish newspaper, *The Forward*. From such biographical details as her age and the street on which she had lived, Levin assumed this Rosa Raisa must be her childhood friend Raitza Burchstein. Bertha wrote to Maestro Campanini asking if her assumption was correct. Raisa sent her front-row tickets for the Boston opening of *Aida* on February 18. Backstage after the performance, the two friends, breaking protocol, embraced in a tearful reunion before Raisa shook hands and exchanged pleasantries with the governor of Massachusetts and the mayor of Boston.

Maliella in I Gioielli della Madonna, *1917. The Neapolitan girl from the slums was one of her most popular roles. Moffett Studio, Chicago.*

The Chicago Opera's presence in New York produced a level of excitement that even helped the Metropolitan Opera in terms of attendance. After the eastern tour Campanini told the *Musical Leader,* "One evening I ran into Otto Kahn at the Lexington and we had a very pleasant chat together. He told me that he knew something of the difficulties under which I had labored and that frankly he had not believed I could overcome them, but added that there was no questioning the fact after being present at the performances at the Lexington." About the element of competition with Kahn's Metropolitan Opera, "He also told me that it had been a good thing for the Metropolitan, for it had stirred up the interest of the public so that their receipts had never been so large as during our visit to the other opera house." This phenomenon is well known in marketing; competition and the inevitable press attention work to everyone's advantage, especially when both products are of roughly equivalent quality.

In addition to her operatic appearances in New York and Boston, Raisa embarked on a concert career in those cities and other major music centers in the United States. She had already given some concerts in Chicago, and she now felt ready to show her comfort with, if not her total mastery of, this more intimate medium before the very severe New York critics who thought her only a large-scale opera singer. In one eight-day period in New York she sang before a total of 15,000 people in two Hippodrome concerts and one at Carnegie Hall. The Hippodrome was hardly an intimate theater; it was in fact a huge arena that also hosted vaudeville, circuses, and Sunday night concerts for the masses. For her Hippodrome concerts Raisa programmed *arie antiche,* operatic arias, duets with Rimini, and Russian and Yiddish songs; for the more fastidious audiences at Carnegie Hall she presented some of the same elements but also some French and American art songs. Max Smith in the *New York American* summed up Raisa's New York operatic and concert activity thus:

> After yesterday's experience I am inclined to go even further—though it may be at the risk of being accused of exaggeration—and to assert that her voice is the most marvelous, the most glorious voice of any

kind or character, barring none, which has come under my observation in many a year. Certainly I can think of no voice of the present day that combines in itself so many notable traits, sheer beauty of timbre, largeness of scope, uniformity of quality, power and delicacy, elasticity, and expressiveness. Nor can I think of any singer who manages his or her resources with greater poise, with greater ease and with fewer manifestations of physical stress and strain.

The New York City Hippodrome on Sixth Avenue and West 43rd Street had a flexible seating capacity of between 5,200 and 6,200, depending on the seating configuration. More than 1,000 stage seats were available if needed. The prices for the Sunday night concerts "for the masses" were inexpensive, thus making it possible for the city's large immigrant population to attend. For attractions such as Raisa, Galli-Curci, Ruffo, Tetrazzini, McCormack, Alma Gluck, violinists Eugène Ysaÿe and Efrem Zimbalist, and the Vatican Choir, for example, promoters were able to sell enough tickets to make a profit even after paying the stars their high fees. A very young Sol Hurok started his American career presenting celebrity concerts in this large theater, often advertising them only in the Yiddish, Italian, and Russian press.

Of Raisa's Carnegie Hall recital Richard Aldrich noted that "Olive Fremstad and Sophie Braslau were among those who heard, with shining eyes and shouts of approval, the first exhibition of Raisa's great dramatic talent applied to the little lyrics of the more intimate sort, Russian songs by Arensky and Rachmaninoff, and many encores in the singer's native tongue." Commenting on the audience's behavior, Aldrich added, "The galleries shouted also for the Hebrew 'Eili, Eili,' which they did not get. . . . Miss Raisa has before now proved herself a singer of remarkable natural powers. Her sustained phrasing and wealth of golden tone earned an ovation for the great air, rarely attempted, of the 'Casta Diva' from *Norma*."[7] Henry T. Finck chimed in: "Rosa Raisa's singing in concert halls has proved a delightful surprise even to those who admired her most as an operatic artist. Her voice has the luscious flavor of a ripe Brazilian pineapple. It seems in turn a real soprano and a mezzo, while in Mozart's 'Voi che sapete' it had the true contralto quality, combined with ingratiating warmth of expression." He happily noted that "One of the songs she had to repeat was Weckerlin's [arrangement of] 'Jeunes filletes,' which was indeed the most agreeable surprise of the afternoon. By the beauty of her tones and the arch delivery of this number she reminded one strongly of Marcella Sembrich." In later years Raisa and Rimini often closed the first half of their joint concerts with the sparkling duet from *Don Pasquale*.

Chapter Five

NORMA

AFTER her operatic and concert successes in the eastern United States Raisa went to South America for her third season. It was wartime and she sailed to Rio de Janeiro on a small Swedish boat, a trip that took almost a month. From Rio she sailed to Buenos Aires on a more conventional, larger ship. Gino Marinuzzi had asked her to prepare for *Il Tabarro, Hérodiade,* and *Norma.* The *Tabarro* was not given, and Yvonne Gall sang Salomé in *Hérodiade.* For the season Raisa gave *Norma* ten times in Buenos Aires alone, with Gabriella Besanzoni, Catullo Maestri/Paul Franz, and Gaudio Mansueto; Marinuzzi conducted. At the time, the impresario Walter Mocchi recalled these performances of *Norma* as being the greatest events in his long career presenting opera.[1] *Aida, Falstaff, Un Ballo in Maschera,* and *Don Giovanni* were her other assignments for the season, all performed with stellar casts. *Musical America*'s Buenos Aires correspondent wired, "*Norma,* which was probably given at the request of Rosa Raisa, was simply loved by the audience. The last act was good due to the dramatic singing of Raisa and Besanzoni. In this act Raisa indeed surpasses herself. The high, dramatic angry notes rang out wonderfully and her low chest effects were also grand." Raisa herself in retrospect counted these first *Norma*s among the highlights of her career, recalling that members of the chorus had tears in their eyes, and audiences nearly went crazy with frenzied ovations.

In one of the few detailed descriptions of her performances included in her memoirs, Raisa recalled,

From the moment I came out on the stage I knew that I was in complete control of the situation. Despite the critical audience and

Before leaving for Argentina in 1918, Raisa took her designer costumes to Mish-kin's studio in New York for her first Norma photos, which would become famous. (Metropolitan Opera Archives.)

fully aware of the difficult task ahead of me, I was completely at ease and sang my part with imposing authority. Majestically I commanded my people (the Druids) urging them with regal dignity to "peace." There was sincerity and conviction in my bearing as well as my song, while giving full value also to the pauses, which are so essential for conveying fully the dramatic message. And when I finished with an A-flat "Il sacro vishio io mieto," making a *messa di voce*, I could sense the approval of the hushed assembly. This was like the visiting card of introduction to the audience in order to acquaint them with the kind of Norma they were to meet that night. I felt that great moments were in store for me. The public was already at my command, for I sang the "Casta Diva" reverently and prayerfully as though I had been transported and transfixed as I stood there facing the assembled Druids. I knew that I had everyone entranced. And when I finished the cadenza that Barbara Marchisio had taught me, just as her sister Carlotta used to do, a different cadenza than any in use—with a trill on the F-E resolving with an F pianissimo, swelling and then descending again, pianissimo, the applause was deafening. I remained motionless under the influence of the great moment and inspiring music without bowing. At this point I was thoroughly convinced that I had conquered. Then came the "allegro," after which I walked off the stage in regal splendor with the high C. I could sense the warm reaction of the public and I anticipated the tremendous ovation that was to follow. This was truly a tremendous ovation. It was then that general manager Mr. Mocchi came backstage exclaiming: "From now on you may do as you please; the public is at your feet." In the second act, the duet and cadenza went off perfectly. It was just as though one voice were singing. And the high D natural which I used to insert at the end of the second act consummated a crescendo of triumphs for both Gabriella [Besanzoni] and myself. And this was carried over by us into the third act, after which we were triumphantly acclaimed; while at the end of the entire performance we were given a standing ovation. The public would not let us go, and the casueleras in the fifth row of the balcony, the most enthusiastic of the spectators, called us again and again by our individual names, while showering flowers upon us in appreciation. I was so deeply touched that my thoughts went out in gratitude to God, to my wonderful teacher Barbara Marchisio, and my father who could not be present at this memorable evening. ੭ᚴ

This account tells us things about Raisa and her performing style and interpretation, and even more about her sense of proportion, occasion, and values.

After Buenos Aires, she performed in Montevideo, Rio de Janeiro, São Paulo, and Recife; she returned to New York and then left for Chicago for the 1918–1919 season. In Chicago she repeated several of her roles, and added *Tosca* and *La Gioconda* to her growing list of operas. *Musical America* concentrated on her visual presentation of Tosca:

> She is a most severe critic, and thus when she undertakes a new part it is only because she knows that the part is well suited to her. Miss Raisa was again right, as her Tosca lived up to expectations. In the first act, all in green, she was regal to the eye, while in the second act she dazzled in her gorgeous evening gown and sparkling diamond diadem and was a vision of grace and beauty. She had no doubt made a close study, as her Tosca was certainly original in many ways. It was seductive, alluring, jealous and courageous. Raisa's Tosca was never afraid of any Scarpia. She fought the aristocratic chief of police before pleading with him. She grabbed him by his coat lapels and shook him as though he were a vulgar malefactor, and only when she found out that her valiant attitude irritated her antagonist did she employ other tactics. Scarpia to her was only a chief of police, a man who would accept graft, but when she found out the villainous design of the brutal inquisitor, she flaunted her rage and, though near complete collapse, her brain worked fast and her mind was made up as to what the ending would be—his death. She knew not how. Would she strangle him? Would she beat him? But murdered he should be, and when her glance fell on the shining knife she knew that her salvation would come. In the third act she appeared radiant, jubilant, unafraid, expectant, and once more she vibrated with love and passion. Her singing of the role can easily be compared to the very best, and her delineation equaled

that of the most famous actresses [Sarah Bernhardt?] who have appeared in the drama.

Raisa's first Chicago *Tosca* featured other notable histrionic elements that continued after Scarpia's death. Alessandro Dolci's superb voice was matched with the most insufferable tenor posturing and attitudes. Raisa made her point in the Third Act, as Edward Moore recounts in his history of the company: "Raisa managed to fling herself in such a way [over the supposedly dead Mario's body] that two vigorous elbows bored into what can be best described as his equatorial line. With a grunt that could be heard out in the lobby, Dolci's feet went up in the air and he deflated like a burst football." Moore continued, "Even that was not enough for Raisa, for in getting up to run over to the parapet before jumping over it, she quite by accident, of course, stepped on his palm with the sharp heel of her shoe. The audience burst into a shout of laughter, and Polacco nearly had a fit because his line of vision was cut off by the top of the stage and he could not see what was happening further back."[2]

Of her first Gioconda, Frederick Donaghey in the *Tribune* wrote, "Often when I have written of Raisa as the most gifted of the dramatic women in opera, I am asked if I remember Destinn: and always do I wonder why anybody, having heard the former, should regard the latter as concerned in the comparison." He went on: "Nobody else is able to take a role like the ballad singer of this piece and in all ways makes so much of it as does Raisa. Saturday's was her first encounter with it; and she was immense in song and in drama, and an enchanting person to see. She vitalized every scene she touched."

A great moment in Chicago musical history came on Sunday night, December 26, 1918, the night after Christmas, when Campanini gave a performance of Rossini's *Stabat Mater* at the huge Medina Masonic Temple, with Raisa, Ruth Lutiger Gannon, Dolci, and Journet. In the "Inflammatus," in addition to the written high C's, Raisa added a stentorian high C at the conclusion. The *Chicago Journal* reported:

> If you do not believe that Rossini's sacred music has in it all the elements of emotional enthusiasm, you should have heard Miss Raisa

To Goldie Stone, her surrogate mother, from Mexico 1919. The inscription reads "fool of love" rather than "full of love"—Raisa often spelled English phonetically. Pertilla Studio, Mexico City. (Collection of the late Beatrice Balter.)

sing the "Inflammatus" last night. It was by a wide margin her high point of the season in singing, with all the enormous power of her voice pouring out in the number, but better controlled, more refined and more charming than in any of her operatic performances of the year. . . . The solo was a revelation in what singing of the first order can be. It moved Campanini to greet her with a chaste, artistic salute, and it moved the audience to disregard entirely the injunction that, in the interests of art, encores are to be excluded. In this case there was no exclusion. Miss Raisa sang the number again, this time a little more feelingly, a little more movingly than she had before. Anything that came after must have been a letdown. She had reached the pinnacle.[3]

The *Musical Courier* reported that the ovation she received was "the most spontaneous and longest demonstration ever accorded any singer at the Auditorium, and shouts of bravos, mingled with the stamping of feet, and thunderous plaudits, which lasted fully ten minutes."

At twenty-six, Raisa suffered her first major illness; she was rushed to the hospital on January 11 for an emergency appendectomy. She had to cancel her participation in the new production of *Loreley* that was being mounted as a vehicle for her, scheduled for January 17, as well as the remainder of the winter season in Chicago, New York, and Philadelphia. Anna Fitziu replaced her in the *Loreley*. Raisa later accompanied the troupe to New York and visited with many of her Metropolitan Opera friends, including Caruso and Rosa Ponselle. Her "mother," Goldie Stone, who took care of her during her convalescence, recalled that "Mr. Rimini met us at the station in Philadelphia. He greeted us most warmly. 'I have reserved a box for you. Mary Garden is singing in *Thais.*' No sooner had we entered our box when the audience focused its attention for several minutes on Raisa, bowing their effusive welcome on her return to the theater. Raisa acknowledged the compliment by bowing in return. The performance itself was interrupted for several minutes while Mary Garden stepped from the stage to extend her hand in welcome." Raisa was fully recovered the next week and sang her reentry *Trovatore* in Pittsburgh on March 13. She and Rimini returned to Mexico for a two-month sea-

In Mexico in 1919, relaxing with her good friend and colleague Gabriella Besan-zoni. Pertilla Studio, Mexico City. (Collection of the late Giulietta Segala.)

son. *Aida, Gli Ugonotti, Un Ballo in Maschera, Tosca, La Gioconda,* and *Norma* were her Mexico City offerings at the Teatro Esperanza Iris and the Plaza del Toreo alfresco performances. The Mexicans were as enthusiastic as the Argentinians and Brazilians had been for her Norma with Besanzoni. Many attendance records were broken that season.

The composer Italo Montemezzi in 1919 rehearsing Alessandro Dolci, Raisa, and Rimini in his spectacle, La Nave. *Chicago Opera photo.*

After the Mexico season Raisa returned to Italy for the summer, visiting family and friends and preparing new roles for the upcoming Chicago season. With the composer Italo Montemezzi she studied the role of Basiliola in *La Nave*, which had been chosen to open the 1919–1920 season. In his music memoirs, *First and Last Love*, the writer and opera historian Vincent Sheean recalled this rarely performed opera and his clear aural-visual memory of a huge ship center stage and Rosa Raisa in blue brocade "emitting notes of an awe-inspiring power."[4] *La Nave* had the distinction of being one of the most expensive productions in the history of the Chicago company. The innovative set designer Norman Bel Geddes designed its elaborate scenery, including the huge vessel Sheean vividly remembered. The opera was performed only twice. Another critic wrote of Raisa's Basiliola:

From the time of her second engagement with the Chicago Opera Company she has been a singer whose match is not to be found, a voice that hesitated at nothing in the dramatic repertoire, a beautiful woman, an intelligent artist. Last night she projected a definite compelling personality as well. She is a glory to the Company and a glory to Chicago, is this lithe, slender woman. Never in a generation was a voice so ringing and powerful. Now that it is overlaid with color, now that she uses it to express emotion as well as to interpret music, now that it reflects the play of expression in her face and the pose of her body, a singing actress has become a different person."

(While a college student in Chicago Sheean ushered at the Chicago Opera. Raisa was one of Sheean's first important singers, along with Mary Garden and Galli-Curci. He went on to cover the period from Raisa to Callas. In 1962 I asked him for additional memories of Raisa, and he wrote, "Her Norma remains in my memory the best I ever heard." He also thought that there were sounds in her voice that reminded him more of Leontyne Price than of Rosa Ponselle, to whom most people compared her. Regarding Raisa's stamina and extravagance, he said, "She tended to throw everything away with the utmost abandon and then throw everything else after it—and the astonishing thing was that there was always something else left to throw!")[5]

In March Campanini heard Cantor Yossele Rosenblatt in concert in Chicago. He was impressed and felt Rosenblatt's voice was of operatic caliber. He formed the idea of presenting the cantor as Eléazer in *La Juive*. At Rosenblatt's request Campanini wrote on March 21, 1918, to the president of his congregation outlining ideas for the engagement. There were to be no Friday night or Saturday matinee performances, he wouldn't have to shave off his beard, and nothing "would reflect in a negative way on the orthodox Jewish faith." And the "role of The Jewess would be sung by Rosa Raisa, who is a Jewess, a native of Odessa [sic]." Rosenblatt declined this unique offer; Raisa waited until the 1922–1923 season to present her much-anticipated Rachel. Rosenblatt's son, in his memoir of his father, recalled Raisa's visit in 1918 to a synagogue on Watkins Street in the Brownsville section of Brooklyn: "She was determined to hear the little chazan who had made so deep an impression on Maestro Campanini, even though she had to stand throughout the service. And stand she did—in prominent view of the women's gallery, with the eyes of a large part of the assemblage glued on her as she followed every note of the cantor's recitation of the Mussaph prayer."[6]

The 1919–1920 season started with a three-week tour of the Midwest; Raisa sang *Aida* nine times in nine different cities in a nineteen-day span. In Milwaukee she took over the Amelia in *Ballo* from an indisposed Ema Destinnová, who was scheduled to perform a similar feat by singing on the in-between days; thus Raisa sang ten times in nine cities and Destinnova a mere eight! (The Czech nationalist Emmy Destinn, after the Great War, preferred to be known by the Czech form of her name, Destinnová.)

Puccini's *Il Trittico* was to be a major Chicago offering in that season, with Carlo Galeffi in two assumptions: the title role in *Gianni Schicchi* and Michele in *Il Tabarro*. *Suor Angelica* was for many the centerpiece of the trilogy. Back in Italy Puccini had been given reports on the viability of his new work. He wrote to Sybil Seligman, "In New York with Farrar, who has no voice left, it had a great success, and then the part was taken up by Raisa and sent the public of Chicago into a delirium of enthusiasm."[7]

Campanini's health, which had been deteriorating at the beginning of the season, finally failed, and he died on Friday, December 19. His funeral was held on the stage of the Auditorium on Sunday, December 21, with the Act III *Parsifal* set as backdrop. The *Tribune's* account of the service read:

> Thousands who packed the theater scarcely breathed as the velvet curtains of the stage were slowly raised, revealing the casket containing the body of the maestro lying in state beneath a blanket of violets. . . . There were flowers everywhere, tributes from friends and admirers . . . the orchestra pit was filled with them. Great set pieces and large bouquets filled the maestro's private box and overflowed into four adjacent boxes. The orchestra, concealed behind the stage setting, broke

Raisa in 1919 as the nun in Suor Angelica. *Of all her Catholic heroines this is the only role in which Raisa wore a cross on stage. Daguerre Studio, Chicago.*

the spell with the opening chords of the prelude from Saint-Saëns' "Deluge" with Charlier conducting. More silence. A great wind made the candles flicker and carried the scent of the flowers to the closely packed devotees in the auditorium. Bonci's voice intoning "Verdi's Requiem" ["Ingemisco"] floated from behind the stage settings. De Angelis was conducting. Silence reigned once more—someone dropped a small coin and the noise seemed thunderous—then Rosa Raisa's voice intoned the Rossini "Stabat Mater" ["Inflammatus"]. The fourth movement of Tchaikovsky's "Pathetique" marked the close of the musical service. Marinuzzi conducted both numbers, unseen, as were all the others.[8]

A Mass was held the next day at Holy Name Cathedral and at that service Galli-Curci sang "Ave Maria," presumably the Schubert. In 1920 the company presented a Campanini memorial concert and Raisa again sang the "Inflammatus." Years later Raisa recalled the funeral service: "It was a very moving experience, overwhelming in its sorrow and sadness. To this day I do not know how I managed to go through with this performance, probably the most difficult of my entire career, overcome as I was with emotion and the sense of irreparable loss. I shall never forget those terrible moments." Edward Moore thought that "this number was peculiarly appropriate and peculiarly touching, for almost a year before Campanini had conducted the *Stabat Mater* one Sunday night at a concert in the Auditorium [actually the Medina Masonic Temple], and Miss Raisa had been fairly ablaze as she sang the excerpt. At the end, and while the audience was doing its collective best to raise the roof with applause, Campanini stepped off the stand, kissed Raisa on both cheeks, and then stepped back and repeated the number." Moore continues on a more personal note: "There it is now . . . an ornately sculptured stone memorial to his honor [in Parma], for which, though she declines to talk about it, Miss Raisa is largely responsible. For among other deeds in his busy life, Campanini discovered Raisa when she was very young and very poor, driven out from Poland into Italy. Having found her, he and Mme. Campanini [Eva Tetrazzini] gave her advice, instruction, material aid, and the encouragement to take the place in opera which she afterwards occupied. And Raisa is not the person to forget." [9]

Campanini's death, Raisa recollected,

શ shocked me violently since he was not only a splendid artist but he had also been so good to me, following my career with utmost devotion, affection, and pride, having been the first to give me the great opportunities of my career. I was heartbroken at losing so good and true a friend and benefactor to whom I owed so much for his faith in my talent. A great man of the theater, he had his performances always under complete control and in masterful fashion, and he also displayed a great ability in managing the Chicago Opera for many years with many innovations. He injected new life by introducing operas of the French repertoire and bringing over artists like Mary Garden, Geneviève Vix, Lucien Muratore, Hector Dufranne, Vanni-Marcoux, Georges Baklanoff, and several others of equal merit. ટ

Campanini was much loved by the musical press corps, and it is from his candid interviews over the years that we know of his unshakable belief in Raisa's potential to eventually become one of the great dramatic sopranos of the era. For her first season he announced her, surprisingly, as Linda in *Linda di Chamonix* with Ruffo. In later seasons he announced his plans to produce Pacini's *Saffo*, Mascagni's *Le Maschere*, Tasca's *A Santa Lucia*, and even Verdi's *Don Carlos* as Raisa vehicles. In late 1918 he told the press he was trying to secure first performance rights to Strauss's new opera *Die Frau ohne Schatten*, saying that he understood that there were good roles in this work for Raisa and Garden, clearly the Empress for Raisa and Barak's Wife for Garden. This tantalizing project reveals that Campanini considered Raisa capable of appearing in modern "singing actress" parts alongside Mary Garden, the "doyenne" of singing actresses. That none of these projects materialized is less important than that they were being seriously considered.

· *Chapter Six* ·

MARY GARDEN

CAMPANINI on his deathbed designated Gino Marinuzzi as his successor. Marinuzzi immediately assumed the music director-ship of the company, but it was to be a very difficult assignment. Mid-way through the following season (1920–1921)[1] he gave up his lead-ership post after nearly suffering a nervous breakdown because of the company's poisonous internal politics. The straw that broke the camel's back was the Walska affair. Ganna Walska was a Polish beauty and collector of extremely rich husbands and at that time the love of Harold McCormick, the heir to the farm machinery fortune and the principal benefactor of the opera company. Harold McCormick was at the time married to Edith Rockefeller, John D.'s daughter; the two would later divorce and he would marry Walska. Walska thought of herself as a potentially great opera singer, and her Chicago Opera de-but was to be in Leoncavallo's *Zaza* on December 21, 1920. Early in the rehearsal stage it became clear that Marinuzzi could not work with Walska, and he turned the opera over to conductor Pietro Cimini. The new maestro asked Walska at one of the rehearsals to sing in her natu-ral voice. Offended, she cried out, "Pig, you would ruin my perfor-mance!" She left the stage in a huff, ran into the business manager's office, and told Herbert Johnson and Marinuzzi, "Gentlemen, I am packing my bags, and at the end of the season you will be packing yours."[2] Mary Garden became the director (the "directa," as she pre-ferred to be called) at the behest of McCormick. She agreed to take the job for one year only, but the singers were not told this. It was Garden's wish to keep the length of her tenure secret in order to keep the artists in line. Raisa, Rimini, and many other artists of the Italian wing of the company were unhappy and very nervous with the pros-

Mary Garden (on the telephone) and Edith Mason in Garden's office at the Chicago Opera, 1921. Moffett Studio, Chicago. (Metropolitan Opera Archives.)

pect of Garden running the organization; they wrongly assumed the devaluation of Italian opera in what they felt was now to be an essentially French company. Garden in her autobiography rightly notes the impossibility of directing a viable opera company in America without a strong Italian presence. She also indicates that she thought the Italian singers foolish children.[3] Actually, in Garden's one and a half seasons as "directa" Raisa sang more performances than had been her average up to then.

An important event in Raisa's career was the unveiling of her Norma in New York City. The first performance, planned for opening night, was delayed a week because of a stubborn bout of flu. New York's operatic public eagerly anticipated this presentation, which sold out immediately. In 1920 America, Italian verismo and the modern French works favored by Mary Garden were the rage. *Norma* was considered an impossibly old-fashioned, almost hurdy-gurdy work that could be justified only if the title part was taken by a very special, almost a supreme singer—one who had all the requisite vocal, technical, and dramatic skills. The critics were prepared to savage an opera they considered passé, and its protagonist, if she was less than perfect. Dated or not, the music was considered sacrosanct. Raisa's great success in this opera in South America, Mexico, and Chicago counted for next to nothing. For most critics, Lilli Lehmann's Norma a quarter of a century before was the touchstone. Additionally, Chicago's annual visits to New York were becoming something of an irritant to the establishment; New York felt it didn't need to be taught any lessons or shown up in any way by what some considered the upstart company from the Midwest.

The opera opened on February 3, and was reviewed in rather lukewarm terms by the great critic and writer James Gibbons Huneker.

Your reporter of musical happenings heard Rosa Raisa for the first time. We still gape with astonishment over the length, breadth, and thickness of her voice. Surely such an organ could have come only from Russia, where she-basses are the most sonorous in the world. Here is a soprano that is extraordinary in quantity, though not in quality. Evidently the handsome young woman has been suffering from a cold; its traces misted the shining surface of those steely tones. But there was an immense reserve, enough to supply ten sopranos. Years ago Katrina [Katharina] Klafsky came over to join Walter Damrosch's company. She looked like a cook but sang like a choir of angels, very large, muscular angels. And then there was the Hoboken Foghorn, so nicknamed because when the wind was favorable you could overhear her in the wet little New Jersey town. She sang at the Metropolitan and was drowned with her husband, Theodore Bertram, the baritone, off the Hook of Holland. Never mind her name [Fanny Moran-Olden]. Her voice too would have paled before the voice of Miss Raisa. But there are qualifications to be made. The niceties of vocal art are not hers. She relies on the bellows concealed in her person. She employed half a dozen tone productions in "Casta Diva," abused the glottis stroke, abused nasal resonance, allowed her lower tones to be unsupported, and shrieked above A natural. There is a well-defined break between her F and G. Her coloratura is full of joints, metallic, heavy, never suggesting airiness or limpidity. She delivers them by sheer strength, and her climax in Act I was a prolonged scream. This unpleasant, strident quality masks the native brilliancy of a glorious voice that ought to roll forth with the mellowness of a French horn. But it doesn't. It is too frequently forced. . . . However, Miss Raisa is a prime favorite, and if she does give too prodigally, at least she has the vocal material. She is striking looking, a stately Norma, but of the grand manner she has no idea. She is voice, and nothing but voice.

Yet the *Post*'s Henry Theophilos Finck had a very different reaction: "Who is the greatest opera singer of the day, next to Enrico Caruso? There can be only one answer to this question: Rosa Raisa is her name. Last night she returned to the Lexington and as Norma in Bellini's masterwork electrified a crowded audience, giving the most glorious, the most thrilling exhibition of vocal art heard in New York from any woman singer in two decades." And Finck goes on: "Rosa Raisa has no rivals. She stands alone. No other singer of our day could do Norma half as well as she did last night." Finck was a very sound and serious critic and musician, both a champion of and an authority on Wagner, but when he was very taken by and enthusiastic about an artist his quotable prose could read like a press agent's.

William J. Henderson, now if not then considered the dean of New York's critical fraternity, later chastised his fellow critics, many of whom dismissed Raisa by invoking Lilli Lehmann as the "gold standard" for heroic coloratura. He reminded them that

> If Miss Raisa's Norma was not in accord with all the traditions of its school nor faultless in the matter of style, it was none the less an imposing and impressive performance when measured by the standards of contemporaneous operatic art. The soprano's voice is one of the most beautiful dramatic organs ever heard by this public. Her attack is not good, but neither was Lehmann's. She indulges in some exaggerations in nuance and her fiorituri are sometimes ragged, but her best phrases are extraordinarily beautiful. She never before sang anything here with so much genuine art, so much sincerity and so much worthy achievement as she sang Norma, and her assumption of the role added greatly to her stature as an artist.[4]

In a slightly hyperbolic vein, William Murray in the *Brooklyn Eagle* wrote,

> Rosa Raisa's voice is still matchless, though since our last hearing of its tremendous outpouring it has lost some of its original velvet. The singer pounds the life out of her natural resources. These must be the stoutest and thickest vocal cords in the world, otherwise they could not have stood up under the pile-driving pounding. We have never heard so much volume out of a human throat as was poured forth in the two performances of "Norma." Her singing of the role in question recalled to old-timers the heyday of Lilli Lehmann's American career, but we are certain that the great Lilli had not the gifts which God has showered on Raisa. Pressed, we might call it the voice of the age. And what the singer might accomplish were she to be convinced that even in singing discretion is the better part of valor![5]

Interestingly, the young Rosa Ponselle attended the Raisa *Norma* and confided to friends who had been urging her to study the role

that she felt she could not handle it. Of Raisa's Norma she later recounted, "Oh, she was a *great* Norma! When I heard Raisa in *Norma*,
it scared the life out of me. That's how demanding I thought it was. I
never heard so much coloratura for a dramatic soprano—and so many
high Cs!" When asked later to describe the difference between their
voices, she said, "Raisa had a marvelous voice—a big, bright sound,
especially at the top. It was a real dramatic soprano, and her voice was
right for *Norma*. And what a top! She could sing high Cs all day."[6]
Ponselle was already a friend of Raisa's, and for the rest of their lives
they formed a "mutual admiration society," as Ponselle described it.
Although seemingly unlikely, Ponselle would claim that Raisa was
present at her 1918 successful audition for Gatti-Casazza of the Met.[7]
Some years later she asked Raisa to sing Aida to her Amneris, thinking this might make for a wonderful vocal contrast, but contractual
complications prevented this dream from being realized.[8] When Ponselle was asked in 1977 by *High Fidelity* magazine to recall for them
some of the most memorable performances she ever witnessed, she
placed Raisa's performances of Maliella in *I Gioielli della Madonna*
and Norma, although very different from her own, on her all-time
top list. She also listed the great performances of Caruso, Chaliapin,
Scotti, De Luca, Muzio, Rethberg, and Destinn.[9]

In addition to *Norma* in New York Raisa also sang Alice Ford in
Falstaff (with Rimini), *Suor Angelica, Aida, Cavalleria,* and *Gio-
conda*. The company then played Boston, Pittsburgh, Detroit, and
Cleveland. For the first time in her young career Raisa did not sing in
South America or Mexico that summer. She returned to Italy for a
long vacation, and when she and Rimini surfaced in New York in late
September they announced that they had recently married, outside
Naples. Also waiting for Raisa in New York were her father, her stepmother, and her siblings Frieda and Aron; Raisa had lost contact with
her family, stranded in Bialystok during the Great War, and efforts
had been made through diplomatic channels, including the Vatican,
to help locate them. Now twenty-seven, Raisa was a married woman
with her family safely residing in New York. Another major event
was her signing an exclusive recording contract with Vocalion. She

was to be the featured singer of their new classical catalogue, which also was to include her new husband, Rimini, Marguerite D'Alvarez, Evelyn Scotney, Giulio Crimi, and Virgilio Lazzari. Her first Vocalion lateral records were recorded earlier in the year and issued in the autumn. (She had recorded five titles for Aeolian-Vocalion two years before.)

In her memoir Raisa details the process employed to bring her family to the United States:

After the First World War, a delegation was formed in Chicago consisting of Judge Harry Fisher, Mr. Neuman, and others to bring to America people whose relatives here wanted them to come over to this country. I immediately contacted the committee and gave them a considerable sum of money for my father to come to the U.S. with the other members of my family. When my father learned of this in Bialystok, he went to see them at once, armed with a photograph of myself as Tosca as proof of his identity. At the committee headquarters in Bialystok he was confronted by a long line of people waiting their turn to apply for admission to the U.S. He took his place at the end of the line. After standing there for some time he was told to come back the next day. He decided to take advantage of the fact that his daughter was a renowned celebrity in America and sent my picture of Tosca to the head of the delegation. The money that I entrusted to them was given him and he began preparations to come to America without delay. When my father arrived in New York, unfortunately I could not meet him at the dock, because I was then on the ocean returning from Italy. Before his arrival, however, I had purchased a house for him and had it completely furnished and equipped with every conceivable appurtenance, to a "T." All he had to do was hang up his hat!

Upon my return from Italy I went straight from the boat to my father's house to meet him and my brother Aron, my sister Frieda, and my stepmother. Many years had elapsed since we were last together and it was a great shock for him to see me after so long a time. Altogether it was a very touching family reunion. And my father and I would sit for hours and talk about my mother. He told me that I resembled my wonderful mother, and I was just as fine and noble as she had been. And he wanted to know whether I, too, always had cold feet as my mother used to have! My husband upon hearing this, would interrupt to say that they could not have been any colder than mine! And since he did not understand Russian [probably Yiddish] and therefore could not make out the substance of our dialogue, he was curious to know what there was so much to talk about! It seemed to him that we had an inexhaustible reservoir of material to draw from for our endless conversations.

My father would come regularly to Chicago and Boston to visit with me and to hear me sing. True Russian that he was, he always had a samovar on the table from which he would draw fresh tea—good, he thought, for any and all ailments. This he used to feed me with lemon, incessantly! But drinking tea with lemon would tend to make me still thinner than I already was, and at that time I needed extra weight! When my husband would catch him in the process of serving the tea to me, he would grab the glass from his hand and stop me from drinking. Poor father, he could not understand how anyone could object to tea with lemon! It just couldn't hurt anyone, it could only do good! ๛

Raisa's announced marriage to the "divorced" Rimini in Italy in the summer of 1920 is puzzling, because on November 10, she and Rimini were married (or remarried?) in a civil ceremony. They obtained their marriage license in nearby St. Joseph, Michigan, across the lake from Chicago, and later that day were married by a justice of the peace in the living room of Mrs. Stone. There seems to be no sensible explanation for this "second" marriage; perhaps this was their only marriage. In any event, their union was now legalized and they remained one of opera's first couples for the rest of their lives. A few days later, the press reported, a big reception was given for the new couple in the Elizabethan Room of the Congress Hotel, jointly hosted by Mrs. Rosenwald and Mrs. Rockefeller-McCormick, representing different branches of Chicago society.

The November 10, 1920, marriage license was applied for at the

Raisa with her father, Herschel, in the early 1920s. Raisa spent as much time with her adored father as her professional duties allowed. de Gueldre Studio, Chicago. (Collection of the late Frieda Goldenberg.)

County Clerk's office in Berrien County, Michigan. On the application James Rimini correctly asserts that he had one previous marriage; Raisa Burchstein indicates no previous marriage. This suggests that the announcement of their September marriage in Italy was not entirely candid. The best possible explanation is that they decided upon their return to America in the autumn to live openly as a married couple. It was obvious to most people who knew them that they had been living together since 1916. Rimini's friend Nicolas LoFranco and Raisa's adopted "mother," Goldie Stone, witnessed the marriage documents. After Rimini died in 1952, his daughter, Rafaella Bettei, sued for a substantial share of Rimini's estate. In the court papers she claimed that the November marriage was not legal, as Rimini was still married at that time to her mother, Delizia, although evidence was produced that Rimini had obtained a divorce in the United States in April 1920. Clearly Rimini could not have obtained a divorce in Italy, given Italian law at that time. There was no reference in the court documents to a late summer marriage to Raisa in Italy. In April 1920 one of Rimini's support payments to Delizia was returned by the postal authorities as "undeliverable." Rimini went immediately to the American courts claiming that his wife, Delizia, was "not found" and on the basis of that claim was awarded a divorce. This would clear him legally to marry Raisa.[10]

Raisa and Rimini usually spent the month of April in New York, where they attended opera performances and socialized with their many friends from the Metropolitan. Raisa's brother-in-law, Irving, recounted that in the 1920s he vividly remembered Beniamino Gigli, Schipa, Hackett, and Martinelli at various times attending as honored guests the Passover Seders at her father's home on Jessup Avenue in the West Bronx.

The 1920–1921 season started with a tour of six midwestern cities. Raisa did her Santuzza in *Cavalleria* coupled with *Pagliacci* starring Marcella Craft, Forrest Lamont, and Ruffo. *La Traviata*, with Frieda Hempel, Bonci, and Rimini, was the other offering. Raisa's new roles this season were Desdemona in *Otello* and Elsa in *Lohengrin*, sung in English. In 1914 Raisa had done an act of *Otello* as part of a gala at the Paris Opéra, and she had sung Elsa in German in Seattle. Charles Marshall was to make his debut as Otello, and for the next twelve seasons he would be the company's leading heroic tenor. He often sang with Raisa, as their dramatic repertory included the same operas.

Raisa as Elsa in the bridal chamber scene in Lohengrin, *1920. This German opera was given in English in the aftermath of the first World War. Of a 1922 German-language* Tannhäuser *in New York, the critic Oscar Thompson thought Raisa's German "came to the ears as a new language." H. A. Atwell Studio, Chicago.*

Raisa spoiled a planned public relations coup by informing some members of the press that in the *Otello* rehearsals she was thrilled with Marshall's remarkable and powerful voice; it was the company's plan to spring Marshall on the public as a great discovery. Of her first Maliella in *I Gioielli della Madonna* of the season, the *Post* critic noted:

> Rosa Raisa had an opportunity last evening and her singing was extraordinary. She fitted right into the spirit of the music and sang with warmth of tone quality as well as with astonishing brilliance of those high-sustained phrases. Just as a stunt her trill on the F-sharp, as she was mounting the stairs, followed by the high C, held out solid and dazzling as a rock of diamonds, if you can imagine such a thing, without any accompanying orchestral support, was a thing to talk about. Walking upstairs is not supposed to be the best preparation for the diaphragm when it has such a feat of virtuosity to perform, but Mme. Raisa acted as if such trivial details did not concern her in the least. She played the part with dramatic power and greater elasticity than usual.

When the company returned to New York in late January 1921, *Norma* was the opening-night opera. The qualms the old guard New York critics had expressed the season before were reinforced. Henderson stated: "Miss Rosa Raisa was defended when she first sang the title role on the ground that she was in a new field. Last night she revealed the fact that she had made no progress whatever. She displayed the same splendid voice and the same ignorance of the style of the work. Her phrasing of 'Casta Diva' covered the stage with the *disjecta membra* of vocal art." Henderson continued, "She made sad work of the florid passages in the great first scene, but she was very good to see." It is interesting to juxtapose a judgment such as Henderson's with the fact that Toscanini, who attended this performance and was surely as aware as Henderson of her imperfections, invited Raisa to give *Norma* and *La Wally* under his baton at the reopened Scala in December 1921. Toscanini was on tour in the United States with the Scala orchestra and he attended the sold-out performance as a standee;

Raisa was not able to accept this complimentary offer because of con-
flicts with her Chicago Opera commitments.[11] Having found his near-
ideal Norma and not succeeded in obtaining her services, Toscanini
was never to conduct this sublime opera in the mature twentieth-
century portion of his long and distinguished career.[12]

This season the tour took the company to the west coast. In addition to singing five times in two weeks in San Francisco, Raisa also
sang a noontime open-air concert at Lotta's Fountain, the scene of
Tetrazzini's famous concert several years previously. Newspaper reports and photos show an estimated 20,000 happy Californians at
this event.[13] So successful was this happening that the following year
(1922) it was given there twice. And in Los Angeles Raisa performed
a similar concert in Pershing Square. When a newspaper reporter
asked her about singing in the open, she said: "It is absurd to think
that the human voice is injured by singing out of doors. Do not the
birds sing in the free air? And do not ordinary individuals? Why not
then great singers, whose vocal equipment is so much stronger and
better developed than ordinary mortals?"[14]

The blistering criticism by some of the most distinguished New
York critics regarding her vocal form and aggressive performing style
brought about some public soul-searching. About her *Norma* Herbert
Peyser in *Musical America* thought that "the title role made plain that
Miss Raisa has one of the greatest dramatic voices in the world and
one of the most devastating vocal methods. What the future holds in
store for her unless she can be counseled to heroic technical reforma-
tion one hesitates to picture." Mary Garden had created a public incident when she indicated to the press her concern about Raisa's tendency to give too much by singing too prodigally in her performances.
She was very specific when she remarked, "This season Raisa's voice
already has begun to go back, and I cannot accurately foresee its fail-
ings of next year and I dread them."[15] (Raisa initiated legal action and
Garden then denied having made the comment, but the newspaper
reporter involved insisted Garden did make that assertion. The con-
tretemps then blew over, as "theatrical" litigation in those days fre-

quently did.)[16] This widespread criticism of her work in New York forced Raisa to consider seriously the state of her instrument and art. She and Rimini retained Russian-born Lazar Samoiloff, a prominent voice specialist with a studio in New York. They coached with Samoiloff for three seasons, with stress on vocal refinement. He accompanied Raisa and Rimini on their 1921 season in South America. There Raisa repeated her Norma, Aida, and Tosca in Brazil, Argentina, and Uruguay, and added Ilara in Gomez's *Lo Schiavo* to her repertoire. She sang this Portuguese-language opera in Italian in Rio and São Paulo. A young Claudio Arrau heard Raisa's Norma at the Coliseo in Buenos Aires, and many years later for *Opera News* the Chilean pianist recalled, "Another singer [he had already discussed Muzio and Dalla Rizza] I heard there was Rosa Raisa—a fantastic Norma, the best I think I ever heard. The melodic line was ravishing, every tone marvelously produced, with all the registers equally good. The pitch was perfect, the coloratura fantastic, the acting marvelous. She was also a beautiful woman."[17] The critic of Rio's *Artes e Artestas* waxed ecstatic:

> In her portrayal of the title role of Norma yesterday, Rosa Raisa once more demonstrated her exceptional vocal qualities. To her lovers of bel canto and pure melody were indebted for moments of artistic ecstasy not often experienced. Her elegant and majestic stage presence, her unconstrained and energetic gestures, her admirable acting formed a wonderful foundation for the glorious triumph scored by her as a singer. Her voice, so justly admired by us, has the same beauty of color, obeys the same securely established rules of vocalization, retains the same vigorous dramatic expressiveness which make her Norma of 1921 not one whit inferior to her Norma of 1918.

When one considers such diverse opinions one has to speculate whether the New York critics had an agenda and were overly exacting, or the South American critics were totally lacking in standards. As in all such cases the truth probably lies somewhere in between. Raisa's singing was not nearly as unschooled as some New York critics wrote and was not as nearly perfect as the South Americans believed. As a general proposition American and English writers on things operatic tend to favor style and musicality over sheer power and technical brilliance, although ideally all four elements are considered desirable. This dichotomy—perhaps not so evident now as then—between Latin-country operatic observers and Anglo-Saxon critics and audiences is an interesting subject with a very long history that goes far beyond Rosa Raisa. It explains in part why many artists, particularly female singers and tenors, who achieve great success in Italy and South America fail to impress equally certain powerful English-speaking critics and audiences.

Raisa must have been very proud to have a wing at Buenos Aires' Hospital Israelita named after her. On October 5 she gave a concert at the newly opened Teatro Cervantes to benefit the hospital. Raisa also received various honors and awards from the Argentine government over the years. The president of Argentina, Victorino de la Plaza, and the leading statesman of Brazil, Rui Barbosa, were reported to be among her greatest admirers, hardly ever missing one of her performances in their respective capitals.

⚜ It was in Rio, in this fantastically beautiful city that the cable came reporting the death of Enrico Caruso. What a shock! Not only the loss of the greatest artist of all, but a friend and a wonderful man who passed on at such an early age, 49! Indeed, the whole world mourned this great loss! We had visited with him at the Waldorf [Vanderbilt] before he left for Sorrento, near Naples, with his wife Dorothy and his little daughter, Gloria. And the year before in 1920, I recall when after playing some of his recordings for us he suddenly destroyed a couple of them, being dissatisfied with their infidelity—which we thought was a sacrilege, for these were wonderful recordings, but it seems they were not up to his expectations, and that his artistic sense was outraged by their failure to meet his meticulous demands. I still think that many of the recordings of this great artist made during the early days are a magnificent exposition of his beautiful singing. To this day I can not restrain the tears that roll down my cheeks as I listen to them and I am deeply moved by his appeal to the human heart. ⚜

Raisa was still nervous about the Garden directorship, and as late as July 30 she contacted, through an intermediary in Rio de Janeiro, Gatti-Casazza of the Metropolitan to offer her services and determine what Gatti could offered Rimini in the upcoming season. She was upset that early Chicago plans called for several *Tannhäuser* performances in German, a language she preferred not to sing.[18] The 1921–1922 Chicago Opera season was the one famous for the loss of over a million dollars under Garden's management. Garden had engaged many new singers with big European reputations, including Claire Dux, Maria Ivogün, Nina Koshetz, and Tino Pattiera, and she even planned to bring back Johanna Gadski. Garden, however, followed the general formula of past seasons, scheduling two performances a week for both herself and Raisa, and for Galli-Curci when she was not at the Metropolitan, thus leaving very little room on the calendar for her new additions to the company. This poor planning had artists being paid not to sing, and in Gadski's case prompted a lawsuit over failure to live up to contractual obligations. Thus Raisa ended up singing often, as the substantial cutback of Italian opera feared by the Italian-wing singers never materialized (although there are several *Tannhäusers* in Raisa's totals for the season).[19]

Although they were colleagues and had professional respect for each other, there was no real love between Garden and Raisa. When John Gutman, in a 1962 Metropolitan Opera broadcast intermission interview, asked Raisa to share her memories of Garden, clearly expecting glowing recollections, she stated that Garden had mentioned her in her 1951 autobiography as a "lady of great charm" and expressed her feeling for Garden with a "ditto!" Raisa was clearly hurt that Garden mentioned her only "in passing" with that dismissive phrase in her book. This hurt attitude contrasts with the feeling she expressed publicly when a reporter asked her in January 1922 about Garden's ability as "directa": "Woman is a much maligned creature at times. As for Mary Garden—well here is an exceptional woman, typically American, with all the high qualities of the women of this great country, ability, imagination, resourcefulness, and tact. I, myself, am a Russian. I am proud of my nationality, of course. But, I know what

American women can do. Your women have so much more freedom, and they develop their intelligence so. Why should not a woman be able to properly conduct an opera company? What difference does it make—Mary Garden or Gatti-Casazza. Women or men? The question is not, is she a woman; it is does she know her job? I think Mary Garden does." To another interviewer at about the same time who queried her about Garden's abilities, Raisa replied: "If she wanted to, she could be President of the United States. Brains, my dear sir, count, and she has them developed and knows how to use them. I could not be an impresario, but she can. She has the stuff of which big generals are made." These "politically correct" answers to provocative questions suggest Raisa herself very early on had figured out how the media worked and gave them good quotes that complemented the "spin" of the moment, that Garden was some sort of "super" woman.

A note about a diva's responsibilities: when Raisa and Rimini went to South America in 1921 they had thousands of sepia photos printed and packed in their trunks; these would be distributed to their fans, often autographed. Raisa loved to meet with admirers in her dressing room after performances. She tried to speak to everyone who visited and often signed their programs and gave them photos. It is fortunate that Raisa loved trains, because she spent many months on them on her various tours of North and South America; probably if one added up all the mileage during her career she could have circled the world many times. In addition to performing on tour, singers like Garden, Muzio, and Raisa were usually photographed stepping off trains; they often posed for group photos and granted interviews. The stars frequently met the local sponsors of the tour and were expected to attend post-performance parties. These public relations duties were regularly featured on newspaper front pages and, in the case of parties, on the society page.[20]

Elisabeth in *Tannhäuser* and Minnie in *Fanciulla del West* were Raisa's new roles for the season. Chicago was developing a German wing, including the tenor Richard Schubert and the baritone Joseph Schwarz. The Greek tenor Ulysses Lappas played Dick Johnson in *Fanciulla*. Both operas were taken to New York and to several other

Raisa as Minnie in La Fanciulla del West, *1922. Critic Henry T. Finck thought Raisa put more heat into her performance than Puccini had put into his score.*

cities on the long tour to California. Henry T. Finck was moved to write:

> Mme. Raisa has done many fine things in this town, but none that quite equaled her *La Fanciulla del West*. . . . In the second act, Mme.

Raisa showed how far Emmy Destinn, with all her glorious voice, fell short of doing justice to the Belasco-Puccini creation of Minnie. Her card scene was equal to that in *Carmen* as done by Emma Calvé, who, by the way, sat in a box last night and led the applause after the second act. The passionate vehemence of her acting and her singing were thrilling. I have seldom, in forty years, heard dramatic singing so emotional. Great is Rosa Raisa! The applause following the act was, with the exception of that bestowed repeatedly on Chaliapin at the Metropolitan, the most enthusiastic I have heard this season. A great shout went up from the whole audience—a shout as thrilling in its way as the performance itself, for it was equally emotional.

In those days contemporary operas such as *Fanciulla del West* were always being reevaluated, and Finck later thought, "It seemed to me, as it did to all the critics, far inferior to its predecessor, *Madama Butterfly*. I still think so, as far as the first and the third acts are concerned; but the second act, as sung by Rosa Raisa and conducted by Polacco, now loomed as the biggest thing by far that Puccini had ever done. Rosa Raisa had previously convinced me that Bellini's *Norma* is a far more dramatic and stirring opera than I had supposed."[21]
Pitts Sanborn in the *New York Globe* editorialized:

All the more acute, therefore, is the pleasure that comes from hearing in these times a voice like Rosa Raisa's. . . . But she does possess a voice like unto no other that we hear today—a voice of liquid gold, uttered with a prodigal and full-throated ease. She has been schooled as a singer in the great Italian bel canto, and when disposed she illustrates that entrancing art brilliantly. Moreover, she has temperament and brains, and her effective singing is not limited to any one kind of part or style of music. But the listener has a right to his preference. Mme. Raisa is a singer so absolutely out of the common run that it would be a great satisfaction to hear her only in parts that give such singing play. As Norma, as Aida, as Desdemona she has proved here the superlative value of her voice and art. One longs to hear her again in those roles, and in some of the florid operas of the Italian repertory of the palmy days that are neglected now because nobody dares to sing them, *Se-*

miramide for example or *Lucrezia Borgia.* . . . The kind of ability Mme. Raisa possesses is so precious that one hates ever to find its treasures expended on the operas that many another singer of lesser ability can encompass, if not so well, at least well enough for all general purposes.

Raisa's work with Samoiloff had started to pay dividends, and in early 1922 it was again Sanborn of the *Globe* who noticed, after a New York City recital,

> Rosa Raisa sang in a way that tempts to swollen and purple prose. Miss Raisa has one of the most glorious voices of our time. When she is at her best her singing is worthy of her voice. Unfortunately, when appearing in New York she has not always sung at her best. But last evening she did. Save for an occasional trace of the glottis stroke in the lower part of the scale there was scarcely a flaw discernible in all her singing. Such vocal poise, such fluidity and spontaneity of tone, such command of breath, such purity and grace of legato, and such a regal ease made one believe that this gifted woman could sing anything.

Unmistakably referring to Samoiloff's tutelage, in May 1923 Henderson wrote in the *Sun* after a New York concert, "Miss Raisa's voice is now in full flower and it ranks among the beautiful voices of the day. The remarkable power and plenitude of it have gone through a beneficent process, and there is a refinement now in her use of it which gives its prodigious coloring the highlight of ease. Rimini too has rebuilt and cemented his voice considerably."

Henderson, ever the patrician and balanced critic, happened to be a personal friend of Samoiloff. Evidence of this friendship is his reported attendance at some of the Sunday afternoon receptions Samoiloff gave for his artists.

Mary Garden relinquished her directorship at the end of the 1921–1922 season. She confessed that "my place is with the artists, not over them." A business manager, Herbert Johnson, was reengaged to handle the financial and everyday affairs of the company, and Giorgio Polacco was named artistic director. Raisa and Rimini returned to Italy in the summer of 1922 and bought a villa in the town of San Floriano near the shores of Lake Garda, outside Rimini's home city of Verona. This elaborate estate became the couple's summer home. The house was renovated, and American comforts were installed. At various times the villa was called GiacoRosa or Villa Raisa. The grounds had a swimming pool, tennis court, stables, garages, gardens, and facilities for making Valpolicella wine. Every summer friends from America and Italy visited and enjoyed the couple's generous hospitality.

When the Chicago Opera first presented a long season in 1918 in New York, the company enjoyed exhaustive press coverage, mostly on its merits, but also because of the novelty of another major company presenting opera "day in and day out" in New York on a scale comparable to that of the Met. It was as if the old Oscar Hammerstein Manhattan Opera had not stopped presenting opera in 1910! From 1910 to 1913 the Chicago-Philadelphia Opera Company did give some performances at the Metropolitan Opera House on Tuesdays, when the Met itself was performing in Philadelphia. Thus, singers such as Garden, Muratore, and Vanni-Marcoux sang in New York, often under Campanini's baton. In many ways, organizationally, physically, and conceptually, the Chicago Opera was the successor to Hammerstein's Manhattan Opera. The 1919 and 1920 seasons were also covered by the press in considerable detail. Of course, Raisa was ill in 1919 and missed the opportunity to "consolidate" her accomplishments from the previous year. The 1921 opening-night *Norma* drew substantial coverage partially because this opera enjoyed a special aura—it was considered almost sacred, and many critics were curious as to whether Raisa had improved upon her 1920 showing in this work. The 1921 and 1922 seasons were not as well attended by the leading critics, and consequently by the public, and this provoked some irritation in Chicago. There was great interest in Chicago as to how the company was being received in New York. There were charges that New York's critics and operagoing public were envious that Chicago was able to present works such as *Norma* and *Otello* that the Metropolitan could not at that time mount. Opera companies (not just the Chicago Opera) visiting New York, and musicians in general, always wanted the approval of New York's famous critics and discriminating audiences. On February 24, 1921, the *Musical Leader*, a Chicago-based journal, editorialized:

The company is neither wanted by the public nor respected by the press. The attitude of the latter is unexplainable. During the first weeks of the Company's engagement the critics were aligned in condemnation, the late James Huneker even up to two or three days before his death finding much to censure and little to praise, with, of course, the one exception, Miss Mary Garden (this, however, was but a continuation of an old story). In contradistinction to what happened in Chicago, those artists and conductors who had failed to please the critics of the western metropolis were treated with much greater consideration than some of their more distinguished colleagues. Mme. Raisa, Mr. Muratore, Mr. Baklanoff, Mme. Gall and Mr. Schipa who had been the delights of the Chicago public and had made "star" headlines were either damned with faint praise or roundly criticized. The Chicago company can not feel elated at the attention given by the New York reviewers. There has been a considerable amount of mud slinging, and spilling of good ink without any valid cause. On the other hand, Mr. Marinuzzi and Mr. Morin [*sic*], who had not been altogether happy in Chicago, were in New York received quite favorably, and Mme. Galli-Curci, after it was announced that she would be a member of the historic house on Broadway, was hailed gloriously. Recent doings of the Chicago company at the Manhattan has been reduced to four or five lines, merely a record that such and such an opera had been given. Fortunately for all concerned, the one hundred or more million over the country are competent to form judgment, and it matters little whether the fourteen daily papers (irrespective of Jewish or foreign) view the Chicago company favorably or otherwise. The company is of sufficient importance for Mr. Higgins of Covent Garden to covet it for the London season of 1922, and its American popularity is such (America and New York not being synonymous) that already negotiations have begun to retake it to the various cities in which it is to appear during the next two months.

It is an irony that the Met was subjected to similar treatment when visiting Chicago on its spring tours in later years. One reason the Met dropped Chicago from its tour itinerary was very tough criticism of its offerings, especially by the powerful Claudia Cassidy of the *Tribune*, much like what the Chicago Opera had experienced a generation before in New York.[22]

· Chapter Seven ·

LA JUIVE

THE 1922–1923 Chicago season saw the contours of the Chicago company begin to change. Because she was now singing part-time with New York's Metropolitan Opera, Galli-Curci's appearances were becoming less frequent. Feodor Chaliapin, also on the roster of the Metropolitan, joined the company and presented his classic creations in *Boris, Mefistofele, Faust,* and *Il Barbiere di Siviglia.* Claudia Muzio, no longer with the Metropolitan, was engaged to sing with the company, and her arrival in Chicago reduced Raisa's workload somewhat and introduced an intriguing element of competition. Over the next decade the two shared Santuzza, Aida, Tosca, and the *Trovatore* Leonora. Muzio became beloved as Violetta, Manon Lescaut, Nedda, and Loreley, while Raisa continued her hold on the heavier roles of Norma, Amelia, Maliella, Rachel, and Gioconda. Even when performing the same roles, the two artists represented completely different operatic values. One writer framed their differences this way: "Given a choice of Raisa or Muzio in, say, *Aida,* one's favorite depended upon whether one preferred dramatic sweep and a voice of phenomenal power, or a smaller-scaled version sung with delicacy, simplicity, and warmth."[1] On a personal level their relationship was proper and professional, though not particularly warm. They really did not like each other. Critics over the years often made diplomatic comparisons between the two sopranos. The headline after Muzio's debut that she was the "Best Italian-born Aida of the present time" makes this fine distinction—Raisa, though Italian-trained, was not Italian-born. At the Congress Hotel, across the street from the Auditorium Theater, Muzio's apartment was directly above the Riminis'. On rare instances

Raisa admiring her jewels in this early 1920s portrait dedicated to Beatrice and Morris Balter. Beatrice was the daughter of Mrs. Stone. Raisa had bought the jewelry collection of a Russian émigré family and wore these strands of pearls the rest of her life. Underwood and Underwood Studio, New York. (Courtesy of the late Beatrice Balter.)

of indisposition they spelled each other. Although only fragmentary salary information is available, it appears that Raisa was always paid slightly more.² While Muzio was establishing herself as a Chicago favorite, Raisa was expanding her repertoire. She added Leonora in *La Forza del Destino* and Rachel in *La Juive*, done in Italian in Chicago and always advertised as *The Jewess*. *Forza* was not destined to be one of her favorites; she sang it only twice. Muzio enjoyed more success in this opera. Rachel in *La Juive* was to be a role in which Raisa was definitive;³ her success with the role was similar to that of her Maliella in *I Gioielli della Madonna*.

Glenn Dillard Gunn in the *Chicago Examiner* penned a very personal review. He admitted that he never bought into Raisa's greatness, and he felt that his friend Campanini was wrong when he predicted that

"Miss Raisa will one day be the greatest of dramatic sopranos. I know voices and hers is a great one. You will hear." I confess I thought the maestro quite wrong; that hers was no great voice; only a loud one and crude. I am afraid I wrote things to that effect. . . . Mme. Raisa forced it upon me last Sunday night by her singing of the music allotted to the part of Rachel in Halévy's "La Juive" which I protest is the greatest example of the dramatic soprano's art that I have heard since Mme. Nordica was in her prime, twenty-five years ago. It was great in its vocal aspects. It was no less great in its spiritual impulse. . . . [Refering to singers whose voices carry at all dynamic levels:] On this foundation of tonal vitality she is able to impose whatever color the dramatic situation demands. Thus her voice, repressed and restrained in the final scenes of this fine old melodrama, expresses terror; or it is the very voice of scorn; or it is ennobled with dignity. By voice alone she can encompass all the emotional requirements of the part. Again, she was obliged to compete with the clarinet, carrying a bravura scale throughout the splendid range of her voice. No coloratura soprano living could have done it with more precise articulation; not even the great Tetrazzini. In other ways has Raisa developed. Last Sunday, and again yesterday one saw her a queenly beauty, moving with dignity, each gesture a lesson in graceful pantomime, singing as Mme. Nordica may

In "eastern" garb as Rachel in La Juive, *1922.* La Juive *and* I Gioielli della Madonna *were Raisa vehicles in Chicago for much of her career. de Gueldre Studio, Chicago.*

have sung the part. You can never tell about these ugly ducklings. Here's another that became a swan.

Potential activities abounded as Raisa made her plans for the summer of 1923. As early as March 1922 it was advertised that Raisa and Rimini had accepted a thirty-concert tour of Australia for summer 1923.[4] Then there were reports that Raisa would go to Salzburg in the summer to study Isolde and the Brünnhildes with Lilli Lehmann, apparently in response to suggestions that her dramatic soprano should be heard in the great Wagner roles.[5] In July there was an announcement that the couple had accepted an engagement to sing at the Verona Arena, and that Ettore Panizza, the music director, had given Raisa the choice of either Norma or Rachel. Raisa opted not to perform over the summer, but Rimini did sing in *Il Re di Lahore* at the Arena. Ester Mazzoleni sang Norma. Rumors surfaced that Toscanini had selected Raisa for the Asteria in Boito's posthumous *Nerone*, planned for 1924 at La Scala. Then the rumors shifted to speculation about the rising Italian soprano Isora Rinolfi as the planned Asteria. The ultimate selection of Raisa for this honor was confirmed only in February 1924, three months before the actual premiere.

The 1923–1924 Chicago season opened with Chaliapin in *Boris Godunov*. Raisa's new role this season was to be Selika in *L'Africana*— new to Chicago, but she had already sung this role in Mexico and South America. *La Juive*, *Il Trovatore*, *Aida*, *Otello*, and *Cavalleria* were her other operas for the season.

The 1924 tour took the company to the Pacific Coast again. The pattern of Chicago Opera tours at that time was to take sixteen different operas to Boston for a two-week season just after the close of the big season in Chicago. Then the repertoire was trimmed to five or six operas for the remainder of the tour. It included Mary Garden, Chaliapin, and Raisa vehicles, and usually something appropriate for Edith Mason. The company gave *La Juive* eleven times in as many cities on this tour. The box office for the Halévy opera was not as potent as for the Garden and Chaliapin operas; one explanation offered was that the title *The Jewess* was off-putting to many people in America at this time, especially in the South and West.[6] In Salt Lake City the company gave a concert of scenes from operas at the Tabernacle. This season and the next one were the only instances in which Chaliapin and Raisa were members of the same company. They were friends and communicated in Russian. Chaliapin remembered having heard Raisa twelve years earlier, when she was still a student in Naples. She had been taken to Capri to audition for him during one of his visits with his close friend Gorky; she remembered singing the big aria from *Pique Dame* on that occasion.

On the 1924 tour, critics were unsparing in their praise of Raisa and their placing of her current attainments in some perspective. On January 29 the *Boston Herald*'s Henry Parker noted, "Mme. Raisa, richly endowed by nature, seemingly not content with the beautiful quality and the golden power of her voice, often forced it and sang with distinctive abandon. It is a pleasure to state that last night this voice was generally controlled artistically; that she sang with true expression, with a dramatic feeling that gave character to Selika in her moments of joy and anguish." The critic of the *Cleveland News* on February 15 wondered about her Santuzza: "If there is a more violently tragic figure on the operatic stage, a more correct impersonation than Raisa as the Sicilian heroine of ancient drama, I have not seen it. And I make comparison with vivid recollection of Eleanora Duse in the dramatic version." Two days later in Pittsburgh the critic of the *Gazette-Times* noted:

> In "La Juive," undoubtedly the most "singing" of the trilogy given by the Chicago Opera Company, the emotional effects are obtained by three singers who dominate the five acts. The first of these, by curtain calls and all other gauges (including one large bouquet of American Beauties), is Rosa Raisa, whose death in the cauldron above the flames surpasses that more classical death shown by Mary Garden as Cleopatra. Where Garden touched the emotional purse, and took quite a part therefrom, Raisa gets the last pennyworth; Raisa singing her ante-mortem, anti-Christian, adieu created about her an illusion of

As Rachel in the last act of La Juive. *de Gueldre Studio, Chicago.*

suffering so intense that half her audience was in tears. Her voice is complete. Nothing better, feminine or otherwise, was in the three casts. Her Rachel was nothing short of superb.

On March 6 the Los Angeles *Evening Herald* commented, "Some of Raisa's tones were of the quality long since lost to the opera. She is a songbird of rare genius, but exaggerated timbres push on out into regions of the unbeautiful at times and spoil what otherwise would be near perfection."

· *Chapter Eight* ·

TOSCANINI

IN late February 1924 came the official announcement that Raisa was Toscanini's final choice for the Asteria in *Nerone*. A front-page "exclusive" in the *Musical Digest* of February 12 reported, "Toscanini has not yet made up his mind about the singer for Asteria. He still hopes for Rosa Raisa who is with the Chicago Company until the end of March. *Nerone* is scheduled for the second week of March. It is whispered that Mme. Rinolfi, first chosen for the part, was excluded because of her work in *Aida*." Rinolfi sang nine *Aidas* under Toscanini in November and December 1923; apparently she was not satisfactory, for her Scala career began and ended with these *Aidas*. (The *Nerone* premiere was rescheduled for March 27, then pushed up to April 20. In the event, the premiere was delayed until May 1.) The elaborate production was already in progress. Raisa's problem was timing, for there was no way she could be available for rehearsals until mid-April at the earliest. It was a point of great pride to Raisa that Toscanini wired, "I will wait for you!"[1]

The Chicago Opera tours, which usually extended well into March, were also complicating factors in Raisa's 1925 and 1926 Scala engagements. Her Chicago contract included the annual tour. The backers in the various cities visited needed the potent names of Garden, Raisa, and Muzio to successfully guarantee these costly visits. Raisa finished the 1924 tour in Denver on March 18. She traveled to New York by train, and then took a steamship to Genoa. On board she studied Asteria with Maestro Panizza. Siegfried Wagner and his wife were on the same voyage. While on the Atlantic Panizza's wife, Fulvia, died and was buried at sea. Toscanini had asked Panizza and Raisa to work as much as possible in non-public areas, as he didn't want outsiders to hear any of the *Nerone* score until the final general rehearsal. This presentation of *Nerone* was a major event; Boito had worked on this epic opera off and on for the better part of forty years and was plagued with self-doubts and never completed it. Toscanini promised Boito on his deathbed that he would give the opera, and he himself along with Antonio Smareglia and Vincenzo Tommasini composed those parts of the score left unfinished by Boito. In the teens it was even rumored that Caruso would be awarded the title role of the opera if Boito ever finished it.[2] In 1912 Boito had written to Caruso, "To increase my burden, there is the thought that I am compelled to lose an opportunity that would have afforded me the fortune and fame of having you as the interpreter of my work." Toscanini believed so strongly in Boito's opera that he gave it one of the most opulent productions in La Scala history. The cast of the May 1 opening night included, in addition to Raisa, Luisa Bertana, Pertile, Galeffi, Journet, and Ezio Pinza. The premiere was broadcast on Italian radio, and it was reported that Mussolini, Pope Pius XI, and indeed much of the country listened to this heavily hyped performance over the airwaves.[3] Today one wonders how an early (1924) radio transmission must have sounded, especially of a large-scale opera. No matter what the sound quality, we can only regret that "off-the-air" recording devices had not yet been invented!

The role of Asteria is not exceptionally long, but her four big scenes contain very dramatic writing in a very high tessitura. The critics of Milan had been anticipating Raisa's return after an eight-year absence and were generally ecstatic about her performance. The critic for the *Corriere di Milan* wrote:

> Only one who has examined closely the unspeakable difficulties of the part of Asteria can judge adequately the excellencies of the interpretation of Rosa Raisa. Rarely have I had the pleasure of hearing a more beautiful, a more robust dramatic soprano voice with a broader range. It is a voice of exceptional volume and finely trained, which does honor to the great Marchisio, who was her teacher and also to the pupil who with such intelligence knew how to make the most of that instruction.

Raisa, torch in hand, as Asteria (the role she created) in Nerone, *Act I. Her suc-cess in this opera led to her selection as the creator of Turandot. Castagneri Stu-dio, Milan.*

And equal to her vocal gifts was her ability as an actress in the expressiveness of her face, in her diction, her gestures and movements. We spoke of great difficulties and we enumerate them, an alarming tessitura, intervals that would seem to have been written in order to endanger the best placed voice, the insistence on lofty tones . . . and in a word, passages which are the ultimate tests of the ability of the artist undertaking the role. Yet Raisa met and conquered all of these difficulties superbly.

A theme that ran through many of the reviews was that Raisa's brilliance was the result of her sound early Italian training. In late March, just before sailing to Italy, Raisa and Rimini placed ads in *Musical America* and *Musical Courier* publicly requesting that Lazar Samoiloff cease using their names as endorsers in his advertisements. They did not deny that they had worked with Samoiloff, but they wanted to stress that he was not their "teacher." They emphasized that their only "teachers" were Barbara Marchisio for Raisa and Amelia Conti-Foroni for Rimini. Samoiloff rebutted the Raisa-Rimini ad with one of his own claiming that they were ingrates who now wanted to reestablish themselves in Italy as exclusively Italian-trained singers. His secretary and others wrote letters, reproduced in his ad, testifying to all the hours the Riminis spent with him and the large sums of money they paid for his instruction.[4] Given the substance of the *Nerone* reviews, with their emphasis on the wonders of Marchisio's training, it is clear that Raisa and Rimini were correct in thinking that in Italy it was important to make the exquisitely fine semantic distinction between their basic Italian training and subsequent American polishing. At what point does coaching become teaching? In fairness to them, Raisa and Rimini may also have been irritated by Samoiloff's constant use of their names as his prime clients in his relentless self-promotion. (From summer 1921 to March 1923 Samoiloff regularly advertised his voice studio in both *Musical America* and *Musical Courier*. Raisa and Rimini's names always headed the list of his clients and endorsers in bold letters. Other artists on his list included Gabriella Besanzoni; Claire Dux; Julia Claussen; Curt Taucher; Angelo

Minghetti and his wife, Lulu Hayes Minghetti; Maria Louise and Consuelo Escobar; Bianca Saroya; Julius Bledsoe; Sonya Yergin; and Aline Sanden of Leipzig. An examination of Samoiloff's client list suggests that he named every singer of note who ever took even one session with him.)

Raisa offers her own account of the *Nerone* experience:

When the day of the first performance of *Nerone* came, I awoke at six in the morning noticing that I was hoarse. I immediately awakened my husband to give him the shock. He asked me very wisely to fall asleep again. "You are just nervous," he said, and "don't worry." But these kind words did not help me for I was in agony from six to eight when I finally got up and went to the balcony, which was just opposite La Scala, and there I noticed people, already at that early hour, forming long lines and waiting patiently for gallery seats to the performance of that night. Then a reaction set in and I suddenly realized that if these people were willing to wait thirteen hours to hear the premiere, I must *not* disappoint them. And I naturally did not want to disappoint Maestro Toscanini, who had chosen me for the role, and I thought of my American friends who were so proud of the honor bestowed on me. So I pulled myself together telling myself that it might indeed be "nerves." Nonetheless at ten in the morning, when the office opened, my husband called the management to tell them that I was not feeling well, and to be ready in any event for replacement if necessary. At eleven A.M. Maestro Toscanini came to my apartment at the Hotel Regina and told me that he was going to put a wreath on Boito's grave and pray for the success of the first performance that evening. Before leaving he said, "forget about your hoarseness," and "order a good lunch, a large juicy steak and some champagne, and you will be all right." To which I added a dish of spinach with a little olive oil and lemon, a baked apple and soup with rice—my usual menu on the day of a performance [throughout] my whole career. After such a meal anyone could sing!

At four in the afternoon I tried my voice and at this time I was certain that I could perform. At six I could not resist. I went to the

La Scala photo of Toscanini at the time of the Nerone *premiere in 1924. Castagneri Studio, Milan. (Robert Tuggle collection.)*

theater to my dressing room to breathe the unique atmosphere of the stage. Slowly I put my makeup on, dressed in my simple costume and looked forward to the performance. Before it started Maestro Toscanini walked in, in a happy frame of mind, to wish me good luck. This certainly was a great encouragement. And, by the way, he did this before every one of my performances. A few minutes later my dear friend Pietro Clausetti [son of Carlo and Margherita], one of the coaches and a great musical talent, came to take me under the stage, near a ladder on which I had to make my entrance with a burning torch in my hand, exclaiming the word "Neron," when Asteria notices him with a bundle in his hand in which was wrapped the head of his mother Agrippina whom he had killed.

The house was packed to the rafters, as the Scala always is on its greatest occasions, and the evening was a triumph in every respect. The performance went on for hours with a crescendo of enthusiasm after each act as we were recalled again and again to take bows with the Maestro. Not only the singing and the acting, but the mis-en-scène was fantastic, such as only La Scala could afford, with its enormous stage and hundreds of supers, horses, chariots, chorus, and scenery. I recall in the last act, when the chariots come in, the settings were so realistic and the chariots with the wild horses driven by the gladiators so awesome that the public gasped in fear thinking that they were approaching them.

As for my own contribution, I remember the serpent-like figure of Asteria that I portrayed: a symbolic character, full of strange powers, insinuating her presence with evil intentions and bent on trapping and ensnaring Nerone. Depicting this strange and elusive character, tormented by evil, was not an easy task said the critics. I accentuated the torments of this turbulent figure that strides through the pages of Boito's score like a mirage: mysterious, enigmatic, cruel and ambitious, with magical, mystical powers. This "vagabond bride of serpents," as she called herself, I molded, said the critics, with fine plasticity through vocal and dramatic effects that made real the vague and intangible character of Asteria. With unreserved appreciation they

NERONE

TRAGEDIA IN QUATTRO ATTI

PAROLE E MUSICA DI

ARRIGO BOITO

(Proprietà G. Ricordi & C.)

PRIMA ESECUZIONE

MILANO

TEATRO ALLA SCALA

(ENTE AUTONOMO)

1 Maggio 1924

PERSONAGGI

NERONE	Sig. Aureliano Pertile
SIMON MAGO	» Marcello Journet
FANUÈL.	» Carlo Galeffi
ASTERIA	Sig.ᵃ Rosa Raisa
RUBRIA	» Luisa Bertana
TIGELLINO	Sig. Ezio Pinza
GOBRIAS	» Giuseppe Nessi
DOSITEO	» Carlo Walter
PÈRSIDE	Sig.ᵃ Mita Vasari
CERINTO	» Maria Doria
IL TEMPIERE	Sig. Emilio Venturini
PRIMO VIANDANTE	» Alfredo Tedeschi
SECONDO VIANDANTE	» Giuseppe Menni
LO SCHIAVO AMMONITORE.	» Aristide Baracchi
TERPNOS	» N. N.

MAESTRO DIRETTORE E CONCERTATORE

ARTURO TOSCANINI

Maestri sostituti: FERRUCCIO CALUSIO - PIETRO CLAUSETTI - EDUARDO FORNARINI
MARIO FRIGERIO - GUIDO RAGNI - EMILIO ROSSI - VITTORIO RUFFO - ANTONINO VOTTO

Maestro del Coro: VITTORE VENEZIANI - Maestro della Banda: ALESSIO MORRONE
Maestri suggeritori: ARMANDO PETRUCCI e EMILIO DELEIDE
Coreografo: GIOVANNI PRATESI - Prima ballerina: CIA FORNAROLI
Direttore della messa in scena: GIOVACCHINO FORZANO
Direttore dell'allestimento scenico: CARAMBA

Scene, costumi ed attrezzi su bozzetti di LODOVICO POGLIAGHI

Scenografo: EDOARDO MARCHIORO colla collaborazione di ALESSANDRO MAGNONI

Rare cast page with signatures of all the leads in Nerone *as well as of Toscanini. The participants signed a small number of first-edition Ricordi scores the night of the premiere, May 1, 1924.*

Rosa Raisa

Luisa Bertana

Aureliano Pertile

Marcel Journet

Mita Vasari

Chiosincha

Carlo Galeffi

Arturo Toscanini

Maggio 934

lauded me for "portraying with great artistry the tormented soul of this tempestuous character." And they praised my successful conquest of this difficult role. ૨ⱥ

Ultimately, from a historic viewpoint, the most important event that occurred during the rehearsals and performances of *Nerone* was an encounter between Puccini and Toscanini. Puccini had slipped onto the stage at one of the early working rehearsals to hear Boito's score. Toscanini ordered him to leave the theater, as it was his policy that no outsiders, even Puccini, should hear the music until the final dress rehearsal, at which time the Milanese opera establishment would be invited to the preview. It fell to Raisa to escort Puccini to the stage exit. Puccini, who had already heard some of the first scenes, told Raisa that he was writing *Turandot*, that it was a role in which "I can just see you and hear you,"[5] and that he wanted her to be its creator. The day after Puccini died, on November 30, 1924, the *Chicago Tribune* rounded up Raisa, Edith Mason, and Polacco, seeking their reactions to the death of the Maestro. "I feel as if I had lost a good friend," said Rosa Raisa. "Puccini acted as if he was completely happy over the prospect of having us, Miss Mason, Mr. Rimini, and myself, engaged for *Turandot*. When I left Italy he was at work on the final duet of the piece, a section of the work in which I was to take part. 'Maestro,' I said to him at the last time I ever saw him, 'be sure and put in plenty of high C's.' He laughed and said he would not forget."

On October 8, 1924 (seven weeks before Puccini's death on November 29), the projected *Turandot* cast was given to the world press. On October 7 Angelo Scandiani, administative director of La Scala, wired Herbert Johnson of the Chicago Opera, "Glad to announce you that Maestro Puccini and Toscanini selected Raisa and Mason for the creation of the two female roles of Turandot which will have the world premiere next April at La Scala stop For the baritone role Rimini stop please communicate Mister Insull regards Scandiani."[6] Other artists would later claim that Italy's acknowledged greatest living composer had promised them roles in this much-awaited opera. It is reasonable that Puccini at different times in the creative process told various artists that he was writing an opera with them in mind. It is undoubtedly true that as early as 1921 he indicated this hope to Maria Jeritza, and had the Metropolitan been successful in obtaining the first performance rights Jeritza would have been the creator. Both Martinelli and Lauri-Volpi were positive they had been promised the role of Calaf. Gigli was uncertain whether the role of Calaf was "right" for him at that time, and he would be in the awkward situation of defying Gatti-Casazza of the Met if he appeared at Toscanini's theater[7]; the then-ascendant tenor Miguel Fleta was given the assignment in his place. As it was, Puccini died of throat cancer, Franco Alfano was asked to compose the final scene from Puccini's sketches, and the premiere was rescheduled for spring 1926, by which time Mason was pregnant and could not accept the honor of creating Liù; a leading La Scala lyric soprano, Maria Zamboni, was her replacement.

About Toscanini's personality, work habits, and the *modus operandi* at La Scala at the time of the *Nerone* rehearsals Raisa had much to relate:

⁊ This was the first time that I had ever sung for this great Maestro. I had heard so much about his being demanding, severe, temperamental, that when I entered the large rehearsal room I confess I was very nervous. But when I saw him come in with his beautiful, smiling, and penetrating eyes I felt at ease and confident. What an inspiration it was to work with Toscanini and he was able to bring out everything an artist had to give! I cannot begin to tell what a joy it was to sing in the presence of this magical artist. I learned so much at every rehearsal! And I could hardly wait from one to the next. . . . The rehearsals continued every day for about a month and Toscanini wanted us to sing and act just as though it were a first performance. This was of course an excellent idea, for with every rehearsal each artist had something new to give of his talent until the part matured and became second nature to him. In the afternoon of the same day we would have sessions with the orchestra.

The custom at La Scala was to arrange two general rehearsals [after the preliminary working rehearsals] before each new opera, an ante-general rehearsal, and a full general rehearsal during which we were all made up and dressed in the costume and the acting and singing took place exactly as in a real performance. Hence, when the real performance came the singers were sure of themselves, having had such preliminary training wherein the integration into a unitary group had been well prepared in advance. We had already passed through the strainer and were ready for any contingency, sure and confident of our individual roles. After we all left, sometimes as late as 2:00 in the morning, it was not unusual for the inexhaustible Toscanini to stay on and direct lighting, working with the electricians and technicians until the early hours of the morning, to make sure everything satisfied his demands. At nine he was ready to go back to the theater for stage rehearsals and at 1:00 P.M. for the orchestra. I often wondered where he got his strength for this ordeal, since I never saw him take any food, except occasionally a date and a cup of coffee. ૨ઙ

Raisa maintained a strong personal connection with the Maestro even after she retired from the stage. She often visited him in Italy, usually at the Salsomaggiore Terme, and at his Riverdale, New York, home.[8]

After her nine Asterias at La Scala, Raisa went to her villa for vacation and study. From autumn 1924 to the end of the 1926 La Scala season, Raisa and Rimini worked virtually nonstop. In the next two seasons Raisa added to her list of roles Cio-Cio-San, the Marschallin in German, Fedora, Turandot, and Toinette in *A Light from Saint Agnes*. Now thirty-one years old and a veteran singer with almost eleven years of experience, Raisa was in her prime.

In the autumn of 1924 *Musical America* ran a lead article titled "What Is the Future of Chicago's Opera?"

It is known that Miss Muzio has made complaint, not only to Mr. Johnson, the business manager, but to Mr. Insull regarding the manner in which she has been cast. The difficulties here plainly have had a connection with the prominence in the company of Rosa Raisa, whose roles and those of Miss Muzio are much the same. There has never been any attempt to disguise the fact that there was a close friendship between Conductor Polacco and his wife and Mme. Raisa and her husband, Giacomo Rimini. They were together abroad last summer and they have continued their close relations in Chicago. Whether there is any justice in the charges that this friendship has worked to Mme. Raisa's benefit and Miss Muzio's disadvantage in the matter of appearances is a subject of dispute, since theoretically at least, Johnson and not Polacco decides on the casts.

By the terms of Mme. Raisa's contract, the Opera Company must also take Rimini. The baritone has been rather severely criticized in the Chicago press and this provision of the Raisa contract is one of a number of details with respect to the engagement of artists that have become subjects of lively discussions. There is no lack of defenders for the singers who have been placed, rightly or not, as of the Polacco group. Chicago is very fond of Polacco, not only as the one really big conductor it has had since Campanini and Marinuzzi, but as a man. Both Polacco and his American wife have made hosts of friends. . . .

[Referring to rehearsal conditions] Where, it is being asked, lies the fault for this condition? With the manager or the musical director? The same question is raised repeatedly as to casts. Friends of Claudia Muzio insist that Rosa Raisa, a close friend of Polacco and his wife, Edith Mason, is not only favored over Miss Muzio in the matter of roles and number of performances, but in that of supporting casts. They point out that, while as much entitled to the honor as Mme. Raisa, Miss Muzio has never been permitted to open a season. That honor inevitably falling to the other dramatic soprano. They ask if Mme. Raisa would have been called upon to take up a role such as Margherita in *Mefistofele,* who has only one important scene, and they regard Miss Muzio's triumph in this work as something of a discomfiture for what they style the Polacco-Mason-Raisa-Rimini faction.

The frequent appearances of Giacomo Rimini in important roles continue to be a matter of discussion. As is generally known, Mme. Raisa's contract requires the company to take her husband also. Indicative of feelings of patrons of the opera, a letter bearing the date of Dec. 4 was published in the *Chicago Tribune,* which did not mention the name of the singer referred to, but which did not need so to be perfectly clear to those who read it. Headed, "The Baritone Who Sings Off Pitch," the letter read as follows:

From left to right: Polacco, Mason, Raisa, and Rimini at the Lido outside Venice, 1924. The close friendship of the two couples was at the root of a power struggle within the Chicago Opera. (Collection of the late Giulietta Segala.)

"Will you permit a grand opera subscriber of six years a word as to the rights of opera lovers? Repeatedly the beautiful operas are utterly ruined by a certain baritone, who has no voice at all, cannot sing on pitch, and while he may act and dress the part, that is not what we pay for. Opera requires a singing voice, not so much the dress and acting.

A number of subscribers have canceled their subscriptions because they drew this supposed baritone so often on their night in years past. If box office receipts are worth considering, it would be wise to keep this artist (?) off the cast. Pay him his salary if he has to be kept on the payroll, but give the public a chance to enjoy opera—Subscriber."

The 1924–1925 season opened with *La Gioconda* with Raisa, Perini, Kathryn Meisle, Antonio Cortis, Formichi, and Alexander Kipnis, and Polacco conducting. Raisa sang Elisabeth in *Tannhäuser*, Aida, Santuzza, Rachel, Maliella, and Desdemona this season. Muzio sang Tosca, Leonora, Aida, Violetta, and Marguerite in *Mefistofele* with Chaliapin. About Raisa's Gioconda, Eugene Stinson wrote, "Of Raisa's magnificent gifts Chicago is well aware. They were abundantly spent upon a role of great latitude if not of equal importance with some others in her repertoire. The amazing volume and richness of her voice are unparalleled anywhere where such things are regarded as worthy of attention, praise and recompense, they are a particular value to the Chicago company and they were of the utmost effective use last night." Glen Dillard Gunn noted, "She is all that Toscanini proclaimed her, the greatest Italian dramatic soprano of the present. I remember Nordica in that role, and the comparison is in no way to Raisa's disadvantage." Regarding her Elisabeth one writer noted, "Olga Forrai was announced to debut as Elisabeth in *Tannhäuser*, but she was not ready for the part and Rosa Raisa got up in it after having left it alone for three years. She always disliked and distrusted German opera for her own voice, and did as little of it as possible, and the world is the loser, for there are parts in the German repertoire which, had she chosen, she could have made her own with few to contest her place."

Raisa finished her part of the 1925 tour in Milwaukee on March 14, then went to New York and sailed from there to Italy. She made her reentry at La Scala as Asteria on April 13. While performing her role in *Nerone*, rehearsed the previous season, she started work on Leonora in a new production of *Il Trovatore*, remarkably last performed in this Verdian temple in 1902. Originally, this new *Trovatore* was to

Caricature of the Trovatore *cast drawn in 1925 by basso Fernando Autori, as it appeared in* Musical Courier *under the caption "A Memorable* Il Trovatore *Performance." Toscanini delayed this important new production from the winter to the spring of 1925 to ensure Raisa's participation. From left to right: Raisa as Leonora, Aureliano Pertile as Manrico, Fanny Anitua as Azucena, Benvenuto Franci as Di Luna, and Fernando Autori as Ferrando.*

be unveiled in late February with a cast of Giannina Arangi-Lombardi, Casazza, Crimi, and Benvenuto Franci. However, Toscanini was "dissatisfied with the cast, which he considers inadequate,"[9] and he put off the premiere until Raisa was available later in the spring. April 30 saw the premiere of this new production, whose massive scenery graced the pages of *The Victor Book of the Opera* for many editions. Fanny Anitua, Pertile, and Franci rounded out the cast. The Milanese critic of the *Musical Courier* wired,

> The first performance of *Il Trovatore* at La Scala this season took place April 30 and was by far the most thrilling presentation of a standard repertory opera this season. The particular feature of the evening was the appearance of Rosa Raisa as Leonora. Her magnificent voice and highly dramatic singing and acting won for her a success which can honestly be described as a triumph. In the first and fourth acts in par-

ticular she was superb. The audience, wildly enthusiastic, interrupted the opera to give her an ovation, and the press praised her extravagantly with one voice. The cast was excellent throughout and the staging impressive. Toscanini gave a vital and moving reading of the old score and shared with Mme. Raisa first honors of the evening.

Despite what letter writers to Chicago newspapers thought, Rimini was a Toscanini favorite, and was awarded all the Falstaffs in two La Scala seasons: 1924–1925 and 1925–1926. Toscanini had taught Rimini the role and had cast him in a run of *Falstaff* at the Teatro Dal Verme in 1915. He was the only Falstaff, other than Mariano Stabile, to sing this significant role under Toscanini during his eight-year tenure as the all-powerful director of La Scala.[10] When Dalla Rizza canceled her May 12 and May 15 performances,

◈ Toscanini was anxious to continue with more performances of *Falstaff* and he looked around for another Alice Ford. My husband happened to mention my name in this connection saying that I had sung this role at the Teatro Colón in Buenos Aires and also with the Chicago Company. I immediately received a call from the management of La Scala that Toscanini wanted to see me. When I arrived the maestro asked whether I would sing Alice with him. My answer was that I would be very happy to do so if I could remember the part after several years during which I had not sung it. The Maestro said "If you knew the part then you should know it for a lifetime, and if you don't remember it means you never knew it." At this my pride was hurt and I asked him to hear me. I said "Maestro, I see the score on the piano, why don't you try me out?" I sang a few phrases and observed with satisfaction that he was pleased and smiling. A rehearsal was ordered the next day for the whole cast for my part alone and the very next night I sang *Falstaff*, a role I adored singing because it was a welcome change, a rest, after all these heavy roles such as Norma, Aida, Tosca, Gioconda, etc. The performance went beautifully, without a single mistake, and I was bubbling over with joy and pride. At the end, after all the curtain calls with the maestro, he hugged me backstage in front of the whole cast saying, and these are his exact words, "Brava la bella Alice," and coming from Toscanini these words meant very much! We continued for more performances [one more]. I was happy also because I had not disappointed the great Falstaff, Giacomo Rimini, who had recommended his wife for the role of Alice. It was a great satisfaction for me to learn that the critics reviewed these performances in glowing terms, saying that I had passed with great intelligence from the dramatic to the lyric to my new role, adapting even the color of the voice to the part I sang, and adding that I was now at the apex of my career. ?

After the La Scala season Raisa and Rimini participated in a rare enterprise, the Italian-French-American Opera at Paris's Théâtre Gaîté-Lyrique. This company was created by the impresario Paolo Longone.[11] Longone was the assistant to R. E. Johnson, a leading American concert manager who listed Gigli, Ruffo, Tetrazzini, and the Riminis on his roster of artists. He had been a classmate of Raisa's at San Pietro a Majella. Longone was once married to the American soprano Carolina White. Later he married Carol Perronot, an accomplished pianist who had studied with Thalberg at the Cincinnati Conservatory. Carol Perronot Longone was often the concert accompanist for Raisa and Rimini in the 1920s and 1930s. I was fortunate to interview Carol Longone in her last years. The Italian-French-American Opera pulled together leading singers of the Metropolitan, Chicago, Paris, and La Scala operas. Mary Garden, Elvira de Hidalgo, Spani, Casazza, Fernand Ansseau, Hackett, Lauri-Volpi, Baklanoff, Didur, Giuseppe De Luca, Lazzari, Luigi Montesanto, Vanni-Marcoux, and of course the Riminis were the featured artists. Roberto Moranzoni and Panizza were the conductors. Representative casts: May 21 opening-night L'Amore de Tre Re with Garden, Ansseau, and Lazzari; May 22 Il Barbiere with de Hidalgo, Hackett, De Luca, and Didur; and May 23 Il Trovatore with Raisa, Casazza, Pedro Lafuente, Montesanto, and Didur. After a repeat of Il Trovatore on May 26, Falstaff was performed on June 1 with Raisa, Casazza, Queena Mario, Hackett, Rimini, Désiré

Defrère, Angelo Bada, and Didur. After a final *Tosca* on June 12 the company folded and the artists went unpaid. Carol told me that she and her husband left Paris in the middle of the night like fugitives in a crime movie.[12] This bad experience, however, did not poison relations between the Riminis and the Longones. Carol was to remain one of Raisa's closest friends until her death in 1963, and Paolo (Paul) managed the Chicago Grand (later renamed Chicago City) Opera seasons in the 1930s, after the fall of Samuel Insull's more luxurious Chicago Civic Opera.

Raisa and Rimini were engaged for the 1925 season at the Ravinia summer festival outside Chicago. This was unusual, as Ravinia routinely featured Metropolitan Opera singers such as Rethberg, Lucrezia Bori, Martinelli, and Danise—singers who did not appear in Chicago during the winter. Although Raisa's large following in Chicago made the short trip to Ravinia to hear her in familiar roles, the festival also offered her in two new ones: Cio-Cio-San and Fedora. There was some doubt as to her ability to successfully sing and act the petite Japanese heroine, as the role had traditionally been sung by lyric sopranos (although early in its life the dramatic soprano Destinn had performed the role successfully in London and New York). The first *Madama Butterfly* on July 2 brought forth some exceptional critiques. Hackett in the *Post* noted,

> Not since the days of Mme. Emmy Destinn's prime has a dramatic singer of such caliber sung this music. But there was in Mme. Raisa's singing of the dramatic moments a whole-hearted sincerity and sheer vocal power such as Mme. Destinn never attained, and it used to be said that vocally Mme. Destinn came the nearest to Puccini's ideal. In the opening scene, Mme. Raisa from the first note of the entrance music used a lightly poised tone which had in it the note of maidenliness and joy. She rose with delightful surety to the climax on the high D flat, which she sustained with satisfying power. All through the act she maintained this light poise with a vocal control finer than anything she ever displayed before. It was a new thing in her singing. Not until the final moment of the duet at the close of the act did she bring forth

the golden opulence of her tone, and even then she did not permit the deeper colors to enter, reserving them for the later scenes. All this with a lightness of touch and an ease that were astonishing. There was no sense of restraint, no feeling that she was holding her voice back so losing something of the essential quality, but rather that she was expressing with just the right tone quality the spontaneous joy of a maiden whose heart had never been clouded by intense grief. In the second act she gave full play to the magnificence of her vocal gifts. The tone had a richness of color with a variety of shading to express the passing mood and when the moment came with a stroke of such downright power as drove the thing home to the last seat. Her singing was but the medium for the revealing of her thought and was always exactly attuned to the unfolding of the story. Dramatic singing in the fullest meaning of the term.

Edward Moore in the *Tribune* confessed,

> For quite a number of years Mme. Raisa has been one of my great admirations in the world of opera. Sometimes, it is true, it was admiration with the reservation that here was one of the world's most magnificent voices which did not always express a warm, human emotion. This performance convinced me that if such a reservation ever became necessary in the future, it would be the fault of the role and not the artist. For here was the same gorgeous voice with all its sparkling bead suddenly becoming emotional, human, sexy, everything that a voice ought to express in a modern part.

And Eugene Stinson of the *Chicago Journal* was amazed by

> Raisa's singing, like her acting, [which] struck new depths in her ability. When has she ever sung with such consistent delicacy, with such unrelenting attention upon what is beautiful and careful and discerning in the use of her glorious but often-lawless voice? As she discovered new graces of characterization, so she had found new refinement of vocal style. As she brought into the role an occasional profundity of tragic force, ever so delicately indicated yet still new to the traditions, so her use of an unmatched soprano gave the score a breadth and fullness it surely has never before known.

Midway through the Ravinia season Raisa received news of her father's sudden death in New York. She and Rimini made the long train trip east for his funeral and burial at Montefiore Cemetery. Family friend Cantor Rosenblatt chanted the committal prayers at the services. Raisa rushed back to Ravinia, taking only forty-eight hours for the round trip and the funeral. Although she was prepared to give her announced performance of *Madama Butterfly* on the night of August 5, she implored Louis Eckstein, the director of the festival, "I have managed to uphold the tradition of the stage tonight [by showing up to perform if "the show must go on"]. Now I must ask you not to schedule me to appear again for a week, at least. The grief of a daughter for a truly beloved father has its rights also."[13] Eckstein was clearly moved by her plea, and *La Bohème* was hastily substituted for the advertised *Madama Butterfly*. Raisa's wish for a traditional "shivah" mourning period was granted. She resumed performing on August 11 in *La Juive*.

On August 1 Raisa presented her Fedora with Martinelli. A young Claudia Cassidy was at this time starting her writing career at the *Journal of Commerce*. Later to become the all-powerful "make or break" critic of the *Tribune*, Cassidy admitted that Raisa was something of a "fetish" with her, and throughout her career she wrote of the soprano in very purple prose. Here is one of the first examples:

Rosa Raisa and Giovanni Martinelli have written some new chapters in the history of opera and the present Ravinia season has launched many of their finest achievements. Greatness is expected of them, and for that reason Saturday night's performance of *Fedora* aroused satisfaction rather than astonishment. . . . To add that Mme. Raisa sang the name part Saturday night for the first time in her brilliant career is but to acknowledge the ideal casting which characterizes our summer opera. Such a performance might easily have dominated the opera to the extent of subordinating the portrayal of Fedora—except for the fact that Raisa was singing it. Her dramatic soprano of astonishing range and lyric charm has evoked so many glittering tributes that the most sincere appreciation hints of plagiarism, but all of them might be repeated by way of justice to her success. Gifted with a fine sense of the fitness of things and with stately loveliness to grace any stage, she rivals Mr. Martinelli in adaptability. "Fedora," like most Sardou melodrama, falls depressingly flat without the appeal of beauty and magnetism contrasted with Romantic appeal. Mme. Raisa was unerringly the great lady. A blond wig chosen with fine discretion, jewels rather than jewelry, gleaming black satin, deep textured ermine, the glitter of crystal against sea green—these were a few of the pictures in an evening of unalloyed pleasure.

After Ravinia, Raisa and Rimini went to California to participate in the Los Angeles Opera season. This was the second year of the new organization; Raisa opened the season with an *Aida* that also featured Meisle, Lappas, Rimini, and Edouard Cotreuil, with Richard Hageman conducting. *Cavalleria* with Charles Hackett and Vincente Ballester was the other Raisa offering in this brief season. Following a short concert tour Raisa opened the 1925–1926 Chicago season as the Marschallin in *Der Rosenkavalier*, with Olga Forrai from Prague's German Opera as Octavian, and with Mason and Kipnis; Polacco conducted. Raisa later said one of the most difficult things she ever had to do was relearn an opera in a different language. In this case she had learned the opera in Italian for South America in 1915, and now she had to master the role in German. *Ballo, Aida, Madama Butterfly, Falstaff, La Juive,* and *A Light from Saint Agnes* were her other operas this season, and she sang *Otello* on the tour. *A Light from Saint Agnes* by the American W. Franke Harling was a one-act opera with jazz elements. Baklanoff and Lamont rounded out the cast of this novelty, which was given a solitary hearing. One Chicago critic wrote, "Miss Raisa found much in the role of Toinette to bring out in an extremely realistic impersonation of a drunken but redeemable creature of misfortune. Much of the part is declaimed in the low soprano register, yet there were opportunities for Mme. Raisa's melting pianissimos and for one of her fearless high C's." Of Raisa's January 15, 1926, Rachel in *La Juive*, Cassidy penned another of her effusions:

Rosa Raisa's portrayal of Rachel is traditional, yet with each hearing it seems to outdo all her former performances. Last night her voice was

Rosa Ponselle, 1925. Ponselle dedicated this photo to her good friend Raisa. Mish-kin Studio, New York. (Collection of the late Giulietta Segala.)

[127]

a golden glory of tumultuous melody, pouring forth in a liquid stream that had neither shallows nor bounds. Mme. Raisa's range is seemingly limitless, and *La Juive* gives her superb opportunities to display the cascading rush of volume which softens with perfect rhythm into sustained lyric song of ineffable sweetness. Last night it was her triumph.

· *Chapter Nine* ·

TURANDOT

W HEN sixty-five-year-old Puccini died in Brussels in November 1924, he left behind the unfinished score of *Turandot*. He was not to be present at its birth. To be human is to know the great masterpieces of art, but these works didn't exist from time immemorial; there was a time before *Hamlet* and the Sistine Chapel. They had to be brought to life, often under stressful conditions, in order to enter our consciousness. *Turandot* was the last major opera to do so. It once existed only as a score in Toscanini's briefcase. He was on leave from La Scala conducting the New York Philharmonic. Commuting from Boston while on tour, Raisa and Rimini called on Toscanini at the Astor Hotel on the afternoon of their January 31 evening concert at Mecca Temple. They were given the *Turandot* score and went over their roles.[1] Little known is that the creator was first handed her score not in Milan but in that hotel room on Broadway. The Riminis completed the tour on March 16 and took a liner to Italy. This allowed little more than three weeks' rehearsal time for *Turandot*, which premiered April 25. In her memoir Raisa admits:

ᐊ I arrived at La Scala two weeks late. Rehearsals had already started with the rest of the cast. As I entered I did not see the Maestro's smile, which meant that he was angry; and he certainly was! But it was not really my fault. I had hoped that the Chicago Civic Opera would release me two weeks earlier so I could go on with the *Turandot* rehearsals, but this was, as I explained, impossible. So I just had to be late! Nevertheless, when the ante-general rehearsal came, Toscanini came to my dressing room telling me how pleased he was with my work. However, I realized that this was quite a loss to the management of

La Scala, a loss for which I felt personally responsible, since they had to give extra performances [of other operas] to fill in until *Turandot* was launched. This troubled me so much that at the end of my seven [eight] performances I turned in my entire fee, which was considerable, to the management. And thus my conscience was relieved and I felt very happy to have done what I thought was proper. And the management was very appreciative of this generous gesture on my part. ❧

In her last years Raisa gave several radio interviews in which she was asked to recall details of the preparations for *Turandot*. Among her vivid recollections were that Toscanini insisted that the artists sing all rehearsals full voice, and that he gave a lot of attention to the Ping-Pang-Pong scenes, trying to find the exact musical and dramatic balance. She recalled that he was tireless in his attention to detail both musical and scenic, that nothing escaped his notice, that he rarely ate anything, and that the artists had no certain advance knowledge that the final duet was to be omitted at the first performance. She suggested that there were rumblings that this might happen, but the artists were never told this officially. Perhaps word had leaked out that Puccini had told Toscanini, near the end of his life when he realized that he would not complete *Turandot*, that he would like an announcement to be made at the premiere to the effect that "the composer wrote so far; then he died."[2]

Having given her description of the night of the premiere hundreds of times over the years, Raisa in her memoir presents her most complete account:

❧ La Scala was in its best dress and offered a marvelous sight. Never have I seen it in such splendor and I could sense the great anticipation of the illustrious audience. It was an electrified atmosphere, with the greatest musicians and critics in the world gathered for this world premiere and listening religiously to Puccini's last creation. At the end of the Third Act [first scene], while the dead Liù is accompanied by Timur, with Ping, Pang, and Pong following, and as the chorus continues to intone the motif of the last aria that she sang, until the whole stage is emptied, Toscanini laid down his baton, and in a voice choking with emotion announced that this is where Puccini left off: "Here is where the maestro died." After a moment of silence during which I, as Turandot, stood motionless in front of the palace, while Calaf, opposite me, equally overcome by the profound sadness which engulfed the entire audience, I could sense the grief of everyone present. Then as the curtains slowly closed, the public burst into applause which soon turned into a grand and interminable ovation. Toscanini himself, deeply moved, remained motionless backstage, so that we had to take the first curtain calls alone. Then, when he had composed himself a bit, he joined us for many more.

The general consensus of opinion was that this was indeed the most difficult task that Puccini ever assigned anyone: to render this difficult and tragic character understandable. And they said that I must have made an exact account of what I wished to get out of this erratic figure, without neglecting the dramatic aspect, vocally and histrionically solving with utmost intelligence the great riddle of this sphinx-like character. Raisa, they said, had succeeded also in solving the problem of the plasticity of this character despite the serpent in her soul. And, that I managed to overcome the great distances of the Scala stage as it then was, which made it even more difficult to convey the message to the public and "requiring an enormous vocal ability to achieve." As a matter of fact, from where I stood high up, at the rear of the stage, Toscanini seemed extremely small and hard to detect. The first ones to come and congratulate us, with tears in their eyes, were Mme. Elvira Puccini and her son Antonio.

I should like to close this account of the first performance of *Turandot* with the following observation regarding Maestro Toscanini's part in this creation. He undertook this task as a sacred duty. Even as he had restored Catalani and Boito, so here again after studying and discussing the score with the ailing Puccini until the details revealed the grand lines of this masterpiece. Toscanini finally plunged into the Puccini score until he could communicate the intense joy of this creation, integrating the many contrasting elements of both the comedy

Two of the four extant solo photos of Raisa as Turandot from the world premiere.
Castagneri Studio, Milan. (Collection of the late Frieda Goldenberg.)

and tragedy of this unique opera, in such a way that Puccini's vision emerged in all its brilliance. Toscanini the artist and master craftsman applied himself to this task with the precision of the mathematician and the gentleness of the poet until the magic of his great art resulted in a perfect performance. ૨*

Milan's newspaper of record, the *Corriere della Sera*, reported,

> Rosa Raisa had the difficult task awaiting her on the stage. Although the role contained many conflicting emotions not once did she shrink from the dramatic demands placed on her nor did she overact. With the intelligence so typical of her she solved the problems of the role. What remained after all is said and done was a complete portrayal that succeeded without betraying the true essence of the character. Her dramatic gifts were matched by her vocal gifts in the struggle with the arduous tessitura of the part. The great demands of volume made in the Second Act of the opera on her voice were handily met and her voice traveled easily from the stage to the far reaches of the gallery. This was especially evident in the long and taxing riddle scene which held no terrors for her voice nor did it for a moment diminish its volume.

Faith Compton Mackenzie, who was present at the premiere, later wrote that "Raisa played the Princess coldly magnificent; Fleta was disappointing as her lover, and Zamboni was exquisite as Liù."[3] The basso Tancredi Pasero, generally no admirer of Raisa's, thought she was superbly cast in the title role,[4] and the conductor, Gianandrea Gavazzeni, thought that casting Raisa as Turandot was "absolutely ideal."[5]

Raisa also expressed the opinion that the final duet by Alfano was not particularly to her liking, and that Toscanini shared this assessment, without being more specific.[6] This was for Raisa the high point of her career; nothing could surpass the honor of creating Turandot. Toscanini conducted only the first three performances before he withdrew, citing a nervous collapse. Some Milanese newspapers even suggested that he needed a long vacation. Panizza replaced him for the

TEATRO ALLA SCALA
(ENTE AUTONOMO)
STAGIONE DI CARNEVALE-QUARESIMA 1925-26

TURANDOT

DRAMMA LIRICO IN TRE ATTI E CINQUE QUADRI DI GIUSEPPE ADAMI E RENATO SIMONI
MUSICA DI GIACOMO PUCCINI
DUETTO E SCENA FINALI COMPLETATI DA FRANCO ALFANO
(Proprietà G. RICORDI & C.)

NUOVISSIMA

PERSONAGGI

La Principessa Turandot . . S'g.ª ROSA RAISA	Ping, Grande cancelliere . . Sig. GIACOMO RIMINI
L'Imperatore Altoum . . . . Sig. FRANCESCO DOMINICI	Pang, Gran provveditore . . » EMILIO VENTURINI
Timur, Re tartaro spodestato . » CARLO WALTER	Pong, Grande cuciniere . . . » GIUSEPPE NESSI
Il Principe Ignoto (Calaf) suo	Un Mandarino . . . . » ARISTIDE BARACCHI
figlio . . . . » FRANCO LO GIUDICE	Il Principino di Persia . . . » N. N.
Liù, giovine schiava . . . . Sig.ª MARIA ZAMBONI	Il Carnefice . . . . » N. N.

Guardie Imperiali - Servi del boia - Ragazzi - Sacerdoti
Mandarini - Dignitari - Sapienti - Ancelle di Turandot - Soldati - Portabandiere - Musici - Le Ombre dei Morti - Folla
A Pekino – Ai tempi delle favole

MAESTRO CONCERTATORE E DIRETTORE
ETTORE PANIZZA
Maestro del Coro: VITTORE VENEZIANI
Maestro della Banda: MARSILIO CECCARELLI — Coreografo: GIOVANNI PRATESI
Direttore della messa in scena: GIOVACCHINO FORZANO — Direttore dell'allestimento scenico: CARAMBA
Costumi e attrezzi su bozzetti di CARAMBA
Bozzetti e scene dipinte da GALILEO CHINI colla collaborazione di ALESSANDRO MAGNONI
Direttori del Macchinario: GIOVANNI e PERICLE ANSALDO

Turandot cast page from a later performance in the initial run of the opera. Toscanini withdrew after three performances citing "nervous exhaustion" and was replaced by Ettore Panizza.

five remaining performances. Toscanini never again conducted *Turandot*. Fleta also participated in only the first three performances; Franco Lo Giudice replaced him.

Tullio Serafin recalled working with Maria Jeritza on *Turandot* for the Metropolitan Opera premiere in November that year. He commented that Jeritza's voice, although pure and rich, was a little short on the very top. At one of the early rehearsals she asked him to "change or transpose down some of Turandot's music." He refused her request and chastised her: "You're nothing but a bluff: you claim that the role of Turandot was written perfectly for you. Raisa claims that, too. But Raisa can sing it as it is written, and you can't." He then related that after his stern rebuke she shut up and blushed, but also that she worked hard, got the top notes, and sang the role exactly as written. Serafin must have heard Raisa in one of the very last perfor-

[135]

mances at La Scala in mid-May, for he was conducting on the Met tour until early May that year.[7]

Some other *Turandot* notes: It was reported that Voce del Padrone (HMV) set up microphones, planning to capture this historic premiere using the new electric recording technology. As it happened, the matrixes were mistakenly labeled "defective" and destroyed when the crate arrived at the Hayes factory in west London.[8] It is also interesting that there is so little photo documentation of this historic occasion. The author knows of only four solo photos of Raisa in her *Turandot* robes; however, there are several rather indistinct full-stage photos of this large-scale production. Raisa stated in a *Musical America* interview in November 1924, shortly after the announcement that she had been chosen to be the creator, that she planned to buy the elaborate Chinese fabrics for her costumes in San Francisco's Chinatown.[9] In the 1925–1926 Chicago Opera programs, the Marshall Field department store advertised that their studios were executing Raisa's Turandot costumes. The Scala program of the premiere credits Scala artist Caramba as the costume designer. Could it be that the Caramba designs were sent to Marshall Field to execute with the fabrics Raisa supplied? Raisa sang Turandot eight times at La Scala that first season, and sang it only six more times in her career—twice in 1929 at the Colón in Buenos Aires with Georges Thill, and four times in Chicago, in 1934 and 1935. Bianca Scacciati, Maria Jeritza, Mária Németh, Gina Cigna, Anne Roselle, and Eva Turner were the most prominent performers of the role in the years leading up to World War II. It is puzzling, and a tremendous loss for posterity, that an important Puccini opera— indeed his last—entering the standard repertory had so little photographic and no surviving recorded documentation of its premiere, as both photography and sound recording were in wide use at that time.

Raisa wrote in Yiddish to her sister Frieda in New York shortly after the somewhat frantic Scala season that she and Rimini were exhausted and were taking a much-needed long summer vacation.[10] What she didn't say was that she and Rimini were planning to start a family. This effort was to last five years, until Raisa succeeded in bearing a child in July 1931. Raisa had a very strong maternal instinct ánd was determined to have a child of her own. She said she would not feel "complete" as a woman until she had a child. To achieve their goal and to reduce the pressures of their usual exhausting schedule, the couple deliberately declined many prestigious engagements and limited their commitments to Chicago and its tours, with very few exceptions. (In 1927 Covent Garden tried on short notice to engage Raisa to sing Turandot when Maria Jeritza canceled, but Raisa did not make herself available for this important engagement.)[11] Between summer 1926 and 1930 Raisa suffered at least six miscarriages. Her fragile condition was a subject of newspaper gossip for five years. Her medical circumstances were well known in certain circles, and on occasion reviewers discreetly hinted at her appearance and compromised vocal and physical strength.

In late September, Raisa and Rimini did accept a short engagement with the Los Angeles Opera, at which they had performed the year before. Raisa gave her now-celebrated Cio-Cio-San, Tosca, Aida, and Leonora in *Il Trovatore*, and achieved her customary success. On the way to Chicago for the 1926–1927 season, she and Rimini gave several concerts. For this season Muzio was finally honored with an opening night: *Aida* on November 8. Raisa offered her Maliella in *I Gioielli della Madonna* the second night. The season included no new roles, but there were repeats of Aida, Rachel, Santuzza, Tosca, and Amelia. On New Year's Eve a new production of *Don Giovanni* was mounted with Raisa, Louise Loring, Mason, Vanni-Marcoux, Schipa, Lazzari, and Kipnis; Polacco conducted. Raisa had already performed Donna Anna in Philadelphia in 1914 and in Buenos Aires in 1918. The controversial production featuring futuristic and cubist sets was not appreciated in conservative Chicago, but musically it was praised. Raisa's performance could only be compared at this time to her own past performances or to Nordica's. Gunn wrote, "The superb Raisa, subdued the splendid power of her voice to match the fragile Mozart melody, and sang with all the detailed attention to shading and phrasing that Fritz Kreisler might expend on the same music." This was a very different Raisa from the twenty-one-year-old singing the *Figaro* Countess at Covent Garden thirteen years before. Arthur Meeker, scion of one of Chicago's first families and an ardent opera lover, told in his 1955 memoir, *Chicago with Love*, of his personal preference for Raisa as the Marschallin and as Donna Anna over her usual Italian roles. Meeker recalled,

> Others spent their best years in Chicago. I think the one we loved the most was Rosa Raisa, who, though born in Russia and long a loyal American citizen, was nevertheless the greatest Italian woman singer of the day. I admired her especially as Donna Anna and the Marschallin in *Rosenkavalier*—roles she herself would rather have avoided: even then I cared more for Mozart and Strauss than for Ponchielli and Verdi. I call her the greatest because there was something invincibly noble about her that shone in everything she did; she was our queen and, modest as she was, looked the part grandly. She still does. I was happy to be able to tell her so the last time we met in Chicago, not so many years ago. She smiled and said, in the soft speaking voice that seemed to have nothing to do with her flame-like dramatic soprano: "Ah! A dethroned queen. . . ."[12]

The 1927 tour featured Muzio in *Traviata* and *Tosca*, Raisa in *Aida* and *I Gioielli della Madonna*, and Mary Garden in Alfano's *Resurrection (Risurrezione)*. A short concert tour after the opera season preceded the Riminis' return to San Floriano for a summer of rest and recreation. In September 1927 Raisa and Rimini gave a rare concert before an overflow audience in Venice's Piazza San Marco. Raisa sang "O patria mia" and "Casta Diva," and the *Gioconda* and *Trovatore* duets with Rimini.

The 1927–1928 season was a long one with many highlights, including the first national broadcasts of opera in North America, or at least the first regularly scheduled broadcasts of performances by a major company.[13] Muzio again opened the season, this time with her famous Violetta, and also performed Loreley, Aida, Santuzza, Tosca, and Leonora in *Il Trovatore*; Raisa sang Aida, Gioconda, Amelia, Alice Ford, and Maliella, and added a new role, Rosalinde in *Fledermaus*. The Johann Strauss masterpiece was presented in English and unveiled on New Year's Eve with Irene Pavloska, Lamont, Hackett, Rimini, and

Raisa with her close friend Toti Dal Monte aboard the S.S. Conte Rosso *returning to America from Italy, circa 1927. (Collection of the late Giulietta Segala.)*

Mojica as a tenor Orlofsky; Toti Dal Monte graced the second-act party scene with the "Carnival of Venice" variations.

La Gioconda and *Fledermaus* were Raisa's broadcast operas this season. These broadcasts presented only the first hour (8–9 P.M.) of the opera being performed on a given night, usually although not always Wednesdays. In fact, in the five seasons of these broadcasts the designated evening was changed several times. An informative newspaper account best describes the technology involved in the November 24 *Gioconda* broadcast:

> Before the [control] "board" are some twenty odd controls, one for every microphone, then for the stage as a whole, one for the orchestra, one for the general mixing pot, and others for uses I could not fathom, but all tuned one way or the other increasingly, above all are indicators showing the pressure and danger mark. These microphones will take just so much, and if the limit is overstepped . . . so the operator must know everything that is to happen on the stage and in the orchestra pit and be ready for it. A man with a score sits at his elbow and tells him of every coming crash for the orchestra and every high note full voice and all the soft passages too, so that all may be in balance. Once Mme. Raisa caught them with an unexpected one which shot the indicator up to sixty, but sixty could be taken, though that is the limit.[14]

On the 1928 tour Muzio played only Boston and Akron, concluding her season on February 15; Raisa finished the complete tour on April 2. Raisa sang Gioconda and Aida six times each as well as Maliella twice, Leonora in *Il Trovatore* four times, and Santuzza twice. Garden sang Katusha in *Resurrection* twelve times, *Carmen* and Massenet's *Sapho* twice each. At the conclusion of the tour Raisa and Rimini retired to their home in Italy.

On January 22, Raisa and Rimini gave the first of several annual concerts for the benefit of the Rosa Raisa Scholarship Fund. The purpose of this fund was to sponsor worthy young musicians for European study. The fund was a project of the Jewish People's Institute, a community house for Chicago's youth and a favorite cause of Mrs. Stone. Mrs. Stone was able to marshal patrons and sponsors from all segments of Chicago society. These annual concerts raised substantial sums.

· Chapter Ten ·

NORMA AGAIN

IN mid-September Raisa cabled manager Herbert Johnson that she would have to cancel in the 1928–1929 season. She was said to be near death in Italy, but *Musical Courier* reported that "it was whispered that Raisa is to become a mother in the spring and her physician forbade the sea voyage. . . . Raisa's cancellation made it imperative to secure another world-renowned dramatic soprano."[1] Muzio had also canceled her season, claiming a need to tend to her mother's illness.[2] Losing its two Italian stars sent the management scurrying to redesign the season. The English soprano Eva Turner was signed, providing coverage for Aida, Leonora, Amelia, and Santuzza. She also participated in a new production of *Le Nozze di Figaro*. A plan had been made to bring Frida Leider and a contingent of established German singers to Chicago for the 1929–1930 season, but this plan was now moved up one year. The Berlin Staatsoper was asked to release Leider in autumn 1928. They reluctantly released her for only three months for Chicago and the Boston section of the tour.[3] Of Raisa's roles she sang Rachel, Amelia, Donna Anna, and the Marschallin; to those she added Isolde and the Walküre Brünnhilde in the Wagner repertory. Maria Olczewska had already been engaged and sang the opening night *Carmen*. Turner and Leider were well received in their assignments, but there was no question that the company was not the same without Raisa and Muzio. As this was to be the last season in the famous Auditorium prior to the opening of the new opera house on Wacker Drive, a chapter was closing.

In early December it was announced that Raisa had recovered from her illness and planned to return in a new production of *Norma* to be unveiled New Year's Eve. In those years a new production could be

Raisa as Norma, 1928. This photo was taken during the short rehearsal period prior to her return to the stage on New Year's Eve after a life-threatening illness. Daguerre Studio, Chicago.

conceived, built, and premiered in less than a month. Coe Glade, who sang Adalgisa, told me that they rehearsed this bel canto opera for only nine days. This performance has become a Chicago Opera legend; no one who was fortunate enough to have been there that night ever forgot it. Thirty-five years later, in a nonmusical professional setting, I met a coworker who waxed on and on about this event; she had been an economics student at the University of Chicago and had the good fortune to be present that night. The brilliant singing and the deeply moving performance were accentuated by the additional element of audience excitement for Raisa's triumphant return. Most of the audience knew about her illness and realized how much they had missed her. Charles Marshall and Virgilio Lazzari completed the cast conducted by an inspired Polacco.

A selection of reviews of that night not only reveals the merits of the performance but also indicates the deep affection Raisa had earned over the years in Chicago. Claudia Cassidy reported:

> Vocal splendor broke over the Auditorium in great waves at the New Year's Eve performance when Rosa Raisa rejoined the opera company and proved in a magnificent display of Bellini pyrotechnics that she is one of the great artists of all time. All that we dream about in a prima donna is Mme. Raisa, of radiant beauty, queenly graciousness and glorious voice. Hearing her "Norma" makes us wonder how we got along without her all these operatic nights of her absence, but she makes up for our loss by coming back in better voice than ever. Her amazing dramatic soprano sparkled with color, flashed with emotion and fairly dazzled by the disdainful ease with which it surmounted one of the most difficult roles of all opera. Truly, having her back gives new zest to the waning season—the entire repertoire takes on fresh interest with her return.

Glenn Dillard Gunn thought that

> in a performance of Bellini's *Norma* which for sheer vocal display was the event of a lifetime . . . all these superhuman tasks Mme. Raisa disposed of with ease. Throughout the evening there was not a mo-

ment that hinted at a tax upon her voice. Its tone remained golden and glorious, eloquent, colored by the mood of the moment, so noble in quality that it is necessary to describe it as the greatest voice of the present, without even a mental reservation.

Herman Devries noted,

> The tone retains a trumpetlike quality and its astounding range and clarity. The execution of the florid passages had the brilliance of the most agile soprano leggiero, and all of her singing was impregnated with the vocal dignity of the great artist. If Mme. Raisa's deviations from pitch are mentioned it is not to blame her but to sympathize with a purely physical condition which no doubt further rest will correct.

Herman's son René, at the time the Chicago correspondent for *Musical Courier*, wrote of the performance,

> Sure of herself, Raisa in fortissimo passages did not hold back any of her strength and her voluminous tones practically shook the edifice to its very foundations. In the last act, so tender was her appeal to Oreveso that Lazzari, who sang the part, was so moved as to permit big tears to erase some of his makeup.

And Eugene Stinson both raved and qualified his rapture:

> It was indeed a pleasure to hear Mme. Raisa employing her familiar breadth and impetuosity of line, her richness of vocal coloring, her heroic declamation and that great vitality of feeling and ambition is of one quality with the spirit of theatrical excitement. . . . For Mme. Raisa has developed authoritativeness of style to a degree impossible to any singer, perhaps, who is not certain of her unfailing sway over a given public, or to any singer who has not the range of conception or the adequacy of vocal gifts which have enabled Mme. Raisa to such singular achievements. In some respects Mme. Raisa's rest has greatly benefited her voice, which has regained its luminosity, its softness and that marvelous technic of production which gives her tone such supreme carrying power even when she sings from the back of the stage. Yet Mme. Raisa by no means sang as perfectly as she should. The vocal line was completely distorted at times, due either to the unguarded

vehemence she poured into her singing or to her indifference to the bel canto style of which the Bellini score is an unrivaled example. And, furthermore, Mme. Raisa has not released her vocalism of a tendency to very incorrect pitch.

The above reviews by five of Chicago's most prominent observers reveal that Raisa's standing as a beloved artist was so secure that the negatives were mentioned only for the sake of accuracy. Raisa later told the *Tribune,* "I could not possibly thank them all and I do want to so much. It was so inspiring, so terribly affecting to me to step out on the stage and to receive that wonderful welcome—to know that Chicago loved me more than I ever thought. Just two months ago I was so dreadfully ill in Italy, and so depressed, and then to come back to Chicago, when I thought I could not be here to close the dear old Auditorium. It's like coming home again. Oh, I love Chicago."

Frida Leider attended the *Norma* performance and later recalled that from a singer's perspective, Raisa's particular advantage was "her completely firm upper register."[4] This observation had been made over and over through the years by Raisa's colleagues. Elsa Alsen, another great Wagnerian, told me that she had heard Raisa in a Chicago *Aida* in the mid-1920s and enthusiastically described how Raisa took the high C in "O patria mia" pianissimo, ballooned the tone to a huge fortissimo, and then made a decrescendo all on one breath.[5] Frequently, great artists have insights that allow them to appreciate the achievements of their peers. Alas, Raisa did not demonstrate on her two recordings of the aria the feat Alsen recalled.

The company's final performance in the Auditorium, on Saturday evening, January 26, was Gounod's *Roméo et Juliette,* the opera that Adelina Patti and Luigi Ravelli sang exactly forty years before at the opening of the historic theater. Mason and Hackett had the closing night honors. The last Saturday matinee was *Cavalleria* with Raisa, Lamont, and Luigi Montesanto. The ensuing tour saw Raisa give her *Aida* in Boston and her *Norma* in Detroit, Birmingham, Jackson, San Antonio, Los Angeles, Fresno, and Oakland. Patterson Greene in the *Los Angeles Examiner* wrote of the March 8 *Norma,*

Raisa in an anguished moment as Santuzza in Cavalleria Rusticana. *de Gueldre Studio, Chicago.*

Mme. Raisa rose triumphantly to the occasion, and supplied such vocalism as we have not heard from her before. Last night it was a new Raisa of gorgeous, appealing tones that had fire, pathos, and loveliness. When she was fairly launched in the great "Casta Diva" it was evident that great singing was to be the order of the evening. She flung forth high C's that were electrical in their effect. In the duet with the contralto in the third act, the fluent, suave, melodic line gave way to a shower of staccati and fioratura that were astounding. Hers was con-

Rimini and Raisa sang Falstaff *together in South America, Chicago, New York, Boston, Paris, Florence, and at La Scala. This late 1920s photo is by Chicago photographer Eugene Hutchinson.*

sistently the grand manner that the role requires, and she was regal to look upon.

Rosa Ponselle, in San Francisco for a March 15 concert, attended the March 16 *Norma* in Oakland. Years later in an interview with the *Baltimore Sun* she recalled that during the first intermission she visited Raisa in her dressing room and asked her, "How many more high C's do you have?" Raisa assured her there were many more, and a high D to boot.[6]

After the tour, the Riminis returned to Italy, where on April 25 Raisa sang the first of four *Normas* at the San Carlo in Naples with Gianna Pederzini, Isidoro Fagoaga, and Tancredi Pasero; Edoardo Vitale conducted. The Naples press carried articles about Raisa's connection with this city, her youth on Capri, and her training at the Conservatory with Barbara Marchisio. Raisa nostalgically recalled that

among the listeners was Maestro Francesco Cilea, who gave me a big reception at the conservatory with some of the outstanding pupils performing [possibly Maria Caniglia? This was Caniglia's final year at the Conservatory]. As I sat there in the very same music hall where I made my first attempts to sing the great operatic roles beginning with *Semiramide* by Rossini at the commencement exercises of this institution, I lived through again those beautiful years of hope and wonder without daring to dream of the great career that lay ahead of me. Was it really I who was sitting there again where I gained my thorough grounding in music, which was to carry me to the great heights I attained? I recalled that my teacher did give me a picture with the inscription: "Youngster, you were born for this glorious art, glory awaits you." And now Maestro Cilea dedicated a score of his opera *Adriana Lecouvreur* to me with the inscription, "To the great artist Rosa Raisa, with admiration, F. Cilea, 4 May 1929," and he asked me to try and get this opera performed by the Chicago Civic Opera. This proved impossible because the management was not inclined to embark upon such an expensive adventure requiring new scenery, costumes, etc., especially in view of the fact that this opera already had been given at the Metropolitan many years before and never repeated.

In fact, the Met had given *Adriana Lecouvreur* three times in 1907 with Caruso and Lina Cavalieri, and it was not a success then. This was not as big a story as was Ponselle's futile attempts to have the

Metropolitan mount this opera for her in the last years of her great career.

Raisa and Rimini accepted an engagement at the Teatro Colón in Buenos Aires for the 1929 season. It had been eleven years since Raisa last sang at the Colón in 1918, and eight years since she last sang a season in Buenos Aires, at the Coliseo in 1921. Buenos Aires had been the scene of some of her greatest triumphs. Raisa was again not well this season, being in the early stages of yet another pregnancy. The plans called for her to sing *Turandot, Norma, Aida, Il Trovatore,* and the South American premiere of Ottorino Respighi's *La Campana Sommersa.* The composer and his wife had traveled to Buenos Aires, and Raisa went through many of the rehearsals with them, but canceled at the last minute; Rautendelein was instead assigned to Marthe Nespoulous. The May 29 *Turandot,* Raisa's first since the La Scala premiere season of 1926, was a successful reentry to the Colón. This was not the Colón premiere of the opera; that had taken place in 1926 with Muzio and Lauri-Volpi. This season Georges Thill made his Buenos Aires debut as Calaf; he would sing four additional seasons there during the 1930s with great success.

The official history of the Colón indicates that the Raisa of 1929 was still a very great singer, but that the voice had lost some of its splendor since she last sang there in 1918.[7] The much anticipated first of seven *Normas,* on June 11 with Bertana, Pedro Mirassou, and Pasero, Capuana conducting, brought back old times for many. One critic wrote,

> Rosa Raisa returned to revive the exceptional memory which we hold of the great Russian artist and her interpretations at the Colón and the Coliseum. Why is it that these memories still live? Because Rosa Raisa gives a fundamental dramatic accent to her interpretations, a force and a motivating power which few voices are capable of. Last night we were able to admire her other than by her voice—through the integrity of her great interpretative qualities. Raisa gave an unsurpassable version by reason of her artistic vision with realizations, and furthermore by

the secrets of the technic of a rare school of singing. . . . What a harmonious tragic line in her gestures and figure; what nuances in her expressions, and what manner of penetrating the musical and dramatic life of this role!

Another writer added,

It was a night of delirium and remembrance. . . . When Rosa Raisa appeared on the scene, she seemed enveloped by a halo of glamour, and in the modulations of her singing to her face, her voice acquired an exquisite form. However, the great artist passes in the following acts from the idealistic poetry of her first singing to the passion which devours and dominates her in reality. Rosa Raisa gave the impression of having defined the psychology of the character she was impersonating, giving her a note of profoundly human emotion. All this she permitted to progress in the transformation which culminated in the final act, and which enveloped the public in an intense artistic emotion. A unanimous warm and enthusiastic ovation conferred on Rosa Raisa a magnificent triumph.

The seven *Norma*s Raisa sang this season, added to her previous fifteen in Buenos Aires, meant that she sang twenty-two of her seventy-three *Norma*s in this one city. Three *Aida*s with Rosette Anday from Vienna, Mirassou, Vincente Sempere, Rimini, and Pasero/Journet, Panizza conducting, and a single *Trovatore* with Bertana, Sempere, Apollo Granforte, and Pasero, Panizza conducting, rounded out Raisa's season. Rimini sang Sharpless, Figaro, Falstaff, Germont, and Amonasro. This was to be Raisa's farewell to South America, the scene of almost one-sixth of her career and an even higher proportion of her genuine triumphs. Once in Chicago when she was chided for her tendency to sing too forcefully, she replied, "Oh, you should hear me in South America where they really like loud singing!"[8]

Chapter Eleven

THE NEW OPERA HOUSE

PREGNANT again, Raisa returned to Chicago for the honor of opening the new multimillion-dollar skyscraper opera house on Wacker Drive November 4, 1929. The move from the old but acoustically superior Auditorium to the new "state-of-the-art" theater was the culmination of Chicago Civic Opera president Samuel Insull's dream to put his opera company on a sound financial footing. The idea was simple and logical: the rentals from the forty-plus floors of office space above the theater would provide the long-term subsidy needed to sustain the company. No longer were there to be endless campaigns raising money from the wealthy in order to keep the opera afloat. American democracy and civic pride were to be the underlying supports. There was just one serious flaw in the plan. The stock market crash just days before the opening night, and the ensuing Depression, would make this dream unworkable.

The nationally broadcast *Aida* featured, in addition to Raisa, Van Gordon, Marshall, Formichi, Lazzari, and Chase Baromeo, with Polacco conducting. The account of the occasion in *Musical America* read:

> For aside from the suitability of the music, it permitted the casting of a group of singers whose rise to glory has been coincident with that of the Chicago Opera. Chief of these was Rosa Raisa, who literally grew up with the company and has endeared herself to this public as but few singers ever have or ever will. Raisa is distinctly Chicago's own. Triumphs elsewhere on the globe can never erase Chicago's proprietary attitude toward her. Of course, as the Ethiopian slave girl, she was in her element. The powerful voice, with its depth and richness of color, soared to the heights of Verdi's melodic line with all its accustomed

thrill, and with perhaps an added emotional impulse redolent of the occasion.

The opening week of the 1929–1930 season also showcased the company's casting strength: *Iris* with Mason, Cortis, and Rimini; *La Traviata* with Muzio, Hackett, and Richard Bonelli; *Roméo et Juliette* with Mary McCormic and René Maison; *Tristan und Isolde* with Leider, Olczewska, Theodor Strack, Bonelli, and Kipnis; *Il Trovatore* with Muzio, Van Gordon, Cortis, and Rimini; and a Sunday matinee *Norma* with Raisa, Glade, Marshall, and Baromeo. Raisa also sang *Falstaff, Tosca, La Juive, La Gioconda,* and, on New Year's Eve, the first of three performances of Zandonai's *Conchita*. The Zandonai opera had been given in Chicago in 1913 with Signora Zandonai, Tarquinia Tarquini. The opera's title role was a good choice for Raisa, as she could do a Spanish dance and sing her high D. The reporter for the *Musical Courier* noted,

> Though the part is very trying she never floundered; she fought valiantly for a cause that seemed to us unworthy; she defended the opera with the best she had in her; she carried away the public; she had them in the palm of her hand; she caressed them with lofty tones; she stunned them with the magnitude of her voice and made them believe that poor music can be made good by great interpreters. If Raisa's singing of the part left nothing to be desired, her portrayal too, was much admired.

Over the years Raisa was often asked her opinion of the acoustical properties of the new Civic Opera House. She recounted that after the last *Aida* rehearsal and again after the first few weeks of performances Insull asked for her evaluation of his new theater. The skyscraper opera house was often referred to as "Insull's throne," as the shape of the building resembled that of a throne. She told him that from a singer's perspective the new house was a failure because, unlike the beloved Auditorium, the singers felt no connection with the audience. The oblong shape of the hall, with the boxes at the rear, meant that the artists could not sense how their voices were traveling. Also, as the building was still so new, and had yet to dry out, there was something disturbing about the way voices reverberated against the walls. The comparison was with the Auditorium, which Raisa always called the "Stradivarius" of opera houses. While on the stage of the bowl-shaped Auditorium the singers could actually see specific prominent bejeweled Chicagoans, such as Mmes. Rockefeller-McCormick, Palmer, and Meeker, in their boxes on the sides of the theater, and felt, as Raisa said, "radium" emanating when they were performing their best. The new 3,600-seat opera house was planned as a statement of social equality, for it had only a limited number of boxes in front of the first tier at the back of the hall. It was suggested at the time that this made it difficult for status-conscious operagoers to check the fashion statements and jewelry of the social climbers who inhabited the opera world. In her last years Raisa was enlisted, happily from her perspective, to serve on the committee formed to restore the Auditorium to its former glory. The 4,200-seat Auditorium had ceased being used as a theater during the Second World War, when it was converted into a recreation center for servicemen.

Norma, a second *Aida*, and *La Juive* were Raisa's broadcasts this season. In the course of the season, Raisa lost her baby. On the 1930 tour Raisa sang Aida in Boston as well as a return to Elisabeth in *Tannhäuser*, this time with Frida Leider as Venus. *Il Trovatore* and *Norma* were her other tour operas. At the end of the tour Raisa and Rimini went, as usual, back to Italy for a summer of travel, recreation, and rest. In late May Raisa returned to Bialystok for the first time in twenty-three years, primarily to visit her mother's grave. Her plan was to go "incognito" and not draw attention to herself; but alas this was not to be.

*While we were standing in the courtyard and meditating on the irretrievable past, there came a man, an old friend of my father's who used to come occasionally to visit and play a game of cards while I stood against the warm oven during the cold winter nights to keep warm. I recalled that when he noticed me there he would turn to my father and say: "She is such a dreamer. Something will come of this

In May 1930 Raisa returned to Bialystok for the first time in almost a quarter of a century. She replaced her mother's tombstone with this grander one. The Hebrew portion of the inscription reads: "Here rests Mrs. Frejda Leja Bursztejn, daughter of rabbi Israel Halevei Krasnatawski, died on 20 Nissan [1899]. May her soul rest in peace and be protected." The Yiddish reads: "dedicated by her daughter Rosa Raisa, 1930." (Collection of Louis Stein.)

girl someday." It was this man who noticed us and recognized me immediately. "You are Raisa," he said. And before long the entire city knew that I was in town. I had gone there in order to relive some of my youthful memories and visit the cemetery. But once the news of my presence got around, people came in bunches to see me and they all claimed to be cousins or other relatives, and, of course, asked for help—in American dollars. I am happy to say that I did not refuse a single one, I helped them all generously. ৯

Raisa was depressed by the appalling poverty and squalor she found in Bialystok, and Rimini chided her, "I thought you came from the Russian Czar's family!" At the cemetery she was saddened by the run-down state of her mother's gravestone, so she commissioned a leading local stonecutter to replace the stone with a grander one of black onyx, worthy of Rosa Raisa's mother. This stone survived the World War II devastation of the Jewish cemetery.[1] After the trip to Bialystok Raisa returned to San Floriano; her villa was now developed to the point that Raisa could almost boast about all the features and activities that made her summer vacations there so precious:

৯ We watched our silkworms grow, bottled our delicious wine (Valpolicella, the best in Italy, of which we had, along with other wines, a large cellar-full and which we and our guests enjoyed to the utmost). Then too we attended to the stable, milking the cows and collecting the fresh-laid eggs from our famous breed of Vendome chickens. We erected a special house for the pigs and one for the rabbits (hundreds of them), all of which we kept in first-rate sanitary condition (the pigs were washed every day) so that the sausages, lard, and salami that the caretaker used to preserve tasted unusually well. And these we would distribute among our friends. But overeating on these delicious meats caused some of them to complain, "Raisa, your meats tasted so good you gave me liver trouble." We also had several rows of tobacco leaves that the dogs would sometimes chew up so that when the finance inspector would come he would ask us to account for the missing leaves. This proved so annoying that we finally gave up raising tobacco alto-

Raisa with writer and friend Maxim Gorky in Sorrento, 1930. Gorky (center) is flanked by cousin Pavel Vigdorchik and Raisa in this press photo. (Courtesy of Giorgio Segala.)

gether and added instead more vegetables, including seedless tomatoes which we would import from America as we did with all the vegetables in our immense vegetable garden. When Edith [Mason] would visit with Mr. Ragland [her fifth husband] during the Arena season [after World War II] she and I would pick these huge tomatoes and other vegetables and relish their fresh and delicious taste. And there was our horse ZaZa which Mr. Rimini rode every morning for exercise while I went to the village on a bicycle. ❧

About her rich life and her successful career Raisa recalled that there was still something very important missing:

*Ş to complete our happiness all we needed was a child. Unfortunately, several times, as I was about to become a mother, which I frequently desired, I lost my unborn babies. Not having a mother's love this desire for a child seems to have been an unusually strong instinct in me, and besides I always loved children. But, between the leaps from the Castle Saint Angelo in *Tosca*, being thrown I do not know how many times as Santuzza in *Cavalleria Rusticana*, the terrible fall I had to do in *La Gioconda*, and being boiled in oil in the big kettle in *La Juive*—how could I survive those ordeals without injury? I always assumed a realistic attitude toward each of my roles, unmindful of the consequences, that this was inevitable. One fine day, however, my doctor announced that I was going to have a baby again. This time, with fifteen inches of snow on the ground, I went to bed and stayed there for seven [actually five and a half] consecutive months until my child was born in the hottest July. During that time I allowed myself only one friend to visit me each day, my only other diversion being reading and conversational language study with a special teacher, and of course, planning our future in anticipation of the "blessed event." ӡ*

In the 1930–1931 season Raisa did sing Maliella, Norma, Amelia, and Santuzza, performing up until mid-January. She gave birth to Rosa Giulietta Frieda Rimini on July 7.[2] The baby was named for her mother, her maternal grandmother, and the heroine, Juliet, of Rimini's hometown, Verona. Telegrams poured in from opera luminaries all over the world congratulating the couple on Raisa's success in giving birth at last. Her nearly five years of trials and tribulations had been well documented in the Chicago press. Much newspaper coverage was given to mother-and-daughter photos, and "human interest" pieces abounded detailing how Raisa and Rimini were handling their new roles as parents. The couple's happiness was turned to dread when their "celebrity status" elicited extortion notes from a madman demanding large sums of money to protect their baby from being

The happy parents with their daughter, Rosa Giulietta (Jolly) Frieda Rimini, born July 7, 1931. Jolly told me that seven was her lucky number, as she was born on the seventh day of the seventh month and was Raisa's seventh pregnancy. (Collection of Suzanne Homme.)

kidnapped. This trend in American life culminated a few months later with the infamous Lindbergh case. On April 19, 1932, months after Raisa's successful resumption of her career, the Associated Press summarized the blackmailing incident and reported that "Andrew Matzukewich, 40, who claims to be a disabled war veteran, has confessed to Federal officials he threatened to kidnap Rosa Giulietta, infant daughter of Giacomo Rimini and Rosa Raisa, Chicago Civic Opera stars, last fall. Several letters were received by the Riminis at that time, threatening the baby girl unless the writer was paid sums ranging from $500 to $10,000." The account continued: "A special guard was placed outside the Congress Hotel by the police and Mme. Raisa refused to permit the baby to be taken outside for her customary outings, remaining herself a virtual prisoner in the hotel."

Being a mother brought out a philosophical bent; Raisa told the reporter Jone Quinby, "Motherhood gives a woman a greater capacity for love, for unselfishness, for all the emotions that are tinged with beauty, and which are worthwhile. It is a great art. All the others fade into insignificance before it. And the most miraculous thing about it is, that it is an art which is within reach of most women. Unlike music or painting, it has not been given to just a few. It comes into the lives of the rich and the poor, the intelligent and ignorant, and beautifies their existence and those around them."[3]

Raisa returned to the stage December 21, 1931, as Rachel in *La Juive*. The public naturally wanted to know if motherhood and enforced inactivity had harmed her voice in any way. Glenn Dillard Gunn, who so lavishly praised her first Rachel in 1922, wrote of her reentry,

For there never was a voice in opera that in magnitude as sheer physical splendor equaled the voice of Raisa in her prime, and it was the great soprano's good fortune to prove to the thousands of her loyal friends and admirers in Chicago that when one speaks of Raisa's prime one must use the present tense. Ill health and sorrow took their inevitable toll of this great voice last season and the season before. But last night one heard again the Raisa whom Chicago discovered and has been linked with the operatic history of this city. A goodly part of that history in latter years has been concerned with her triumphs, so happily revived last night. She is by all odds the greatest interpreter of the frightfully difficult music Halévy wrote for the dramatic soprano role in his one surviving opera. Raisa has kept it in the repertoire here because of her power to lend to its technical problems, so taxing to range and facility, a quality of excitement that no other soprano has evoked. Its musically empty cadenzas become so many stimulating adventures which Raisa has the gift to make the listener share. When last night she soared to a high D of such brilliancy that the full sonority of chorus and orchestra were overshadowed the audience was swept by a thrill such as comes all too rarely in opera. The public expressed its approval in no uncertain manner. The remainder of the season will be more interesting because Raisa is with us again.

Musical America's critic wrote:

After a period of prolonged rest and realization of her heart's desire, in the form of a baby daughter, Raisa returns in full command of her former vocal glory. The voice has regained its incomparable luster, its prodigious, overwhelming power, its inescapable appeal to the emotions. . . . She sang with greater technical security than for many seasons past. There were no lapses from pitch. The voice was flexible and under perfect command at every moment. The high tones were dispensed prodigally and with complete ease, with a high D to climax the series. It was a triumph such as one rarely witnesses in a theater.

Santuzza and Gioconda were her only other roles of the season, and she did not join the tour. Preliminary plans drawn up by the newly installed general manager, Herbert Witherspoon, for 1932–1933 did not include Raisa and Rimini. The plan was for Muzio, Iva Pacetti, and Rosetta Pampanini to carry the Italian wing of the reconstituted company. Also on the drawing boards was an attempt to bring in Mária Németh of the Vienna State Opera for the Raisa repertoire.[4] It seems that the tension between the Riminis and Insull, which had been growing since the economic crash of 1929, forced the new man-

agement to largely overhaul the company and in the process to eliminate the expensive Raisa and Rimini contracts. The company did play
its two-week season in Boston, and this marked the very end of the
great Chicago Civic Opera. The company collapsed under the weight
of the Depression and Insull's mounting legal and financial problems.

Chicago's salary information is not as reliable as that of the Metropolitan Opera, whose pay books and contracts are lovingly kept in
the archives. Mary Garden, of course, was always paid the highest salary—in 1921 it was rumored that she commanded $3,000 per perfor-
mance and Lucien Muratore $2,800. Raisa's salary was rumored to be
brushing $2,000 at that time, and it climbed to $2,500 per performance
in the mid-1920s.[5] Figures for the last season, 1931–1932, do exist
in Herbert Witherspoon's files in the Met Archives. In that first
post-Garden season (she retired from the Chicago Opera in February
1931), and after Depression-related salary cuts, the salaries were: Tito
Schipa, $2,000 per performance; Raisa, $1,900; Muzio, $1,700; Vanni-
Marcoux, $1,100; Frida Leider, $1,000; Lotte Lehmann, $1,000; Con-
chita Supervia, $1,000; Antonio Cortis, $1,000; John Charles Thomas,
$700; Alexander Kipnis, $625; and Giacomo Rimini, $600. Earlier in
his career Rimini had been on "weekly" salary status.

Insull's flight from the United States to Greece in October 1932, his
arrest in Turkey in 1934, his repatriation to the United States, and his
trial were front-page stories at this time. Insull was one of the most
important figures in American industry and finance. Many informed
people throughout the country and many politicians blamed the 1929
national financial collapse and the ensuing Depression on the "trend"
he established with his questionable leverage methods. When his financial empire had crashed so also did the dreams of Chicago's opera
lovers and the fortunes of many of the company's members. Raisa and
Rimini had invested their considerable savings in Insull securities and
were totally wiped out. Their loss, on paper at least in the range of
almost a million dollars, was an enormous sum of money in the early
1930s. In December 1933, the Associated Press published Raisa's most
complete account of her financial loss:

Rosa Raisa, great opera star, said Monday that Samuel Insull, Sr. persuaded her and her husband Giacomo Rimini, baritone, to invest their life savings and their earnings in now worthless stock of his utility financing companies. When they refused to buy more, she said, they were ostracized from the Insull controlled Chicago Civic Opera, their appearances cut off, and "life made hell for us." Their stock was not delivered to them until after the crash, she said, and then only with the stipulation that they would not sell it. Mme. Raisa said that at one time Insull showed her "paper profits" of $500,000 and assured her that she would be a "very, very rich woman." She said a "very prominent Chicago business man" came to her in 1926 as Insull's representative and asked her to buy Insull stock. At that time she was at the height of her operatic career here. "I felt very honored that Mr. Insull should send his 'confidential man' to me," she said. "Everyone looked upon Mr. Insull as the god of American business. I went to Mr. Insull's private office and gave him a check for $100,000. He told me I would become very wealthy. Every year after that my husband and I put $50,000 or more, all my earnings, into stock. One year, I don't remember which one, he asked me for more money to invest. I told him I had no more money, but that I had $50,000 in Liberty bonds. He smiled and said, 'good, good, they are just like gold.' So I invested them too." The opera star said she and her husband invested more than $500,000.[6]

Frida Leider in her memoir describes the pressure the artists were put under to invest in Insull securities. "We singers would often receive a courteous letter from one of Mr. Insull's secretaries inviting us to buy a few shares in one of his enterprises. On principle, I threw these letters straight into the waste-paper basket. My colleagues kept urging me to take advantage of these offers, for it was said that Insull rather liked to see part of the generous salaries he paid, flowing back into his own pocket." Leider had had a foretaste of that unpleasant aspect of life when her father's modest wealth was wiped out in pre–World War I Germany.[7] Coe Glade told me that she was so thankful that her ignorance of finance prevented her from indulging in Insull's "get-rich-quick" schemes. Glade indicated that failure to buy left one

Early 1930s photo of Raisa and Rimini, with their Cord, at their San Floriano villa outside Verona. During World War II the Germans appropriated the villa and used it as a communications station.

out of the important social events and parties that surrounded the opera company.

Instead of appearing with the Chicago Opera in Boston, Raisa and Rimini sailed with their young daughter for Italy. They had never before been at their Italian home in February. On March 9 Raisa sang the first of a run of six *Normas* at the Reale in Rome with Ebe Stignani, Alessandro Dolci from her 1920 Chicago *Normas*, and Giacomo Vaghi, with Marinuzzi conducting. Stignani sang with more important Normas than anyone else in the twentieth century. In addition to Raisa she sang the role with Mazzoleni, Tina Poli-Randaccio, Iva Pacetti, Muzio, Scacciati, Arangi-Lombardi, Vera Amerighi-Rutilli, Gina Cigna, Maria Caniglia, Maria Pedrini, Gabriella Gatti, Catarina Mancini, and at the end of her career, Maria Callas.

Raisa was not able in late April 1932 to participate in the Columbia complete recording of *Falstaff* with Rimini, as she was again pregnant; this time she lost a baby boy.[8] Pia Tassinari replaced her as Alice Ford in the acclaimed recording. Raisa was sufficiently recovered to participate at the end of the summer in an open-air concert at Piazza San Marco in Venice and in two performances of *Tosca* at the Vittorio Emanuele Theater in the Adriatic resort city of Rimini with Gigli and Rimini. She was then inactive professionally until January 1933, the last year in which she had a reasonably full schedule in top-level venues. The combination of the Great Depression, the loss of her fortune, motherhood, and undoubtedly some diminution of her powers dictated the less than stellar look of the last five years of her career. Rimini, however, continued working steadily in Italy until 1936, mostly in such leading roles as Falstaff, Don Pasquale, Boris, Don Giovanni, Scarpia, and Jack Rance—roles in which the acting is almost as important as the singing.

On January 19 Raisa added a new role, and a world premiere: Manuela in *Una Partita* by Zandonai at La Scala. With her in this one-act opera were Nino Piccaluga and Piero Biasini; Sergio Failoni conducted. Rimini was featured on the double bill with his Gianni Schicchi. *Una Partita* was performed three times that season and rarely thereafter anywhere. Later in January Raisa sang her first performances at

Genoa's Carlo Felice Theater; in the five *Toscas* were Alessandro Ziliani and Rimini. In early May, Raisa and Rimini participated in two *Falstaffs* at the first Maggio Musicale in Florence. This Festival also featured Ponselle in her only Italian stage appearances, *La Vestale* with Stignani. Other operatic offerings were *Nabucco* with Gina Cigna and Galeffi, *La Cenerentola* with Conchita Supervia, and *I Puritani* with Mercedes Capsir and Lauri-Volpi. With the Riminis in the *Falstaff* were Mason, Casazza, Dino Borgioli, and Badini; Victor De Sabata conducted. A young Desmond Shawe-Taylor, reporting on the Festival for *The Gramophone*, wrote,

> But the real distinction of the performance was due to the women, all of whom could hardly have been bettered. Rimini's wife, Rosa Raisa, was an enchanting Alice: such verve and gaiety, allied with a fine voice and accurate musicianship, are rare anywhere today, doubly so in Italy. But then she has had long experience with the Chicago Opera, as also has Edith Mason.

The Riminis went to London at the end of May to participate in the short International Season at Covent Garden. With Queen Mary sitting in the royal box, Raisa's onstage partners in *Tosca* were Angelo Minghetti and Formichi, former colleagues from the Chicago Opera. The *Times* reported:

> Mme. Rosa Raisa never let dramatic intensity destroy the musical qualities of her singing. She was sensitive to the gentler aspects of the character, an artist in everything she sang and did, from the petulant jealousies of her first scene to the despair of the beginning of the monologue, "Vissi d'arte." Her movements in the difficult scene with Scarpia excited admiration, and its melodramatic ending has never been better managed on the stage of Covent Garden.

The critic of the *Musical Times* was less impressed:

> Rosa Raisa in the name part wore marvelous dresses, and looked lovely enough to inspire both the manly devotion of Cavaradossi and the less reputable attentions of Scarpia. Singers who wear marvelous dresses and look lovely are usually suspect as singers. They aim to blind the

eye and cheat the ear. You would have enjoyed Raisa's singing if she had been clad for hiking. Stridulous tones, misshapen vowels, tortured phrases even, made the performance less than perfect. It could be avouched that it was by good acting, rather than good singing, that she insinuated herself into favour. Be that as it may, it must be conceded that her soft tones were very beautiful, and that she had the necessary ability to make the most of a big moment. That she did not always do so is another matter. The penultimate phrase of "Vissi d'arte," for instance, came out in a rare burst of tone, and the top C in the last Act was something to remember. She jumped up the ladder of tone with the vehemence of a lion leaping to its kill.

Rimini later that week sang Posa in *Don Carlos* and Iago to Lauritz Melchior's Otello. Following her return from London, Raisa went to the Conservatorium of Milan, where she made recordings of four verismo arias for Voce del Padrone (the Italian wing of HMV) with the Scala orchestra under Franco Ghione. These were to be her last commercial recordings. At the end of July she participated in five performances of *Gli Ugonotti* at the Verona Arena in a spectacular production featuring Lauri-Volpi, Adelaide Saraceni, Pederzini, Rimini, Umberto Di Lelio, and Pasero, with Antonio Votto conducting. In her memoir, *We Followed Our Stars*, Ida Cook recalled an evening at the Arena: "The purple night sky of Verona overhead, pierced by a thousand purple stars, the gorgeous voices of Raisa and Lauri-Volpi to enchant our ears . . . it was indeed another night to remember."[9] Rumor has it that recordings were made of these performances, and that they are (or were) in the late Lauri-Volpi's private collection. A 1933 movie starring the tenor includes his first phrases of the love duet. Raisa several years later told Francis Robinson, "I will never forget when I sang this with Lauri-Volpi in the Arena of Verona, he was all the time practically in [on] the prompter's box while he would leave me a mile away from him—can you imagine this love duet?"[10]

· *Chapter Twelve* ·

TOSCA IN BERLIN

A MOST unusual engagement for the Riminis was the early October 1933 stagione in Berlin by a group of famous Scala artists. This was not an official visit but rather a group of distinguished artists who were advertised as being from La Scala. Dal Monte, Stignani, Arangi-Lombardi, Formichi, and Gigli were in this ensemble headed by Panizza. Hitler, Goebbels, and Hess sat in a loge for the October 13 *Tosca* with Raisa, Gigli, and Formichi. Obviously the Nazis had not done their customary biographical research, and the leaders, sitting in a prominent box, applauded Raisa. They attended this sold-out gala as much to hear the Berlin favorite Gigli as to hear *Tosca*. The critic Herbert Francis Peyser, who had so brilliantly chronicled Raisa's first performances in New York fifteen years earlier, reviewed her Berlin Tosca for *Musical Courier*:

> To me hers is one of the supreme Toscas of this generation, an impersonation extraordinarily distinguished and noble, all the more gripping because it so pointedly eschews cheap sensationalism. For the most part one forgot more matters of vocalism in contemplating this magnificent embodiment, which really deserves a column of detailed study. The adroitness with which Mme. Raisa adapted her action to the awkwardly arranged second act settings they use at the Städtische Oper is something which only an expert can properly value. Every layman, on the other hand, could appreciate the grace of her movements, the intensity of her expressions and the sculptured beauty of her poses.

(Peyser was one of the great critics and stylists of his time. He penned probing critiques of Raisa's first New York *Cavalleria Rusti-*

1. Akt: Gigli (Cavaradossi) und Raisa (Tosca)

Caricature from a Berlin newspaper in 1933 showing Gigli and Raisa in Act I of Tosca. Hitler, Goebbels, and Hess applauded the Jewish artist! (Collection of the late Giulietta Segala.)

cana, Aida, I Gioielli della Madonna, and *Norma* for *Musical America* in the late teens and early twenties. At that time he thought Raisa possessed the preeminent dramatic soprano voice of the era, but he was often alarmed by the rough edges in her vocal method and her assertive portrayals.)

This presentation had obvious political overtones. A performance in front of Hitler by a Jewish artist inevitably drew comment. Raisa received harsh criticism from Jewish groups for this politically insensitive engagement.[1] This was the first time her own people had ever criticized her career decisions and it must have hurt her deeply. My own rationalization is that in late 1933 Raisa and Rimini, who had been living entirely in Italy since early 1932 (except for two weeks in

London in 1933), had their information about world events, especially what was happening in Germany, filtered through the Italian media. It is quite possible, even probable, that they were not then aware that Jewish artists and their supporters were already boycotting Germany. The Riminis in 1933 were financially strapped, and this was a well-paid engagement. Perhaps Raisa was politically naïve, but she cannot be accused of insensitivity to the plight of her own people, as she continued in the years to come her longstanding tradition of performing before Jewish, labor, and socialist groups in the United States. Almost exactly two years later she sang a concert in Chicago for the benefit of Jewish refugees from Germany. Ultimately, the real irony is that the Nazi leaders attended and applauded her performance. The memory of this performance stayed with Gigli himself. In a page of his postwar memoirs devoted largely to the listings of operas and places where he sang them, he breaks in to single out the key figures of that October 13 evening. Perhaps he was aware that what had then been the merely incongruous would soon become the impossible. His own career in the Third Reich continued through 1942, when no one could mistake the nature of the regime. My information, from members of her family, is that Raisa in the 1920s, like many Italians, approved of Mussolini's transformation and modernization programs. Italy had not yet instituted its anti-Semitic policy; that came much later, under German pressure. Mussolini and Rimini were known to each other. There is, for example, a September 1924 gossip item in *Musical Leader* about Rimini: "He drives seventy—eighty—ninety—a hundred miles an hour. There are no speed laws. If there were Rimini would be in jail nearly every day. No one drives as fast as he, according to reports, except, perhaps Mussolini. Mussolini is another speed demon in a fast car. Rimini and Mussolini raced into Milan the other day from Lake Como over washboard roads. Mussolini won the last lap. 'He had the better car,' Rimini said."

Back in Italy, Raisa sang *Tosca* at the Teatro Nuovo in nearby Verona before going to Treviso November 4 for three *Giocondas*. In December she returned to America "on money expressly advanced" to sing with the reconstituted Chicago Grand (later renamed Chicago

City) Opera Company, now under the management of her longtime friend Paolo Longone. This new organization only partially resembled Insull's grander Chicago Civic Opera. The singers were from the Metropolitan, the old Chicago Civic, and the touring San Carlo Opera, rather than forming a group that was uniquely Chicago's own. Scenery and costumes were from the warehouse of the old Chicago Opera. For the Chicago premiere of *Turandot* the Metropolitan Opera sold Chicago its elaborate 1926 production for only $3,000.[3] Raisa used her own Turandot costumes. Salaries were one-third to one-half of what they had been in pre-Depression times. Jeritza, no longer attached to the Metropolitan Opera, opened the season December 26 as Tosca. Rethberg in *Madama Butterfly* on December 27 and Mason in a *La Bohème* matinee December 30 preceded Raisa's reentry as Aida on the evening of the 30th. The Amneris was the new Mrs. Longone, Eleanor La Mance; the American tenor John Pane-Gasser was Radamès, Claudio Frigerio the Amonasro, and Papi conducted. Gunn observed of Raisa's reentry to the Chicago musical scene, "The voice is still the most opulent and imposing of all sopranos, a limitless reservoir of power so ample in every resource and so splendid in every quality."[4] *Tosca* on New Year's Day and *Cavalleria Rusticana* on January 3 preceded the Chicago premiere of *Turandot* on January 10. Marion Claire and Aroldo Lindi appeared with Raisa in the *Turandot*. The press was full of claims by Jeritza and Raisa, each asserting Puccini had created the title role for her. This piqued some audience interest and irritation. Claudia Cassidy, who didn't much like the opera, wrote about the second performance,

> *Turandot* says nothing that Puccini has not already said a thousand times better—even the pageantry becomes mere dumb show in the absence of music to be sung. Normally a curious person, I have never been stirred to the faintest excitement by Turandot's enigmas. The princess strikes me as a bad tempered damsel, and that princes are willing to lose their heads for her sake I put down to the spirit of adventure. Something that seemed like a good idea at the time. Another thing that perplexes me about *Turandot* is why Mme. Raisa

and Mme. Jeritza stage the perennial argument about the title role, [each] insisting that Puccini wrote it for her. Were *Turandot* Puccini at his best, there would be reason for battle, but why argue over an opera which counteracts the decorative glories of a fabulous train with some of the most fiendish music ever written to plague a soprano? Turandot's famous question scene is just plain shouting in the upper register, and the fact that Mme. Raisa sang it with opulent tone, brilliant attack, and superbly focused projection does not alter the fact that it may irreparably damage the voice which remains to me the most beautiful voice ever heard. . . . But why not stick to music worthy of her gifts?

This *Turandot* was Paul Hume's first encounter with Raisa. He later became the music critic for the *Washington Post*, and was especially famous for his encounter with President Harry Truman over his dismissive review of Truman's daughter Margaret's vocal abilities. Almost thirty years later he wrote of Raisa that "her voice was the largest I ever recall hearing. . . . I remember how at the end of the second act of *Turandot*, with total ease, she poured out a sound that covered the entire augmented chorus and orchestra." He related that for the big high notes Raisa's method was to put her diaphragm under the note and open her mouth as wide as it would go, and that the sound she produced was "utterly unforced." He also remembered that "Raisa nights at the opera were uniformly occasions of the most gala atmosphere," explaining that "it was a voice that could bring a house to the wildest cheering imaginable or hush it to a silence as it hung in the air in seeming inexhaustibility."[5] This was to be the beginning of Hume's devotion to Raisa, about whom he, like Cassidy, penned the most extravagant and loving praise.

Three nights after the *Turandot* premiere, Raisa did the first of her last two *Trovatores* ever, with La Mance, Lindi, and Carlo Morelli. *La Gioconda* on January 20 was her last role of the season. Interestingly, Rimini did not return to Chicago for the season, electing to remain in Italy performing his special repertoire. On February 6 Raisa joined a new enterprise, the New Boston Opera. Like the new Chicago Grand

Opera, its artists were drawn from the Metropolitan, the old Chicago, and the San Carlo operas. Maria Jeritza and Elsa Alsen starred in *Die Walküre*, Carmela Ponselle and Sydney Rayner in *Carmen*, and Josephine Luchese and Claudio Frigerio in *Rigoletto* with this new company. Raisa's *Aida* on February 6 also featured Dreda Aves, Aroldo Lindi, and Mario Valle, with Cesare Sodero conducting. The February 10 *Cavalleria* promised Raisa, but started an hour late as Raisa refused to go onstage "because she had not been paid according to her contract."[6] Such was the state of regional opera in an America dealing with the fallout of the Great Depression.

Returning to Italy in June, Raisa participated in three *Giocondas* at Fabriano commemorating the Ponchielli Centennial. A rather strange engagement comprised two performances of *Tosca*, six weeks apart, at the Vichy Casino—strange in that the July 15 performance featured Ziliani and Formichi, and the repeat on August 26 a totally different cast including Lauri-Volpi and Domenico Viglione-Borghese.[7] On January 9, 1934, Raisa wrote to a friend, the New York artist's manager Bruno Zirato, regarding her current career plans: "Another offer has come to me from Hurok for performances with a company which is being formed for a theater tour of Russian operas. As there was a lack of guarantees regarding the seriousness of the offer, I hastened to reply with an equally kind refusal."[8] Raisa never performed professionally in Russian operas, although she did sing Lisa's big aria from *Pique Dame* in concert throughout her career. Although she was fluent in Russian, it would have been a large undertaking to learn several new roles in a totally new operatic idiom.

No record of other professional activity by Raisa has been found for the balance of 1934. She resurfaced in 1935 with a touring company singing *Tosca* in Madrid on April 14, with Alessandro Granda and Rimini. Later that month she sang her last ever *Norma*s at the Teatro la Fenice in Venice. With her were Nini Giani, Antonio Melandri, and José Santiago-Font; Franco Capuana conducted. She sent a postcard to Carol Longone indicating happiness with her successes in Madrid and Venice. Six months later Raisa went back to Chicago for

As Silvana, with Chicago contralto Sonia Sharnova as Agnese, in the North American premiere of Respighi's La Fiamma *at the Chicago City Opera. Silvana was Raisa's next-to-last new role.*

Cavalleria, Turandot, Aida, and a new production of Respighi's *La Fiamma.* With her in the *Fiamma* were Sonia Sharnova, a Chicago contralto who had studied with Jean de Reszke, and the Oklahoma tenor Joseph Bentonelli (his real name was Benton). Stinson in the *Chicago Daily News,* explaining the convoluted story in which Silvana, the wife, at one point cannot utter a sound, elaborated:

> Mme. Raisa, it must be admitted, was fully capable of uttering sound up to the point of her librettist's prohibition, and the sound she uttered was prodigious in its tone, beautiful in its texture and stimulating to the palms of her adorers. Mme. Raisa in her career has been in good

voice or in bad; she has never failed to make a good job of it when she has had material suited to it. The title role of *La Fiamma* is suited to her and she gave a magnificent account of herself.

Stinson's evaluations of Raisa are significant, as he could be both a sharp critic and an admirer. He was often his most ecstatic when evaluating large soprano voices, especially those with brilliant upper ranges. He could at times be carried away by this enthusiasm, and thus he heaped hyperbolic praise on both Eva Turner and Florence Austral over the years.[9] However, it was to Rosa Raisa that he returned again and again. In reviewing her concert of December 22, he waxed a bit mystical:

There was not an extra inch of space at the Auditorium last night when Rosa Raisa resumed a practice she has abandoned for too long and appeared in recital. The program was given under the auspices of the Jewish Labor Committee for the benefit of refugees from Germany. Mme. Raisa and her associate, Mischa Mischakoff, were greeted by a house preponderantly Jewish. She is, to be sure, the pride of her people; well may she be and well may her people take delight in having offered the world of music the unique dramatic soprano of her day. Mme. Raisa's program was varied and in the little space at my disposal I shall confine myself to the best part of her excellent performance, her songs in Russian. These were but two, the marvelous aria from Tchaikovsky's "Pique Dame" and its encore, Rachmaninoff's "Cease Thy Singing Maiden Fair," for which Mr. Mischakoff provided the violin obbligato. Mme. Raisa has attained to a line which it were folly for another soprano to attempt. She has been helped to it with the prodigious volume of her voice and the extraordinary fineness of its texture, especially at pianissimo. But she has been led to it by the depth of her feeling and last night I wondered if her operatic repertoire, much of it as she has singled out to be irrecapturably her own and no other's, has actually been sufficient to her temperament. There are persons of natures whose depths are inscrutable to them, and the blue-eyed Raisa is too indefinably guileless, I am sure, ever to have plumbed the depths of hers. That is why Russian music is curiously suitable to her, why it evokes from her and enhances in her a quality, a magic she hardly so fully possesses in any other musical literature. For the Russian nature expresses itself by transposing its mood from what has engendered it to what may relieve it. When the Russian is sad he laments something other than the cause of his sadness, and when that cause comes close to being clear and recognizable, he still insists upon eluding it by becoming merry. Mme. Raisa is too simple and too direct—and she has had too definite a training in the correctness of the Italian school—ever to distinguish between feeling and style. She has attained to a style of arresting dimensions, even so, but this style has not permitted her to express herself fully. It is when she enters into the mysticism of the Russian that one hears, in addition to the magnificence of her outward voice, the voice that must sing always in her sweet and tender soul.

While in New York in 1936 Raisa attended the February 29 performance of *Die Walküre* that featured the return to the Metropolitan Opera stage of Florence Easton as Brünnhilde. Easton had not sung at the Met since 1929. Raisa's companions at that sold-out, popularly priced Saturday night presentation were Ponselle and Carol Longone. Even with all their connections they were not able to secure seats, and they attended as standees. This unusual situation was reported in the press. The presence of these two stars in standing room can only mean that Easton was highly regarded as a "singer's singer." Carol told me that before the performance, over supper, Ponselle asked Raisa if she could clarify for her some of the unusual plot relationships, such as who was whose father, mother, husband, wife, brother, sister, son, and daughter. Like Ponselle, Raisa was also unclear in her mind regarding the libretto's intricacies and gladly referred the questions to Carol, who was the most knowledgeable of the three.

In May that year Raisa undertook her last creation, Leah in Lodovico Rocca's *Il Dibuk*,[10] sung in an English translation as *The Dybbuk*, under the auspices of the Detroit Civic Opera. After a performance in Detroit, the company took the opera to Chicago and New York. In New York the opera was given at Carnegie Hall in a semi-staged version with the artists in costume and with the elaborate settings used in Detroit and Chicago adapted to Carnegie's shallow stage. The think-

As Leah in Rocca's The Dybbuk, *given in English, with Vassily Romankoff as her father. The Detroit Opera gave the work its North American premiere and then took the production to the Chicago Auditorium and New York's Carnegie Hall. Raisa felt she intuitively understood the milieu of this story.*

ing was that Raisa in the old Jewish legend would have great audience appeal. She was enthusiastic about this opera, telling Louis Biancolli in an interview just prior to reporting to Detroit, "I love it! It is a very interesting part vocally and dramatically, and I love it. It appeals to me because it is a Jewish part. I love my people, and I am proud that a non-Jew was interested in writing a Jewish opera. I feel happy to be the one to create it in this country and sing it to my people, and I hope they will respond to it as much as I do. . . . It calls me back to my childhood." Here she seems to be alluding to her early days in Russian Poland before she left for Naples with some exiled relatives. "I feel I am delivering a message to my people in my own atmosphere. *The Dybbuk* was written for the Jewish people." The interviewer mentioned Halévy's *La Juive*. "Little more than the name is Jewish," Miss Raisa said. "*La Juive* is pure Byzantine. No, *The Dybbuk* is really the only Jewish opera—and it is by a non-Jew. Rocca, you know, lived in Palestine for five years, taking in the color and the atmosphere. He has caught the spirit of it. I feel it in every bar of the music." Asked how she did the "possession" scene, Raisa explained, "I do it very naturally, the way I feel it. To feel it you must know it. I express it with the eyes, like crazy—this way." Raisa opened her eyes wide, clenched her hands, and stiffened up. "You see, she feels within her the man's soul."[11] Of her May 14 appearance Leonard Liebling wrote in the *New York American*, "Rosa Raisa assumed the role of Leah last evening and sang and acted with intense conviction and effect. Her voice retains its former volume and warmth, and her delivery its art and emotional depth. The striking illusion she created was aided by Mme. Raisa's racial sincerity and appearance."

Raisa achieved her eighth and final opening night in Chicago when she repeated the *Fiamma* success of the previous season on October 31. Santuzza on November 13 and Rachel on December 2 completed her short season. Cast with her in *La Juive* as Eudoxia was the young Vivian Della Chiesa, in only her second role with the company; the Eléazer was the Metropolitan's Giovanni Martinelli. Glenn Dillard Gunn, who had so enthusiastically embraced her Rachel when she first unveiled it in 1922 and when she returned to the stage in late 1931, wrote,

Rosa Raisa, whose art has been identified with the title role of Halévy's ancient melodrama *La Juive*, ever since that opera has been popular in

Chicago, restored it to the repertoire last night, and at the same time re-established herself in the regard of the public. Not for some seasons past has she sung with the opulence of tone and the spiritual abandon that marked this performance. The public had forgotten that a dramatic soprano could achieve such imposing tonal amplitude. In fact, not even in her youth, has she been able to create such towering climaxes as marked the end of the first act and the more dramatic moments of the second act.

At the end of the review Dunn noted, "The opera was announced to be sung in French. Raisa had always sung the work in Italian and saw no good reason to relearn her part for a single performance. The chorus followed her example and the rest of the principals emulated Martinelli in the use of the original text." In 1961 Paul Hume told me about this performance:

Raisa in *Juive*: This was something more than many of her parts. Because you see she was born a Polish Jew in Bialystok, Poland. . . . Well in *Juive* Raisa darkened the quality of her voice, which from her records you can tell is a velvety thing anyway, until it was nearly as black as midnight in "Il va venir." But in the second act, when the Princess Eudoxia has her big scene all full of coloratura, running up to the high D, Raisa would let the light shine back in her voice in order to match the lighter voice's brilliance. One night I heard her singing the opera when the young Vivian Della Chiesa was singing the Princess. And it had not been a good night for Raisa in her first act aria, while della Chiesa was at her best and getting a big hand. Now, Raisa was never jealous of another artist. But she was unhappy that she had not sung well. So when the two sopranos started up their fast scales to the top D, Raisa just sort of let out her girdle a little and after that you simply did not hear Miss D. C. But the great moment that night came in act three, in the duet with Martinelli, who was at his best in *Juive* and *Otello*. He and Raisa were very fond of singing together, and in their duet one has a phrase, then the other has it, and finally they do it together. Martinelli began it, then Raisa came in for her part, and cut the time almost in half, slowing it down so that the top would roll out. It was the kind of thing that just picked the house up and shook it all the way through.[12]

The opera historian Charles Jahant was certain that Victor had planned to record this *Juive* performance and had taken several preliminary steps, but the company's accountants overruled the Artists and Repertory department, claiming such a large-scale recording in 1936 Depression America was not economically feasible—yet another big gap in Raisa's recording career. Given Gunn's and Hume's reports of this performance we can justly feel a sad loss. If this performance had been preserved we might hear for the only time on record Raisa's fabled vocal power in a 1936 "live performance" ambiance.

On October 27, 1937, Raisa gave one of her very last concerts: a benefit for Prothose Memorial Cancer Research. The sold-out concert gave her Chicago critics one more chance to evaluate the current state of her voice and art and, perhaps realizing that her career was coming to an end, to put some perspective on her place in Chicago's rich operatic history. Cecil Smith, whom Londoners were to know in the 1950s as a very sound critic, wrote:

Returning from a summer in Italy Rosa Raisa sang in Orchestra Hall last night taking her audience by storm and precipitating a demonstration of approval reminiscent of old opera days in the Auditorium. Mme. Raisa's appearances in Chicago are not to be taken lightly or tossed off with a few polite words. She has sung over 275 performances of thirty-six operatic roles here and at Ravinia. In the last decade of the Chicago Civic Opera she was one of the major box office assets of the company, ranking with Amelita Galli-Curci and Feodor Chaliapin. She is one of the most important figures in the operatic history of Chicago. I have not heard her sing so gloriously or so easily since an unforgettable performance of Zandonai's *Conchita* eight years ago next New Year's Eve. Her pianissimo and her full voice alike are completely dependable to the very top of her voice. I hope you were there last night to hear her sing a high C-sharp half-voice, staccato, and clean in the Bolero from the *Sicilian Vespers*.[13]

Cassidy chimed in:

by virtue of the most thrilling dramatic soprano of the generation, a poignant voice in color, a deep, lustrous purple, a line so prodigally full that to hear it has been one of the privileges of our time. That voice appeared last night only when Mme. Raisa deserted her printed list for operatic encore, lashing at emotional response with the fury of her tone, dropping cello deep in the urge of drama. I make no bones about Mme. Raisa's voice thrilling me in spectacular fashion no other quite has touched.

Again it was Stinson who assumed the role of Raisa's most committed critic. He wrote:

Interesting as they were—and *Trovatore*, like *Aida* remains peculiarly Mme. Raisa's own property—there were still other operatic examples among her many encores. I took as my own the aria from Tchaikovsky's *Pique Dame*, which I have always loved to hear her sing, but which she has never sung so tellingly or with such subdued but gripping mastery. There was also an interesting performance of the prayer from *Tosca*, sung with a new note of repression, yet with great power; and never in a stage performance of *Tosca* has Mme. Raisa's beauty seemed so magnificent as at her latest recital. . . . As I listened to this most phenomenal dramatic soprano of our times I reflected that of all the musical careers that of the soprano is richest in its possibilities of varied development. Few of the truly great sopranos of the past remained content in their style; they have in one way or another expanded it. Mme. Raisa's own rightful framework is grand opera; the scope of her powers has demanded it and her vocal hearing has actually been conditioned by the accompanying orchestra's richness of overtone. Furthermore, dramatic as it is, her style has been formal; it is unique, as every turn of phrase on Wednesday evening disclosed, but it has not been highly personal. It seemed to me that Mme. Raisa is now searching for the intimate, that she is refining her phrase, that (as her Russian folk songs showed) she is experiencing delight in a legato of quite a different nature from those passages in the third act of *Aida* in which she has never been equaled. There is something more human

in her singing, something more of warmth, and something more of
beauty. We applaud her as of old and with quite peculiar excitement,
and we rejoice in the standard she has maintained. We value the accomplishments of a stupendous vocal equipment. But she is a woman
of rare and unspoiled sweetness, simplicity and feeling, and we feel
that now, in admitting us to the undisguised utterance of her own
heart, she is finding a new and tremendous sway over ours.

A few weeks later Raisa gave her very last stage appearances:
Cavalleria on November 25 and *La Juive* on Saturday evening December 4. Again she had Della Chiesa and Martinelli as her partners
in the Halévy opera. But the opera world was changing, and other
singers were assigned roles thought to be hers. In the weeks leading
up to Raisa's last performances Rethberg sang Aida and Leonora and
Gina Cigna sang Norma. Years later Raisa told Charles Jahant regarding Aida, "that's the role we give up first." Other star turns were Lily
Pons as Lakmé and Lucia, Grace Moore as Manon and Mimì. Lotte
Lehmann sang the Marschallin, Kirsten Flagstad was Isolde and Brünnhilde, and Helen Traubel was just starting her career as a Wagnerian soprano. The fact that many of the new big names of opera were
not much younger than Raisa (Flagstad was only two years younger,
both having made their operatic debuts in 1913) means only that she
had reached the top level earlier and had sung heavy roles sooner
than her contemporaries. Her name was flanked now not by Muzio,
Chaliapin, Galli-Curci, and Garden, but rather by the newer stars
of opera. Although she was only forty-four years old, twenty-five
years and almost a thousand performances had taken their inevitable
toll. These last brilliant performances took place in a period of semi-
retirement; their infrequency made them all the more remarkable and
precious.

Six months later she gave her very last public performances. For
the Fourth of July she was invited by the American Legion to sing the
national anthem at their celebrations at Soldier Field, and five nights
later, on July 9, she sang her final concert, a free alfresco event at
Grant Park. Her audience had a chance to hear her in an ambitious

[181]

program, one extremely challenging for an artist of any age, but especially so for an artist on the verge of complete retirement. Again, Stinson was to have the final word:

> Mme. Raisa's selections were the aria from *Norma*, a work in which no one at any period of her career has come close to rivaling her, and the first-act aria from *Traviata*, which she sang, considering the hugeness of her tone, with an astonishing lightness and facility, and without permitting herself the breathing spell taken by virtually all sopranos not coloraturas before the end. With the Bolero from the *Sicilian Vespers*, Mme. Raisa gave an even more dazzling account of her mastery of bravura ornamentation. It was in the florid aria from *Trovatore*, however, that those who have followed her throughout her career must most excitedly have identified this singing as the work of a singularly endowed, an unexampled mistress of dramatic delivery. Mme. Raisa has her own system of tonal emphasis, and if this system seems both costly and perilous, Mme. Raisa's exemplification of it on Friday proved her completely competent in it. She has not in many years sung with such freedom, certainty, and excellence; never have I heard her sing with an easier skill or more elastic and brilliant phrasing. And there remained in her singing, besides its unique richness and hugeness of tone, that crowning mark of her supremacy in her own type, that bold, unmatched and masterly breadth and decisiveness of line by which she has characteristically staked out vocal proportions quite beyond the capacity of any singer known to our generation.

Chapter Thirteen

RETIREMENT

RAISA and Rimini made the inevitable but painful decision to retire from the stage in mid-1938, and they then did what many retired singers do: they opened a voice studio. They worked with young singers and during the summer months took some of them to their San Floriano home for additional study. Their celebrity in Chicago guaranteed a steady flow of young aspirants seeking instruction. Their studio in the Congress Hotel moved to 920 North Michigan Avenue, on the "Gold Coast," when the hotel was taken over by the government during the Second World War. Over the years their studio produced three well-known singers: Giorgio Tozzi (perhaps the most famous), Virginia Haskins, and Gloria Lind. They also started training their daughter for an operatic career. The general plan of the studio was for Raisa to teach the women and Rimini the men. Tozzi remembers his teachers as very lovely and unpretentious, very relaxed and at peace with themselves; on occasion they dined at his parents' home. He recalled that in their teaching they stressed legato and word pointing as much as vocal production. Rimini was his primary teacher; he recalls that Raisa gave him one-on-one lessons only when Rimini was not available, and he has no recollection of Raisa ever opening up her full voice to demonstrate a vocal or technical point. Unlike some other renowned teachers, the Riminis kept their fees reasonable. Tozzi fondly recalled that on April 11, 1947, the Raisa-Rimini studio presented a performance of Cimarosa's *Il Matrimonio Segreto*, a Sunday afternoon presentation at the Civic Theater. Tozzi was cast as Count Robinson, and Rimini, in a rare post-retirement outing, played Geronimo. One of the young artists begged off attending the final Sunday morning rehearsal in order to attend church. Rimini asked the young lady if she believed that "God was everywhere." When she said she did, Rimini assured her that God would be at their studio that Sunday morning![1]

The Riminis became fixtures in the musical life of their adopted city; their attendance at operatic events and concerts was often noted in the newspapers. Celebrities visiting Chicago made a point of meeting Raisa. Edwin McArthur, who had heard Raisa in concert and opera in his native Denver in the early 1920s, told me how pleased Flagstad was to meet Raisa in the mid-1930s, shortly after Flagstad's sensational American debut. This was especially unusual, as Flagstad was famous for avoiding post-concert socializing.[2] When Toscanini and his NBC Orchestra visited Chicago during World War II, he enjoyed a pasta dinner at Raisa and Rimini's home, and he reciprocated the next evening by having the Riminis dine with him at the Drake Hotel. In 1952, with the touring New York City Opera, Tullio Serafin, with whom Raisa had sung only in Bologna in 1915, inscribed his photo with fond memories of those long-ago, "magnificent" Francescas. Raisa, unlike many retired prima donnas, was capable of generosity when other sopranos sang roles closely identified with her. After a December 1940 performance of I Gioielli della Madonna, she greeted the soprano Dusolina Giannini backstage exclaiming, "You did it, you did it, you sent chills down my spine."[3] Raisa on occasion sang in private homes for charities, usually those connected with her home city of Bialystok, not only in Chicago but also in New York. Her father years earlier had made her promise him that she would sing a Bialystok benefit at least once a year. Her brother-in-law recalled that in 1943 she came out of retirement to sing at a political event in New York's Madison Square Garden—a rally that was organized by leftist groups urging the United States to open a second front in Europe to take some pressure off the embattled Soviet Union.[4] This was a far cry from her Tosca ten years earlier in Berlin with Hitler in the audience.

There are so many other ironies in Raisa's biography. In 1940, her nine-year-old daughter Giulietta (now known by her nickname, "Jolly") was baptized into the Roman Catholic faith.[5] The half-Jewish Rimini wanted his daughter to have an easier road in life than Raisa had had; being accepted and identified as Italian and as Catholic rather than as a Jew in these troubling and discriminating times seemed logical from his point of view. Raisa herself was very broad-minded about religion and agreed to this arrangement. Although steadfastly Jewish herself, she always had a fascination with Catholicism through her early years in Italy and through her professional years. Most of the heroines she sang were Catholic: Spanish and Italian noblewomen, a wild Neapolitan girl, and a Sicilian peasant. She had studied the religious gestures of their real-life counterparts to give her characterizations verisimilitude. Only in *Suor Angelica*, where she played a nun, did she feel compelled to wear a cross on stage. Everywhere she went she took with her pictures of her parents, Herschel and Frieda, her Hebrew bible, Star of David, and mezuzah.[6]

Rimini, the son of a Sephardic father (Riccardo) and a Hungarian-Italian Catholic mother (Giulia Sottopera), was raised in his mother's faith. Rimini once told Olga Trevisan, the daughter of Vittorio, the Chicago Opera basso buffo, that when his Catholic mother died in 1913 she was denied a prime burial location in Verona's municipal (Catholic) cemetery because she had married a Jew. He deeply resented this intolerance and felt himself moving toward his Jewish half, especially as he was later married to Raisa. However, he encountered the same bias when his father died and was refused a choice burial location in the Jewish cemetery because he had married out of the faith. He felt that all religions "in practice" had elements of narrow-mindedness.[7] Raisa often told her family and friends that Rimini was "sort of Jewish." Rimini forged a close attachment with his ortho-dox Jewish father-in-law, Herschel. He was very comfortable moving in Raisa's Jewish circle of family and friends, and he always called Mrs. Stone "Mother." From Raisa he learned many Yiddish expressions, not always the most elevated ones, and he used them liberally.

In the couple's home, the two cultures and religions existed easily side by side. In 1923, while the Riminis were in New York for their usual visit prior to embarking for Italy for the summer, they gave a joint concert at the Hippodrome for one of Raisa's Jewish causes. Of a totally different type of concert, *Musical America* reported that "after receiving Holy Communion at St. Patrick's on March 18 over 3,000 members of the police force went in a body to the Commodore Hotel where a concert was given for their special benefit by Beniamino Gigli, tenor, and Giacomo Rimini, baritone."[8]

Raisa visited New York every year and was very generous with her sisters, who lived there. Her nephew Murray recalled that she paid for his summer camp and frequently sent clothing and other practical gifts to his middle-class family. Her nephew Louis remembered with gratitude that Raisa helped to support his family during the Depression, even though she had already lost her fortune. She made the annual visit to her father's grave and she always arranged for Yarzheit prayers to be said for her parents on the anniversaries of their deaths. Over the years she contemplated buying a plot at Montefiore Cemetery for herself, but she never followed through on this. One of her stillborn babies is buried there. When in New York she often visited Toscanini at his home in Riverdale. Toscanini had a belief in the curative powers of "Jewish penicillin" and always asked Raisa to bring jugs of her sister Frieda's chicken soup with her.[9] Raisa's strong sense of family also extended to her maid, Ida Bosi. Raisa hired Bosi in 1915; she came highly recommended by Gino Marinuzzi, her prior employer. Raisa kept Ida on the payroll through the lean as well as the rich years of her career. Ida lived with the Segala family in California until 1969, six years after Raisa passed away.

The late forties were marked by events common to many middle-aged women, not necessarily the experiences of an opera luminary. In 1948 Raisa was diagnosed with breast cancer and underwent a double mastectomy. It must have been very difficult for the handsome Raisa to endure this operation and the subsequent reconstruction. In 1950 her daughter, Jolly, married Dr. Carlo Giuseppe (Pino) Segala of Verona. Nineteen-year-old Jolly had chosen matrimony and family rather than the opera stage for which her parents had been training her. The August 5 wedding at Verona's San Giorgio in Braida Church was a social event that saw many opera luminaries in attendance. Gigli, singing *La Forza del Destino* at the Arena, was a guest, as were Martinelli and Maria Callas, a family friend who lived in the same

Outside Verona's Chiesa di San Giorgio in Braida for Jolly's wedding to Dr. Charles (Pino) Segala of Verona, August 1950. Raisa, second from left, is flanked by two bridesmaids, her good friend Carol Longone, Giovanni Martinelli (with silver hair), and Rimini on the right. A diabetic, Rimini had become quite heavy by this time. (Courtesy of the late Carol Longone.)

apartment building as Jolly in Verona. In Jolly's wedding album there is a rare photo of Gigli and Callas sipping champagne together at the reception.[10]

Two years later everything changed for Raisa:

As my husband and I were in the habit of having coffee together in the morning. One day, March 6, 1952, seeing that he was sound asleep, I decided to let him rest and delayed waking him. But when I noticed that it was getting unusually late and he had not risen, I brought the coffee to his bed. "Giacomo, here is your coffee. Drink it while it is still hot." No answer! I put down the cup and leaned over him and

I found that he was gone, probably dying while asleep, during the night. The shock was a great one even though I realized that he had a most peaceful departure from this earthly life. Just as he would have wished! As the years went by I missed him and his beautiful companionship more and more. To this day I feel the void caused by his passing and the absence of his cheerful, ever-jovial disposition, full of joy and mirth. He had a priceless gift of telling the most interesting stories. Giacomo Rimini was always, in the best sense of the term, the "life of the party," and our many guests and friends still remember his warm and engaging personality. Among the many wires of condolence containing the most beautiful expressions of sympathy, the first was by Maestro Toscanini, whose comforting words were extremely helpful in my great sorrow. Our daughter came from Italy to assist at her father's funeral and to help me get through the terrible ordeal, while our dear friend, Maestro Polacco, took the first plane and came to console us and pay a warm tribute to his devoted friend. He was a fine conscientious artist with an inborn love of the stage and a thorough understanding of its problems. We were a great help to each other and I am certain that it was not easy for him to be the husband of a prima donna. He loved me and respected me as a mother, companion, and wife. ❧

The death of the diabetic Rimini at the relatively young age of sixty-four left Raisa for the first time since 1916 without her life partner. Those familiar with the couple's home and marriage felt that theirs was a great union, despite all the expectable tensions in the domestic life of extremely temperamental artists. Jolly told me somewhat devilishly that a recurrent theme in their home while she was growing up was Rimini often reminding Raisa that "although your star shines brighter, I am still the Sun and you are only the Moon." It seems that Jolly bonded more with her father than with her mother. In the dynamic of their home Rimini indulged Jolly's whims and moods, and it was left to Raisa to be the disciplinarian, a role that did not come easily to her. With the passing of Rimini some of the energy and the "will to live" went out of Raisa, although she kept up a sem-

Publicity photo from 1936, dedicated years later to her "mother," Goldie Stone.
Maurice Seymour Studio, Chicago. (Collection of the late Beatrice Balter.)

blance of normalcy. She went through the motions with her activities and teaching; she lent her name and support to the new Lyric Theater of Chicago and its Opera Guild as well as to the committee established to restore the old Auditorium. Raisa always considered Chicago her home and sang its praises.

I loved Chicago from the day of my arrival, feeling so at home there. Perhaps this was because I had learned English at the Berlitz School in Naples, to make sure I could communicate with the American people and so make friends more readily. The people took me to their hearts, considering me their adopted daughter. Chicago made me and loved me—and still does! My roots, my memories, my friends are in Chicago, and all this is deep in my heart, with endless gratitude. I have many friends there that I love dearly. Among them one who has since passed away, Mrs. Julius Stone, who was a great worker for charities, assisting Mr. Julius Rosenwald, the great philanthropist, and Mr. Max Adler. I still bless the memory of that wonderful lady to whom I could go and open my heart as though she were my own mother. I loved her so much, I don't think I could have loved my own mother more! She was a great comfort to me and a truly wonderful woman.[11]

Raisa, like many artists, was paid by commercial interests for the exploitation of her name. In the early part of her Chicago career she endorsed Mason and Hamlin pianos, as did almost all the members of the Chicago Opera, and she is quoted in their ads in the opera programs: "The Mason and Hamlin piano is, without doubt, absolutely the most perfect piano I have ever known. It is equally ideal in presenting the delicate charm of Mozart or the most taxing of the modern writers." In the early 1920s the Chicago Opera shifted affiliation from Mason and Hamlin to Baldwin, and Raisa was quoted in Baldwin ads: "My Baldwin is a treasure—a treasure of exquisite tone. I like to think of my possessions as superior; but I must admit this is true of all other Baldwins." When a friend of Raisa's, in the mid-1950s, asked her if she was upset when she saw herself named in newspaper items seemingly advancing the careers or agendas of others, she merely shrugged.[12]

Although Barbara Marchisio had cautioned her in her student days that it was not proper for a professional singer to smoke, in the late 1920s Raisa endorsed Lucky Strike cigarettes, saying, "My husband, Giacomo Rimini, prefers Luckies because they keep his throat ever clear and free from irritation. He insisted that I try them and I found that all he said was true. Now we both smoke Lucky Strikes. Not only because they are kind to our throats, but because of their rare flavor." Many opera singers over the years have smoked, and even in our day, when smoking is frowned upon in many circles, there still are singers who have this addiction. Raisa's granddaughter, Suzy, remembered her grandmother smoking Viceroy cigarettes.

Starting in 1956 Raisa divided her time between Chicago and California, and in 1958 she moved from Chicago to the Pacific Palisades in the Los Angeles area to live with her daughter, son-in-law, and two young grandchildren, Suzanne and Giorgio (Suzy and Georgie, Raisa called them). This move afforded her some needed financial and emotional security. She made annual visits to Chicago during the opera season, and she was always treated as an honored guest. And when the San Francisco Opera played a short season in Los Angeles she went to all the first performances. She networked with the opera community in southern California, the home of many famous retirees, and sat as a judge in singing competitions, many under the auspices of the Metropolitan Opera. She was on the panel that recognized the very young and talented Grace Bumbry. Bumbry's teacher, Lotte Lehmann, recused herself from the selection panel and asked Raisa to fill in for her. In a late-1950s interview with a Los Angeles Yiddish-language newspaper, she told the reporter, "I've got a home in Italy, which is the way of American artists. . . . I also have a home in Santa Monica, but my dream is to take a trip to the land of Israel and make my home there." Whether she was serious or this was merely her way of bonding with the paper's readership is a matter of conjecture. Her very full life was capped with a visit East in 1962, where she was intermission guest on the Met's February 24 *Turandot* broadcast. She

A 1953 snapshot Raisa sent to her good friend Dea Cornbleet of Chicago. On the verso Raisa wrote, "three generations, Jolly, Suzy, and grandma." (Gift to author from Dea Cornbleet)

Visiting Birgit Nilsson backstage after a Metropolitan Opera Turandot *performance, February 1962. Raisa loved to visit artists in their dressing rooms. Photo by Louis Mélançon. (Metropolitan Opera Archives.)*

reminisced with John Gutman of the Metropolitan about her participation in that historic premiere. She also visited friends in Boston and spent time with Rosa Ponselle at Villa Pace outside Baltimore. Photographs of the two divas together show a remarkable physical resemblance. The *Baltimore Sun* ran a human-interest article about the two

Rosas in which each complimented the other and the two recalled their numerous professional and social encounters over the years. Raisa wrote to Francis Robinson upon her return to California, "My visit with Rosa was very touching. We sat every night until three o'clock in the morning reminiscing the beautiful past. Her gorgeous home, her lovely friends, her music, and the fourteen poodles all over the place keep her young. She received me like a Princess."[13]

Raisa had marked on her calendar her planned participation in the November 20, 1963, gala at the Metropolitan Opera celebrating the fiftieth anniversary of Giovanni Martinelli's Metropolitan debut. She would have sat on the stage as one of his former illustrious colleagues. Amplifying her connection to Martinelli, she wrote to Robinson, "It seems to me yesterday when I heard him as Johnson di Sacramento in the *Girl of the Golden West* at the San Carlo in Naples during the time I was studying at the Conservatorium in 1910 [1911–12 season]. More than half a century ago—how sad and how I wish I were 25 years younger. Well, I am thankful that I am still here to talk about it. I sang with Martinelli many performances of *Aida, Ballo in Maschera, Trovatore, La Juive,* and *Fedora.* Oh yes, also *Hugonottes* [*sic*]." On a lighter note, she told Robinson, "I hear Giovanni is still popular with the young girls!" Although Raisa was not herself a Metropolitan Opera artist, her participation in the gala evening would not have been incongruous; Dame Eva Turner, herself never a Met artist, also participated. With regard to Turner, in the same letter Raisa thanks Robinson for an article he sent her about a Turner tribute somewhere: "About our friend Eva Turner I was delighted of her deserving honor. She's a fine person, and I have admired her magnificent voice in *Aida* and *Turandot.*"[14]

When in New York, Raisa stayed at Carol Longone's 222 Central Park South apartment. In Raisa's last two years, the Mets' Francis Robinson entered her life as a friend and correspondent. Raisa was so taken with Robinson's friendship that, with the expressed hope that the material would eventually be placed in the projected museum in the new Metropolitan Opera, she gave him, as a token of appreciation, many choice pieces of memorabilia, including her *Turandot* score signed by Toscanini.[15] She also gave him a brooch belonging to Barbara Marchisio that had been willed to her, as well as a letter from Puccini about *Turandot* and the 1916 photo Saint-Saëns inscribed to her. From March 1962 until her death at the end of September 1963 she and Robinson corresponded by letter almost weekly. It is from these letters that many of her opinions about the operatic scene of the day are taken. In June 1962, Robinson wrote to her about Giulietta Simionato's huge success at La Scala in *Gli Ugonotti*. Raisa went back to her memories of her many performances of this opera, recalling her illustrious fellow cast members. About the current Scala performance she wrote,

> I can't understand Simionato (whom I admire greatly) wanting to sing Valentina, one of the most difficult parts in the dramatic soprano repertoire—the tessitura lays so high and low. She would be a beautiful Paggio [Urbano]—the aria in the first act, 'salut a voi cavalieri' she would make of it a masterpiece. I heard her sing two years ago Santuzza in the Verona Arena—and I liked her very much. Corelli with his beautiful voice and so handsome—I am certain contributed to the triumph of the great evening. Naturally Sutherland [must have] carried away the honors with her phenomenal singing.[16]

Raisa was obviously thinking in a very conventional way about the "right" voice for Valentina. It probably never occurred to her that a wide-ranging mezzo-soprano could score a huge success in her old dramatic soprano role. Yet Raisa's own analysis of the many highs and lows of the role suggests Simionato at that point in her career probably had exactly the right voice for the role. Raisa, unlike many retired singers (see Lanfranco Rasponi's *The Last Prima Donnas*), had a generally high opinion of the current stars of opera, finding that many of them were great artists with fine voices. Like many of her age group, she lamented that the pressures of modern life made it nearly impossible for young singers to receive the kind of intensive training she had been given when she was just starting. The need to perform and earn money before one was fully trained was her explanation.

Of the famous singers of the modern era she admired both Callas and Renata Tebaldi. In the early days of the Lyric Theater of Chicago in the mid-1950s Raisa was constantly asked her opinion of these two famous divas; being a friend of both, and not wanting to be drawn into the publicity and hype surrounding their supposed feud, she found diplomatic ways of expressing sensible and noncontroversial judgments. She had a professional's appreciation of their exceptional and contrasting qualities. Raisa knew only too well how fans and partisans create rivalries where none exist simply because of the different qualities and strengths each artist brings to the stage. She too had had to endure in her time aficionados pitting her against Muzio. This said, I think that privately she gave Tebaldi the higher notch, probably because of her opulent and more conventionally beautiful voice, but at the same time she recognized Callas for bringing back the bel canto operas and for her sterling musicianship.[17] She praised Elisabeth Schwarzkopf's performance in *Der Rosenkavalier*, which she thought *"stupendous.* Never have I heard a greater Marschallin, and I doubt I ever will."[18] And further: "She's so pretty and noble as Marie Teresa."[19] Raisa having sung the role herself and surely having heard both Lehmann and Leider in the role in Chicago, this was high praise indeed. She wanted to hear Joan Sutherland's 1962 Hollywood Bowl concerts but was not able to obtain tickets, as they sold out immediately. She had already heard Sutherland as Lucia in Chicago the previous October. "This great artist after her second performance of Lucia in Chicago, in which she thrilled me, expressed to Carol Fox [Lyric Opera of Chicago's general manager] a desire to meet me. I would have gone backstage anyhow to express my great admiration to this phenomenal singer. You know that she never moved until she saw me, and that was to the very end of the performance. This was something that I appreciated more than words can express."[20] Many younger artists of the time who knew anything about opera history knew that Rosa Raisa and Chicago went together. The only word Raisa uses over and over again in her letters to describe Sutherland is "phenomenal."[21]

About some other performers in Los Angeles in autumn 1962 she said, "I enjoyed very much Dorothy's [Kirsten] Floria. She was magnificent, and together with Gobbi they were a 'great treat.'" She thought Tito Gobbi a colossal artist in every respect. ("I love Tito Gobbi's Scarpia, *stupendous*.") About Victoria de los Angeles's Mimì: "What a fine artist! She is also very pretty which does not hurt."[22] Another hearing of Simionato in a Los Angeles *Cavalleria* brought forth the opinion that she "was magnificent. I think she's the *only* Santuzza today!" In the subsequent *Pagliacci* she opined that "del Monaco's Canio was thrilling." Both del Monaco and Franco Corelli were special favorites. Perhaps their Latin movie-star looks created an additional aura of excitement, since she alludes repeatedly to Corelli's appearance in several letters.

The gala concert at Lyric Opera of Chicago in November 1956 with Tebaldi, Simionato, Richard Tucker, and Ettore Bastianini, Georg Solti conducting, was for her a "golden age" evening. She had favorable reactions to Met radio performances by Eileen Farrell, Leontyne Price, Zinka Milanov, Robert Merrill, and Cesare Siepi. When she heard the 1962 *Andrea Chénier* broadcast, she was pleased at how fresh Milanov sounded at that stage of her long career. She was glad that Price had regained her vocal security after the *Fanciulla del West* problems of the year before ("I am happy that Leontyne is in very good shape"). She thought that Leonie Rysanek in *Ariadne auf Naxos* and *Der Flie-gende Holländer* "sounded extremely well." About the February 9 broadcast of *Adriana Lecouvreur*, she said, "I loved Tebaldi and Co-relli." She never missed one of Giorgio Tozzi's performances, as she felt she was deputizing for Rimini, who had been his primary in-structor and had predicted for him a wonderful career. Raisa proudly dubbed Tozzi the "Michelangelo of basses."

In her letters Raisa sounds very positive, hugely appreciating and liberally commenting on the current scene. She attended the Verona Arena opera every summer from the end of World War II through 1961; she also heard opera regularly in Chicago and Los Angeles, and listened every Saturday to the Metropolitan broadcasts. She par-ticularly enjoyed Robinson's acclaimed intermission series "Biogra-phies in Sound." She was moved to tears by his essays on Galli-Curci, Ernestine Schumann-Heink, Calvé, Garden, Schipa, Rethberg, and

Flagstad. She knew, or had at least met, all these artists and was carried away by Robinson's skillful, poetic descriptions. She did tell him that in his Garden biography he had "certainly made a saint out of Mary!" About his essay on Rethberg she wrote, "it was thrilling—what a gorgeous voice and what beautiful singing—alas, you don't hear this singing anymore."[23] Although she claimed to dislike talking about herself, she loved to reminisce about her career and the fabulous era of which she had been a part. She regaled friends with tales about the famous *Pagliacci* performance at she attended Montevideo in 1915 that paired Caruso and Ruffo, claiming that each tried to outdo the other in greatness. ("Both were in great voice, so you can imagine what happened? The public was like *mad*. I thought the theatre was *on fire*.")[24] One wonders if she was equating greatness with volume.

In a 1962 letter to Carol Longone, who was preparing *Pelléas et Mélisande* for an operalogue, Raisa related that years earlier Campanini had encouraged her to attend Garden's famous Mélisande, saying, in words of praise, that "Mary will be giving a lecture." In general she regarded Garden's Mélisande as a masterpiece. Nevertheless, in another letter to Carol she recalled Fanny Heldy and Journet singing the same opera at La Scala when she was performing there in 1925 and 1926. "It was the first time that I heard so much 'singing' from Mélisande. Mary faceva delle conferenze (was always giving lectures)."[25] Here she suggests something dry and academic in Garden's Mélisande. (Carol Longone had, since the mid-1940s, presented monthly operalogues at the Hotel Pierre; these were abridgments of operas about to be revived at the Metropolitan Opera and other venues in the New York City area. Society ladies were the attendees. Carol would narrate the story, give interesting background information, and play highlights on the piano while showcasing young singers in need of an opportunity to perform. Among the young talents over the years were the as yet unknown Beverly Sills and a very young Mario Lanza.)[26]

When she visited New York in 1963 she took with her an early draft of her memoirs and visited potential publishers. Mary Watkins Cushing, who authored the Fremstad biography *The Rainbow Bridge*, was enlisted to help her refine her notes; alas, the manuscript was too short and fragmentary and needed additional editorial work before it could be published. Almost a third of a century later, the present book, with its extensive excerpts from the autobiography, sees Raisa's dream partially realized. Raisa was fascinated by a tape recorder she acquired in her last years.[27] "I vocalize every day. Just to exercise my lungs and also hear how much noise I can still make."[28] In August 1962 she wrote to her friend Carol Longone about the tape recorder experience: "I sing every day. The first day I tried my voice, it sounded awful. Now, after exercising the instrument, I can assure you it is not bad at all. I want to make a couple of recordings for my own pleasure, and if it will be pretty good I will send you a copy—but this will take me a little time—so don't expect it the next day—don't tell anybody about it."[29] The ability to hear oneself and to learn by hearing one's mistakes intrigued her. She thought that if they had had tape recorders in her day her recordings would have been better. It is regrettable that her seventy-year-old voice, singing into a tape recorder, has been lost. Her grandson, Giorgio, remembered returning from school when he was seven years old and hearing her vocalize several houses away! She asked Carol for help in locating the sheet music for Massenet's "Elégie" in the Russian translation—the very first song from the Western literature she ever sang. She was obviously thinking about some of the things that went into the launching of her career many years earlier.

I must interject at this point, because after I heard her on the *Turandot* intermission, I wrote to her in care of Texaco, the sponsor of the Met broadcast. It was the first time I had ever written to anyone famous and I was not sure of the protocol; did the artists actually receive the letters and did they answer them? About a month later I received a beautiful two-page handwritten letter in her bold angular script and an autographed Mishkin Aida publicity photo (circa 1916). She thought it unusual for a young person who had never heard her in person to know so much about her. Her reaction: "You know about me more than I do myself." I had sent her a list I had compiled of all her roles, and a list of her known published recordings. She annotated both lists. She wrote after the Pathé *L'Africana* aria, "this, I never recorded." I had at that time found documentation for forty-three of her forty-nine roles. She crossed out Mascagni's *Il Piccolo Marat*, which I had erroneously included. I had listed several roles within her reach that she may have sung, and she crossed them all out except Margherita in *Mefistofele* and Fedora. However, she did not add Lida in *La Battaglia di Legnano*, the First Flower Maiden in *Parsifal*, Romani's *Fedra*, Iskah in Nepomuceno's *Abul*, and Zina in Gunsbourg's *Le Vieil Aigle*. She could very well have forgotten several of these seldom-performed roles from early in her career. It turned out that her appearance on the *Turandot* broadcast was important to her, as she received a large stack of letters (mine included) when she returned from New York. One senses she felt she was back in the select circle of celebrated singers of the past who still had the attention of the public. In May 1963 I sent her a card for her seventieth birthday and the fiftieth anniversary of her operatic debut at Parma. She wrote me a very kind thank-you note and enclosed a signed sepia postcard of herself as Tosca. We were on the verge of becoming regular correspondents when I read with sorrow in the *New York Times* that she had passed away on September 28, 1963.[30]

I was quite puzzled, when I read in the *Chicago Tribune's* lengthy front-page account of her death, that she was buried in a private graveside service at Holy Cross Cemetery in Los Angeles. I assumed that she must have converted somewhere along the line, but this remained a mystery, as throughout her career she had been so sincerely Jewish in her public persona. In 1983 I had the delight of visiting her now-deceased daughter, Jolly, in Santa Monica. I was able to go through Raisa's remaining memorabilia and newspaper clippings and to discuss her life and career. Although Jolly and I had a comfortable rapport, I deliberately did not raise the question of Raisa's death and burial. Fortunately, Jolly said to me, "I assume you are interested in my mother's last days and her funeral?" She told me that about a month before she died, and knowing that her bone cancer was terminal, Raisa had stated that she wanted to become a Catholic. Jolly asked her, "Why? You have your own religion." Raisa said it was so that she

Raisa's marker at Los Angeles's Holy Cross Cemetery. Raisa's daughter placed her Star of David, miniature Torah scroll, and the photos of her parents, Herschel and Frieda, in her coffin as an acknowledgment of her Jewish heritage. Photo by Bill Ecker, 1999.

could be buried next to Rimini in Verona. Jolly confided that she had placed in Raisa's coffin her Star of David and the pictures of her parents, which she had taken with her everywhere and which she kissed every night before retiring.[31] (Ten days before her death Raisa attended Rosh Hashanah services at Hollywood's Temple Israel [Reformed] to hear a favorite pupil sing.[32] She was greeted warmly by several worshipers who knew who she was, and she was thrilled that she was still so lovingly remembered.) Jolly added that she never got around to moving Raisa's body to Verona.[33]

Many of her closest friends, such as Carol Longone and Claudia Cassidy, had no idea of a change in faith and were confused by the interment arrangements. Her Jewish relatives in the East, and many of her Jewish admirers, were devastated. In fact, Cassidy, in her tribute essay in the *Tribune*, went out of her way to make the point that the Raisa she had known was a "proud Jewish woman" who "once asked my husband if 'there is a Jewish Paradiso?' Irish himself, and not to be stumped by many topics, he said, 'Of course, right next to ours, and we can visit.'" (It is clear that Cassidy's anecdote about Raisa's strong Jewish loyalty came to be published because friends and admirers of Raisa must have asked her, as Raisa's close personal friend, if she was aware of any conversion. She must have felt compelled to state publicly what normally she would have considered a private matter.)[34] The announcement of Raisa's death came just before the October 4 Lyric Opera opening night *Nabucco*; the great chorus of the Hebrew slaves, "Va Pensiero," was fittingly dedicated to her memory.

Raisa the woman could be seen as either a bundle of contradictions or a very simple and uncomplicated person. Depending upon whose company she was in, she presented herself as Raitza Burchstein, Rosa Rimini, or Rosa Raisa the famous opera star. When she was in the presence of her Jewish family, friends, or admirers, Raitza Burchstein came across as a woman who never forgot her humble Polish ghetto origins, conversed in her native Yiddish, and was very knowledgeable about and still observant of some of the customs and traditions of her people. When she was in the company of Italians Rosa Rimini presented herself as a woman steeped in Italian culture and customs, and at times she used very Catholic turns of phrase. In the kitchen she could make borscht, latkes, and raisin and almond cookies, or polenta and lasagna. Before the general American public she revealed herself as a cosmopolitan and sophisticated woman, but one at home with the open and informal style of American democracy. On yet other occasions she could play the role of the great international diva. In her later years she consciously tried to understate her very voluble, ebullient Jewish personal style, but she retained till the end her rather heavy Yiddish accent when speaking English. As Raitza Burchstein she often laced her sentences with phrases such as "Manna from Heaven," and "God forbid!"; as Rosa Rimini, "I don't know what saint interceded," or "my guardian angel" when referring to Margherita Clausetti. She often referred, in a generic way, to angels, shrines, blessings, saints, and miracles. When questioned on occasion about her religious beliefs she would say that she believed in God, period.[35] She obviously wanted to please and to be loved, and therefore she often said the things she thought were expected of her. She was very

charitable and often "gave" both publicly, when her example was useful in encouraging others to give, and privately, when it was a very
personal matter. Near her San Floriano villa, at Valgatarra, there was
a convent and school run by an order of nuns. She routinely sent the
surplus food produced on her estate to this institution, and she even
donated a playroom for the children. She often visited the facility and
played with the children. She was told that the priest in his Sunday
sermons would tell the children that Raisa was an example of "doing
good to others." The roots of this multifaceted personality are in the
various stages of her unusual life's journey.

Notwithstanding these multiple identities, it was with the Jews of
the United States, and especially of Chicago and the Midwest, that
Raisa enjoyed her greatest popularity and almost iconic status. I remember years ago the great Benny Goodman, in an interview with
Dick Cavett, being asked where his musical talents came from; he
spoke lovingly of his Jewish immigrant father, who adored music, especially opera, since in Chicago they had the "opera and Rosa Raisa."
Studs Terkel, who grew up in a tough Jewish working-class neighbor-
hood in Chicago, remembered that in the operas *Aida* and *La Juive*,
"the name Raisa was as Babe Ruth is to baseball,"[36] clearly meaning the
pinnacle of her profession, truly a heavy hitter. Shortly after Jolly was
born in 1931 Raisa and Rimini opened a savings account in her name
at the Liberty Trust and Savings Bank. The president of the bank,
Adolph Holquist, wrote to her: "Situated as we are in the center of the
Jewish district in Chicago, we understand the sentiment and high regard our people have for their most beloved artist, and they join with
me in wishing you further success, as well as a brilliant future for
Rosa Julietta." Raisa must have known that if in her own very personal spiritual journey she left Judaism, her substantial Jewish following would have been confused and disappointed. It would have seemed
foreign to their understanding of her character. Possibly, just possibly,
if there had been a change of religion, this was known to only her
daughter, her son-in-law, and their children. Many of her family and
close friends who obviously knew her intimately were not aware of a
change of faith. If the account her daughter related to me is accurate,

as late as the beginning of the last month of her life no documented change of religion had taken place. Jolly made clear to me when I visited her in 1983 that she was the authority on her mother, and that anecdotes and stories about Raisa from family members and friends other than herself were to be taken with some skepticism.[37]

The mystery surrounding Raisa's religious identity is further complicated by her granddaughter's certainty that Raisa was a Roman Catholic with an interest in Christian Science. Raisa adored Rimini, and a wish to be buried next to him in a Catholic cemetery would not be entirely out of character and might plausibly account for a conversion. Cassidy, who had been so very close to Raisa, felt that after Rimini died Raisa was often just going through the motions of a normal life, for without Rimini something very important to her was missing. Even Jolly, who was not that knowledgeable about Jewish burial customs, felt she had to make some gesture acknowledging Raisa's strong Jewish attachment and therefore placed some of her Jewish artifacts in her coffin. Raisa's body never was sent to Verona, despite the fact that Rimini, his mother Giulia, and Jolly and her husband, Dr. Segala, are all buried in the municipal cemetery there.

Feeling that because Raisa was not given a public funeral something additional was needed to remember the great woman, the Opera Guild of Southern California held a memorial service on October 21, 1963. Plans called for her pupil Giorgio Tozzi and longtime admirer Orson Welles to speak at the service, but unfortunately their schedules could not accommodate this event. Both sent their regrets.[38] A cantor chanted the Hebrew prayers for the dead, and Mario Chamlee and his wife, Ruth Miller, gave eulogies, as did the Los Angeles critics Patterson Greene and Albert Goldberg, who had reviewed her many times in the past.[39] Mario Chamlee in his eulogy recalled: "The first time I heard Raisa was in Chicago in *Aida* when I was en route to New York aspiring to be engaged at the Metropolitan. As I listened to that thrilling Raisa voice and witnessed her most convincing portrayal of the Ethiopian princess, I thought I had chosen the wrong opera company—I thought the Metropolitan could offer nothing to compare with Raisa. The fact is I have yet to hear an Aida to compare with

Raisa's."[40] Ruth Miller remembered one of Raisa's difficult pregnancies: "I was with Raisa and walked hospital corridors with her when she was ordered to do so . . . but the child she hoped to save she lost. Then an overpowering longing displaced all else in her heart. Fame meant little—she the woman longed to be a mother. How many women are willing to leave a life such as her brilliant life . . . to lie flat as she did and she bore a child—her only child, and she felt complete as a human being, she said."

· *Chapter Fourteen* ·

PERSPECTIVE

R OSA RAISA clearly was blessed with a remarkable, dramatic voice and enjoyed one of the great operatic careers of the twentieth century. Her status was dominant at the Chicago Opera and her international engagements were on the highest level. Her being selected for two of the most important world premieres of the century (*Nerone* and *Turandot*) tells us that both Toscanini and Puccini (in the instance of *Turandot*) heard in her the splendor and strength of the ideal dramatic soprano. On only a handful of her recordings does one sense both the personality and vocal power that sent her critics and audiences into raptures. Many veteran commentators thought hers to be one of the most sensual, beautiful, flexible, and powerful voices they had ever heard; in fact, some believed hers to be the most powerful of all.[1] Raisa had to be acknowledged among the greats, along with Ponselle, Destinn, Muzio, Rethberg, and Jeritza. Was there a "best"? Probably not! When one listens to an important and unique singer, one doesn't long for what is missing; one is absorbed in the wonders of what is there. And greatness can "travel." Raisa, like the others, had a city that much adored her, but her vocal glory came through to any public that heard her.

There never was a singer who always had consistently great nights in the theater or concert hall, and Raisa's great nights were probably fewer than those of other artists considered great. The lack of consistency is one of the few problems with her career (insofar as I can reconstruct it from the various and numerous materials I have located). On her best nights few could begin to equal her thrilling voice and artistry, but on her off nights she could be below par. So many elements had to be in place for her to show her best qualities; her physical health and mental equilibrium had to be precisely calibrated in order for the voice itself and its control mechanisms to obey her will. Raisa would confide to trusted friends that she often sang her best after fabulous sex with Rimini. It comes as no surprise that Raisa late in life once told Claudia Cassidy that "when you are up there on that stage, when your voice is right, when everything is right, there is nothing like it in all the world."[2] Cassidy mirrored this sentiment in her own highly embellished style: "Raisa's voice was a royal purple dramatic soprano shot with gold and fire, and if you ever heard it on a great night you know that isn't fancy writing, but a reasonable description of the improbable come true."[3]

Carol Longone, who accompanied the Riminis in many of their concerts, told me that Raisa's voice was both enormous in decibels and gorgeous as pure sound, and that she had a very charming stage presence. She recalled that Raisa often sang as an encore the "Bolero" from *I Vespri Siciliani* with an extraordinary rhythmic impulse and verve. Although one hears some of the technical bravura in her 1920 three-minute recorded version, in person she probably sang it in a slower and more shapely manner, but with similar brio. Carol told me that on occasion Raisa could be a bit slack with musical details, especially counting; some of this carelessness can be heard on a few of the recordings and inferred from some of the reviews quoted. Carol also thought Raisa's to be a Semitic rather than a classically Italian or Slavic voice because the color and the underlying emotional melancholy made it so.[4]

Commentators often singled out Raisa's stage presence as something extraordinary. Her exemplary carriage made her seem tall, even majestic on stage, though she was only 5 feet 4 inches tall.[5] Like most professional singers she was constantly fighting the battle of the waistline, but she was mostly successful. Her relative slimness was often noted by reviewers and is apparent in most photos. Her Semitic beauty was frequently alluded to, and she had a healthy sense of humor about her prominent nose, regularly making jokes about it. She had an instinctive feeling for fashion and elegance, and she was always a beautiful picture in life as in art. Paul Hume wrote, "Her carriage, even as she walked across Michigan Avenue, was innately beautiful. Onstage, she could appear noble or scornful, timid or indomitable by a simple gesture."[6] When Francis Robinson wrote to her in 1962 that a mutual friend in New York had said he thought she strongly resembled the much-photographed Madame Pandit Nehru, she was of course delighted and said the compliment "makes me feel swell headed! You are a dear to put us both on so great a standard."[7] She apparently thought about this praise and in her next letter wrote, "Coming back to Mme. Pandit as you mentioned about her tiny hands, beautiful carriage, and I imagine gorgeous Indian eyes, she certainly can be considered as one of the beauties in the world."[8]

Raisa's musical and artistic taste has been called into question by some observers over the years. The recordings and many reviews suggest that she was not an aristocratic artist, but rather a more basic and instinctive performer whose deepest need was audience response to her thrilling voice and highly emotional presentation. It was very important to her to make big-scale vocal and theatrical points, as these have a way of swaying the public. She was working with an extraordinary voice and she knew the public loved artists who could scale the heights. She had the rare dynamic ability to sing both very loud and very soft, very slow and very fast, very high and very low. With this armory of skills she invited the public to note and respond to her mastery of vocal art. Later in life she told a reporter, "I always had to have the audience in my hand. I always had to get a response. It was the most wonderful feeling." Cecil Smith, in an *Opera* magazine essay in 1952 in anticipation of Callas's London debut as Norma, wrote of the Normas of his experience, and as he had heard Raisa, Ponselle, Cigna, and Milanov, he wrote with authority.[9] He said of Raisa: "she took a showman's attitude, using the music to display the spectacular flexibility and freedom of her voice. Her ebullience was exciting, but she was on the whole undiscriminating both musically and dramatically, although her characterization was well conceived in its externals." These qualities can be heard in her three *Norma* recordings. Unbelievable vocal feats are mixed with uneven and sometimes very unfinished vocalization. Smith's evaluation on many levels meshes with

Raisa's own account of her first Norma in Buenos Aires. The phrases, high notes, cadenza, and trills she singled out as important to her in her performance were obviously show-stoppers, but they speak of details rather than a unified musical realization. In Smith's review of the Callas London debut performance he writes that Callas started out a bit slowly but was fully warmed up by the end of the Act II trio, where "she held for twelve beats a stupendous, free high D. Among dramatic sopranos of my experience, I have heard this tone equaled only by Rosa Raisa. From this point onward Miss Callas held her audience in abject slavery."

Some have wondered why Raisa left the stage at age forty-four, an age that in our time probably would be a dramatic soprano's prime. There is an understandable admiration of those artists who sing into their fifties and beyond. Sadly, this is not always possible. As every artist is intrinsically different, so also is the length of a career. In the nineteenth century many important female artists, not unlike Raisa, started their careers at a very early age and, with the exception of a few like Patti, also ended relatively early.

It is of some interest that Raisa's contemporaries Emmy Destinn, Claudia Muzio, and Rosa Ponselle, the three singers to whom she is most often compared because of common repertoire, also started their careers at about the same age, in their early twenties. Although just out of their teens, those three remarkable stars for various reasons also left the stage after twenty- to twenty-five-year careers. Destinn stopped singing in major opera houses on the international circuit after a twenty-four-year career that included a two-year break during the Great War; after 1921 she preferred to sing only in her native land on a very limited and sporadic basis. Muzio died twenty-six years after her debut, but she was clearly in early vocal decline, although still a treasured and compelling artist. Ponselle retired from public performing after twenty years, but her leaving the stage was as much due to her nerves as to some inevitable vocal deterioration. Of these four sopranos only Destinn and Raisa were particularly famous for their powerful high notes. It appears that Raisa could on occasion in her last outings still summon up superb free ringing high notes, but on her

1933 recordings one detects the beginning of a beat in the very top notes, that telltale indication that deterioration has set in. Had she continued singing into her early fifties, into the 1940s, we would probably have some "off-the-air" or "in-house" recordings. It is likely these could have told us many things about her remarkable voice in her last years on the stage.

Furthermore, although Marchisio had given Raisa a superlative technique, it was a nineteenth-century technique for a dramatic coloratura, that is, a soprano who would sing Rossini, Donizetti, Bellini, and the early Verdi. Raisa brought this superbly trained voice, with its ease in both florid and long-lined legato singing, to roles her teacher may never have envisioned her in: the famous verismo and post-verismo roles of the late nineteenth and early twentieth centuries. These operas, with their heavier orchestrations, greater demands for textual clarity, and sometimes punishing tessitura, may have subjected her voice to demands for which it had not been specifically trained. It would therefore seem that the technique Raisa learned from Marchisio was an "incomplete" technique for the type of repertoire that engaged Raisa's emotional needs. Raisa, above all else, wanted to be "dramatic"—to "cry," as she said, to be "larger than life."

The Italian critic Teodoro Celli, in his seminal 1958 essay, "A Song from Another Century," in which he analyzes the Maria Callas phenomenon, expresses a similar idea. He felt Callas's singing both the operas of Verdi and his predecessors and verismo operas, particularly Puccini, "exposes her voice to grave dangers of a purely physiological nature: the singing of veristic opera, often strongly hammered out, powerfully enunciated often across fiercely intoned intervals, puts a dramatic soprano d'agilità in danger of having her vocal chords imperiled by weakness resulting from muscular damage. When she sings phrases like 'quel grido e quella morte . . .' in *Turandot* or 'Io quella lama gli piantai nel cor . . .' in *Tosca*, she places in useless peril all the precious 'vocal organism' she has won through all the years of the hardest study."[10] While the Raisa and Callas voices are not precisely the same, in both size and organization, there are some similarities. I am only suggesting that Celli's thoughts about the dangers of mixing verismo and the more linear vocal writing of the pre-verismo composers are pertinent to Raisa's case as well.

Then there are the demands placed on her voice simply by the frequency of her singing and her internal need to sing "big." While Vincent Sheean thought her resources were equal to any demands, and that she could have sung Aida every night, in truth Raisa was only human. That said, in an examination of almost everything that was written about her, one detects in the reviews, some cited in this book, that in the last third of her career she tended to be at her most remarkable when well-rested, often after an absence from the stage. One also observes in the body of criticism, good and bad, that when she sang long runs of performances, sometimes three or four times a week in very heavy roles, that a detectable weariness sometimes (but not always) crept into the voice. Conversely, many critics also noticed how fresh she sounded in the last act of an opera after having given so much in the earlier acts. It is indisputable that in the first half of her career she was singing largely on the physical strength of "youth," that her voice was able to sustain a prodigious amount of grinding and pounding. It is clear from both the reviews and the early recordings that Raisa liberally used her chest voice for both vocal and dramatic effect and for the production of the lowest notes. Whether this heavy usage of the chest voice harmed the rest of her instrument and its tractability is speculative. The wear that would inevitably come from departure from the Marchisio technique could be held off, at least for a while, by that youthful strength.

Interestingly, the Raisa projects that did not take place, but were reported as being planned, tell us much about what impresarios and conductors thought feasible. In addition to the previously mentioned *Linda di Chamonix*, *Semiramide*, *Lucrezia Borgia*, *La Wally*, *Hérodiade*, *La Campana Sommersa*, *Il Tabarro*, *La Rondine*, *Don Carlos*, *Le Maschere*, *Saffo*, and *Die Frau ohne Schatten*, there were announcements of *Fidelio*, Goldmark's *Queen of Sheba*, Marinuzzi's *Jacquerie*, *La Navarraise*, and *Carmen*. Extensive tours of Australia, China, and Japan were announced, but never came to pass. Sol Hurok's plan to present her in a tour of Russian operas, Ponselle's idea of the two of them doing *Aida* together with Ponselle as Amneris, Tosca-nini's desire to conduct her in *Norma*, and the plan to study the heavy Wagner roles with Lilli Lehmann are still more "might-have-beens." The range of roles, from the florid Linda to the mezzo Carmen and everything in between, suggests that very levelheaded musicians felt Raisa could do almost anything in the soprano canon.

The quality of Raisa's career is evidenced in many ways. The Chicago Opera in Raisa's day was considered second only to the Metropolitan in the United States, but its overall stature was as one of the world's great opera companies. Its star attractions, especially its sopranos, were second to none in the world. Mary Garden, Galli-Curci, Muzio, Mason, and Raisa would have been big stars in any company, and a repertoire fashioned around their unique capabilities was the general plan of the company. Chicago's male voices, although very fine, were not as impressive as their female counterparts. The critic Cecil Smith recalled that "when you attended the Chicago opera in those days you heard neither the same singers nor, in many cases, the same operas you could hear at the Metropolitan, but you saw performances that were equally well cast, rehearsed, and produced, and frequently more sumptuously mounted."[11] Chicago's publicity did not have the reach of New York's, and the recording industry largely made its choices based on what was being showcased at the Met. It must be noted that in Raisa's time recordings did not have the importance that they now have. There simply was not the realization that voices needed to be engraved in wax for posterity. It is not only Raisa who is underrecorded and less well documented; so also is Mary Garden. In the American Midwest and on the Pacific coast the Chicago Opera was considered the gold standard. Chicago was not an operatic backwater. Even before it had its own resident opera company all the great names of opera that appeared in New York also appeared in Chicago on various tours. As America's second largest city, Chicago was an automatic stop for all operatic endeavors and stars, whether in opera itself or in concert. There is a tone of pride and proprietorship in the writings of the Chicago critics; they did suffer somewhat from "Second-City syndrome," and often their writings have an element of boosterism in making the case that their company was second to none.[12] They were proud of Raisa and were certain there could be no finer dramatic soprano anywhere in the world, and their reviews reflect that sense. Francis Boardman wrote in Henderson's *Singing* magazine in 1926 about the issue of comparative critical standards in New York and Chicago; he found that "Chicago's musical resources and activities are so impressive that no sane lover of art can fail to regard them without respect, and with wondering anticipation of what they predicate for the future. The essential difference, though, is that musical appreciation in New York has already entered the aged-in-the-wood stage, while Chicago must for a while longer, so it would seem, be content with the mere promise of that state of blessedness."

One test of a great star is her power to have operas mounted especially for her, and then repeated over and over, season after season. So, *I Gioielli della Madonna* and *La Juive* were Raisa vehicles for much of her career, and it was unthinkable for any other artist in the company to sing these roles when she was present. Another interesting aspect of the Chicago Opera between 1920 and 1932 is that its roster of artists was totally different from the Metropolitan's. This is completely unlike the operatic scene of today, where at the highest levels there is a worldwide traveling road show with the same stars, conductors, and directors appearing everywhere. Only Chaliapin, Galli-Curci, and Dal Monte sang both in Chicago and at the Metropolitan during the same season as company members rather than guests; all the other artists were linked to one organization or the other. The repertory reflected the singular abilities of its artists. In a sweeping generalization, one could reasonably assert that Chicago welcomed and favored singers who may have been flawed but were more exciting than those in New York. Raisa, Muzio, and Garden were apt to be less "even" as pure vocalists than Ponselle, Easton, and Rethberg, but a strong case can be made that they were more absorbing and fascinating as theatrical personalities. It is worth noting that Chicago welcomed a consequential but imperfect Maria Callas before New York did. It was indeed a rich vocal banquet that both Chicago and New York gave the world.

Chronology

Every effort has been made to document all of Raisa's performances, both in opera and in concert. Day-by-day listings are given with casts, and I have included additional interesting facts and important nonperformance information that give context to events in her career where I deemed it appropriate and useful. Question marks (?) indicate that the information is not concrete—that is, when the date or cast included here is conjectural because I was unable to confirm specifics, but there is some good evidence that the performance(s) did take place. When additional elaboration of "soft" information is needed, I have added clarifying footnotes. First names of colleagues are given on first mention, and last names are used thereafter (except in cases where two or more individuals share a last name; in those cases I will supply first initial as well on all mentions after the first). Names of auditoriums are given when they are known. Official names of opera companies are given, taken from actual programs. Casts of the leading artists are given in the traditional order—soprano, mezzo-soprano, tenor, baritone, bass, and conductor. Any deviations from this format will be self-explanatory. When there is more than one change in a cast, the new cast is listed. Raisa's first assumption of a role is indicated in bold letters. As the Chicago Opera under its various official names is the centerpiece of Raisa's career, and in order to maintain the day-by-day chronology, occasional concert dates that took place during the Chicago company's season or its tours but were not connected with or presented by the Chicago Opera are preceded by an asterisk (*). For the Chicago Opera tours and cast changes, I have relied heavily on the cast listings provided by the late Charles Jahant, who compiled the best list extant of Chicago Opera performances both in Chicago and on tour.

DATE	PLACE	EVENT	CAST AND REMARKS
[1911]			
3 Jul	Naples, Conservatorium S. Pietro a Majella	Graduation ceremony	**RB:**[1] *Semiramide:* "Bel raggio"; *Norma:* "Casta Diva."
[1912]			
12 Apr	Rome, Accademia di Sancta Cecilia	Concert	**RB:** Giuseppe Kaschmann and Alfredo Zonghi. Giovanni Tebaldini. De'Cavalieri: *Rappresentazione di Anima et di Corpo* and Monteverdi: *L'Incoronazione di Poppea: two arias.* With Sistine Chapel Choir.
16 Apr	Augusteo	Concert	Same as 12 Apr plus Cavalli: *Giasone: Medea's Aria.*
? Oct			*Mme. Marchisio takes Raisa to Milan for an audition with Maestro Cleofonte Campanini. RB sings Norma, Aida, and Ballo arias. He engages her for the Parma Verdi Centenary Festival with promise to take her to his Chicago-Philadelphia Opera if successful.*
[1913]			
		VERDI FESTIVAL, TEATRO REGIO, PARMA El Primo Centenario della Sua Nascita 1813–1913 Cleofonte Campanini, director	
6 Sep	Parma, Teatro Regio	*Oberto, Conte di San Bonifacio*	**RB: Leonora**, Nini Frascani; Italo Cristalli, Angelo Masini-Pieralli. Cleofonte Campanini.
8 Sep		*Oberto, Conte di San Bonifacio*	Same as 6 Sept.
16 Sep		*Un Ballo in Maschera*	**RB: Amelia**, Elisa Marchini, Tina Alasia; Alessandro Bonci, Vincenzo Guicciardi, Andrea Perellò de Segurola. Campanini.

1. For events when Raisa sang under her given name, Raisa Burstein (Burchstein), I give the initials "RB."

CHICAGO-PHILADELPHIA OPERA COMPANY
(also known as Chicago Grand Opera Company)
Cleofonte Campanini, General Director

14 Nov	Baltimore, Lyric Theatre	La Bohème[2]	RR:[3] **Mimì**, Mabel Riegelman; Giovanni Martinelli, Francesco Federici, Gustave Huberdeau, Giuseppe Sturani.
20 Nov	Philadelphia, Metropolitan Opera House	Cristoforo Colombo (Alberto Franchetti), North American premiere	RR: **Isabella d'Aragona**,[4] Amedeo Bassi, Titta Ruffo, Henri Scott. Campanini.
22 Nov		Cristoforo Colombo	Same as 20 Nov.
24 Nov	Chicago, Blackstone Hotel	Morning Musicale	Showcase of the new stars of the Chicago opera.
29 Nov	Auditorium	Aida	RR: **Aida**, Cyrena Van Gordon; Bassi, Giovanni Polese, Scott (Ramphis); Huberdeau (King). Sturani.
4 Dec		Cristoforo Colombo	Same as 20 Nov.
8 Dec		La Bohème	Same as 14 Nov except Aristodemo Giorgini for Martinelli.
10 Dec		Cristoforo Colombo	Same as 20 Nov.
31 Dec		Aida	Same as 29 Nov.
[1914]			
11 Jan		Parsifal	Minnie Saltzmann-Stevens, **RR: First Flower Maiden**; Charles Dalmorès, Clarence Whitehill, Alan Hinckley, Hector Dufranne, Campanini.
18 Jan		Parsifal	Same as 11 Jan.
25 Jan		Parsifal	Same as 11 Jan.

2. When asked about her American debut, Raisa would often say either *Cristoforo Colombo* in Philadelphia or *Aida* in Chicago. Although her memory was very good, she never seemed to recall her United States debut as Mimi in *La Bohème* in Baltimore.

3. At this point Raisa adopts the stage name Rosa Raisa, by which she will be known for the rest of her life.

4. In these Chicago-Philadelphia performances of *Cristoforo Colombo*, in the double role of Isabella/Iguamota, the Iguamota scene was not given.

DATE	PLACE	EVENT	CAST AND REMARKS
30 Jan 1914		Gala	*La Bohème*, Act III: RR, Riegelman; Giorgini, Polese. Sturani. *Samson et Dalila*, Act II: Julia Claussen; Dalmorès, Dufranne. Ettore Perosio. *Lucia*, Mad Scene: Florence Macbeth; Attilio Parelli. *Tosca*, Act II: Mary Garden; Bassi, Polese. Campanini. *Monna Vanna*, Act II duet: Garden; Lucien Muratore. Campanini. *Aida*, Act III: Carolina White; Bassi, Polese. Perosio.
7 Feb	Philadelphia, Metropolitan Opera House	*Aida*	Same as 29 Nov.
21 Feb		*Don Giovanni*	**RR: Donna Anna**, White, Alice Zeppilli; Ruffo (DG), Giorgini, Huberdeau, Scott, Vittorio Trevisan. Campanini.
23 Feb		*Cristoforo Colombo*	Same as 20 Nov.
26 Feb		*Cassandra* (Vittorio Gnecchi), North American premiere	**RR: Klytemnestra**, Claussen; Dalmorès, Polese. Sturani. Followed by *A Lovers' Quarrel* (Parelli): Zeppilli; Bassi, Polese. Parelli.
7 Mar	Dallas, Coliseum	*Cavalleria Rusticana*	**RR: Santuzza**; Giorgini, Francesco Federici. Sturani. Followed by *Pagliacci*: Jane Osborn-Hannah; Ottokar Marak, Ruffo, Armand Crabbé. Campanini.
12 Mar	Los Angeles, Auditorium	*Parsifal*	Saltzmann-Stevens, RR; Marak, Whitehill, Hinckley, Dufranne. Campanini.
21 Mar	San Francisco	*Cavalleria Rusticana*	Same as 7 Mar except Polese for Ruffo.
22 Mar		*Parsifal*	Same as 12 Mar.
26 Mar		*Parsifal*	Same as 12 Mar except Claussen for Saltzmann-Stevens.
31 Mar	Seattle, Orpheum	*Lohengrin*	**RR: Elsa**, Claussen; Marak, Whitehill, Hinckley. Campanini.
2 Apr	Portland, Orpheum	*Cavalleria Rusticana*	Same as 7 Mar except Bassi for Marak.
3 Apr		*Parsifal*	Same as 12 Mar.
8 Apr	Denver, Auditorium	*Cavalleria Rusticana*	Same as 7 Mar except Federici for Crabbé.
12 Apr	Kansas City, Convention Hall	*Parsifal*	Same as 12 Mar.

Date	Venue	Work	Details
16 Apr.	St. Louis, Odeon	*Parsifal*	Same as 12 Mar.
17 Apr		*Cavalleria Rusticana*	Same as 7 Mar; *Pagliacci?*
21 Apr	St. Paul, Auditorium	*La Bohème*	Same as 14 Nov except Bassi for Martinelli.
22 Apr		*Cavalleria Rusticana*	Same as 7 Mar except Emilio Venturini for Giorgini; followed by *Pagliacci*: Zeppilli; Bassi, Ruffo, Nicola Fossetta. Campanini.
23 Apr	Milwaukee, Pabst Theatre	*Parsifal*	Same as 12 Mar.
25 Apr		*La Bohème*	RR, Riegelman; Giorgini, Polese, Huberdeau. Sturani.

ROYAL OPERA–COVENT GARDEN, LONDON
The Grand Opera Syndicate Ltd.
Harry V. Higgins, Chairman
Percy Pitt, Musical Director

Date	Venue	Work	Details
19 May	London, Covent Garden	*Aida*	RR, Louise Kirkby-Lunn; Enrico Caruso, Carel Van Hulst, Adamo Didur, Huberdeau. Giorgio Polacco.
30 May		*Aida*	RR, Claussen; Martinelli, Antonio Scotti, Didur, Huberdeau. Polacco.

PARIS: SAISON ANGLO-AMÉRICAINE DE GRAND OPERA
Boston Opera Company and Covent Garden (Joint Venture)
Henry Russell, General Director

Date	Venue	Work	Details
17 Jun	Paris, Théâtre des Champs-Elysées	*Un Ballo in Maschera* (Benefit for the survivors of *Empress of Ireland*)	RR, Felice Lyne, Eleanora de Cisneros; Martinelli, Pasquale Amato. Ettore Panizza. Preceded by *Il Segreto di Susanna*: Maggie Teyte; Jean-Emile Vanni-Marcoux. Panizza.
19 Jun		*Pagliacci*	**RR: Nedda:** Edoardo Ferrari-Fontana, Amato. Roberto Moranzoni. Preceded by *Tristan und Isolde*, Act I: Margarete Matzenauer, de Cisneros; Ferrari-Fontana, Amato. Egon Pollak; *Il Barbiere di Siviglia*, Act II: Lyne, Vincenzo Tanlongo, Amato, Vanni-Marcoux, Luigi Tavecchia. Moranzoni.
20 Jun	Opéra	*Otello*, Act II	**RR: Desdemona:** Ferrari-Fontana, Vanni-Marcoux. Conductor and other cast members unknown.

DATE	PLACE	EVENT	CAST AND REMARKS
			ROYAL OPERA–COVENT GARDEN, LONDON
26 Jun 1914	London, Covent Garden	Mefistofele	Claudia Muzio, **RR: Elena**; John McCormack, Didur. Polacco.
1 Jul		Aida	RR, Marguerite D'Alvarez; Martinelli, Francesco Cigada, Didur, Huberdeau. Panizza.
4 Jul		Mefistofele	Same as 26 Jun.
7 Jul		Le Nozze di Figaro	**RR: Countess**, Zeppilli, Teyte; Scotti, Jean Aquistapace. Panizza.
8 Jul		Mefistofele	Same as 26 Jun.
18 Jul		Le Nozze di Figaro	Same as 7 Jul.
Late July–August			*Concert tour of Jewish centers of Europe under auspices of Jewish organizations. Tour is suspended at the outbreak of World War I. Details unknown.*[5]
Fall 1914			*1914–1915 Chicago season is canceled owing to bankruptcy, reorganization, and the European war.*
			TEATRO MUNICIPALE, MODENA
			Giuseppe Sturani, Music Director
26 Dec	Modena, Teatro Municipale	Francesca da Rimini[6]	**RR: Francesca**; Remo Andreini, Enrico Roggio. Sturani (Zandonai supervising).
? Dec		Francesca da Rimini	Same as 26 Dec.
? Dec		Francesca da Rimini	Same as 26 Dec.
[1915]			
? Jan		Francesca da Rimini	Same as 26 Dec.
? Jan		Francesca da Rimini	Same as 26 Dec.

5. Abraham Cahan, editor of the Yiddish-language *Jewish Daily Forward*, refers to this pre–World War I tour sponsored by Jewish organizations. He was writing in 1918 about Raisa, who was about to make her New York debut, and recalling her past.

6. Raisa is very specific in her memoirs about singing *Francesca da Rimini* nineteen times in Modena under Zandonai's supervision.

? Jan	*Francesca da Rimini*	Same as 26 Dec.
? Jan	*Francesca da Rimini*	Same as 26 Dec.
? Jan	*Francesca da Rimini*	Same as 26 Dec.
? Jan	*Francesca da Rimini*	Same as 26 Dec.
? Jan	*Francesca da Rimini*	Same as 26 Dec.
? Jan	*Francesca da Rimini*	Same as 26 Dec.
? Jan	*Francesca da Rimini*	Same as 26 Dec.
? Jan	*Francesca da Rimini*	Same as 26 Dec.
? Jan	*Francesca da Rimini*	Same as 26 Dec.
? Jan	*Francesca da Rimini*	Same as 26 Dec.
? Jan	*Francesca da Rimini*	Same as 26 Dec.
? Jan	*Francesca da Rimini*	Same as 26 Dec.
? Jan	*Francesca da Rimini*	Same as 26 Dec.
? Feb	*Francesca da Rimini*	Same as 26 Dec.
? Feb	*Francesca da Rimini*	Same as 26 Dec.
? Feb	*Francesca da Rimini* (*Serata d'onore*)[7]	Same as 26 Dec.

TEATRO COSTANZI, ROME
Emma Carelli, Director
Edoardo Vitale, Principal Conductor

10 Mar	Rome, Teatro Costanzi	*Francesca da Rimini*	RR, Flora Perini (Schiava): Aureliano Pertile, Giuseppe Danise. Edoardo Vitale.
13 Mar		*Francesca da Rimini*	Same as 10 Mar.
15 Mar		*Francesca da Rimini*	Same as 10 Mar.
17 Mar		*Aida*	RR, Perini; Bernardo De Muro, Danise, Carlo Walter, Giuseppe Gorini. Vitale.
18 Mar		*Francesca da Rimini*	Same as 10 Mar.

---

7. Following Italian tradition, after a notable success the last performance of this run of *Francesca da Rimini* was a "Serata d'onore," an "evening of honor" dedicated to Raisa.

DATE	PLACE	EVENT	CAST AND REMARKS
20 Mar 1915		Aida	Same as 17 Mar.
21 Mar		Francesca da Rimini	Same as 10 Mar.
23 Mar		Aida	Same as 17 Mar.
24 Mar		Francesca da Rimini	Same as 10 Mar.
25 Mar		Aida	Same as 17 Mar except Pertile for De Muro.[8]
28 Mar		Aida	Same as 17 Mar.
30 Mar		Francesca da Rimini	Same as 10 Mar.
31 Mar		Aida	Same as 17 Mar.
3 Apr		Fedra,[9] world premiere	**RR: Fedra**; Hipólito Lázaro, Cesare Formichi. Vitale.
4 Apr		Aida	Same as 17 Apr.
6 Apr		Fedra	Same as 3 Apr.
8 Apr		Aida	Same as 17 Mar.
10 Apr		Francesca da Rimini	Same as 10 Mar.
12 Apr		Fedra	Same as 3 Apr.
13 Apr		Aida	Same as 17 Mar.
15 Apr		Abul[10]	**RR: Iskah**, Perini; Pertile. Vitale.
16 Apr		Francesca da Rimini	Same as 10 Mar.
18 Apr		Aida	Same as 17 Mar.
? Apr		Abul	Same as 15 Apr.

8. According to Vittorio Frajese's monumental history of the Rome Opera (Costanzi/Reale) with day-by-day casts, *Cronologia degli Spettacoli*, Bernardo De Muro sang all the *Aida* performances this season. However, I have seen a broadside of the 25 March *Aida* with Aureliano Pertile advertised as Radamès. This suggests that even the best-researched chronologies likely contain some errors. This compiler knows he is in good company!

9. This is Romano Romani's opera *Fedra*, performed by Rosa Ponselle at Covent Garden in 1931.

10. Alberto Nepomuceno was the composer of this seldom-performed opera.

GRAN COMPAÑÍA LÍRICA ITALIANA
Faustina Da Rosa and Walter Mocchi, Directors
Gino Marinuzzi, Music Director

Date	Location	Opera	Cast / Notes
18 May	Buenos Aires, Teatro Colón	*Francesca da Rimini*	RR, Hina Spani (Samaritana), Perini; Lázaro, Danise. Marinuzzi.
20 May		*Aida*	RR, Frascani; Caruso, Danise, Giulio Cirino, Berardo Berardi. Marinuzzi.
23 May		*Aida*	Same as 20 May.
24 May		*Francesca da Rimini*	Same as 18 May.
26 May		*Cavalleria Rusticana*	RR, Perini; De Muro, Danise. Marinuzzi. Followed by *Pagliacci*: Maria Roggero; Caruso, Mario Sammarco. Marinuzzi.
1 Jun		*Francesca da Rimini*	Same as 18 May.
2 Jun		*Cavalleria Rusticana*	Same as 26 May.
6 Jun		*Francesca da Rimini*	Same as 18 May.
7 Jun	Teatro Coliseo	Gala (Benefit for Italian war victims)	*Aida*, Act III: RR, Frascani; Caruso, Danise, Cirino. Marinuzzi. Geneviève Vix sings "La Marseillaise."
8 Jun	Teatro Colón	*Francesca da Rimini*	Same as 18 May.
11 Jun		*Aida*	RR, Frascani; De Muro, Danise, Cirino, Berardi. Marinuzzi.
12 Jun		*Francesca da Rimini*	Same as 18 May.
13 Jun		*Aida*	Same as 11 Jun.
17 Jun		*Aida*	Same as 11 Jun.
18 Jun		Gala	*Aida*, Act III: RR, De Muro, Danise. Also *Pagliacci*, Act I: Roggero; Caruso, Sammarco. Arias and ensembles: Caruso, Lázaro, Vix, Frascani, Tina Poli-Randaccio, Gilda Dalla Rizza, Spani; De Muro, Sammarco, Cirino. Dance by La Argentina.
29 Jun		*Aida*	Same as 11 Jun.
6 Jul		*L'Africana*	**RR: Selika**. Mary Melsa; De Muro, Ruffo, Cirino, Teofilo Dentale. Marinuzzi.
9 Jul	Teatro Colón	*L'Africana*	Same as 6 July except Spani for Melsa.
11 Jul		*Aida*	Same as 11 Jun.

DATE	PLACE	EVENT	CAST AND REMARKS
11 Jul 1915	Jockey Club	Concert	RR, Caruso, Ruffo, Vix.
12 Jul	Teatro Colón	*Francesca da Rimini*	Same as 18 May.
16 Jul		*L'Africana*	Same as 6 Jul except Spani for Melsa.
19 Jul		*Aida*	Same as 11 Jun.
24 Jul		*Der Rosenkavalier* (in Italian)	**RR: Marschallin**, Dalla Rizza, Amelita Galli-Curci; Ernesto Caronna, Cirino, Luigi Nardi. Marinuzzi.
25 Jul		*Der Rosenkavalier*	Same as 24 Jul.
28 Jul	Home of Susanna Torres De Castrex	Concert	RR and Caruso.
29 Jul	Teatro Colón	*Der Rosenkavalier*	Same as 24 Jul.
1 Aug		*Der Rosenkavalier*	Same as 24 Jul.
5 Aug	Rosario, Teatro Opera	*Aida*	Same as 11 June except Dentale for Cirino.
8 Aug		*Der Rosenkavalier*	Same as 24 Jul.
11 Aug	Buenos Aires, Teatro Colón	*La Bohème*	RR, Maria Ross; Lázaro, Sammarco, Cirino. Sturani.
12 Aug		*Der Rosenkavalier*	Same as 24 Jul.
13 Aug		Gala	*Carmen:* Vix; De Muro, Ruffo; RR sings Russian songs; *Pagliacci* Prologue: Ruffo. Caruso and Lázaro are also on the program.
17 Aug	Montevideo, Teatro Solis	*Aida*	Same as 11 Jun.
18 Aug		*Der Rosenkavalier*	Same as 24 Jul.
20 Aug		*Aida*	Same as 11 Jun.
23 Aug	Teatro Urquiza?	*L'Africana*	Same as 6 Jul except Spani for Melsa.
24 Aug	Teatro Solis	*Francesca da Rimini*	Same as 18 May.
27 Aug	Teatro ?	Concert	RR and Ruffo.
5 Sep	Rio de Janeiro, Teatro Municipal	*Aida*	Same as 11 Jun.
6 Sep		*Francesca da Rimini*	Same as 18 May.

9 Sep		*Aida*	Same as 11 Jun.
10 Sep		*Der Rosenkavalier*	Same as 24 Jul.
13 Sep		*L'Africana*	Same as 6 Jul.
14 Sep		*La Bohème*	Same as 11 Aug except Caronna for Sammarco.
	São Paulo, Teatro Municipal		
20 Sep		*Aida*	Same as 11 Jun.
28 Sep		*Francesca da Rimini*	Same as 18 May except Rona Francesco for Spani.
29 Sep		*L'Africana*	Same as 6 July except Anita Giacomucci for Melsa.
2 Oct		*Der Rosenkavalier*	Same as 24 Jul.
3 Oct		*Aida* (outdoor popular matinee)	Same as 11 Jun.
	Parque Antarctica		
7 Oct		*La Bohème*	RR, Giacomucci; Lázaro, Caronna. Conductor unknown.
12 Oct[11]		*Cavalleria Rusticana*	RR, Lázaro. Conductor unknown.
	Rio de Janeiro, T. San Pedro		

TEATRO CORSO, BOLOGNA
Tullio Serafin, Music Director

25 Nov		*Francesca da Rimini*	RR; Pertile, Eduardo Faticanti. Tullio Serafin (Zandonai supervising).
27 Nov		*Francesca da Rimini*	Same as 25 Nov.
28 Nov		*Francesca da Rimini*	Same as 25 Nov.
4 Dec		*Francesca da Rimini*	Same as 25 Nov.
5 Dec		*Francesca da Rimini*	Same as 25 Nov.
8 Dec		*Francesca da Rimini*	Same as 25 Nov.
11 Dec		*Francesca da Rimini*	Same as 25 Nov.
12 Dec		*Francesca da Rimini*	Same as 25 Nov.
	Bologna, Teatro Corso		
Mid Dec			*Raisa is introduced to Giacomo Rimini, who is singing Falstaff under Toscanini at the Teatro Dal Verme in Milan.*

11. There is speculation that this San Pedro company played a few performances in Porto Allegre.

DATE	PLACE	EVENT	CAST AND REMARKS
			TEATRO ALLA SCALA, MILAN
			Gino Marinuzzi, Muscial Director
[1916]			
5 Jan	Milan, Teatro alla Scala	*Aida*	RR, Elvira Casazza; Alessandro Dolci, Danise, Cirino, Luigi Ferroni. Marinuzzi.
8 Jan		*Aida*	Same as 5 Jan.
11 Jan		*Aida*	Same as 5 Jan except Emma Barsanti for Casazza.
16 Jan		*Aida*	RR, Casazza; Gennaro De Tura, Giuseppe Montanelli, Ferroni, Dentale. Gabriele Santini.
19 Jan		*La Battaglia di Legnano*	**RR: Lida**; Giulio Crimi, Giacomo Rimini, Cirino, Luigi Manfrini. Francesco Merli (2nd Console). Marinuzzi.
20 Jan		*La Battaglia di Legnano*	Same as 19 Jan.
22 Jan		*Aida*	Same as 16 Jan.
23 Jan		*La Battaglia di Legnano*	Same as 19 Jan.
25 Jan		*Aida*	Same as 16 Jan.
29 Jan		*La Battaglia di Legnano*	Same as 19 Jan.
1 Feb		*La Battaglia di Legnano*	Same as 19 Jan.
3 Feb		*Aida*	RR, Casazza; Dolci, Montanelli, Ferroni, Dentale. Marinuzzi.
6 Feb		*Aida*	Same as 3 Feb.
11 Feb		*Aida*	Same as 3 Feb except Santini for Marinuzzi.
13 Feb		*La Battaglia di Legnano* [12]	Same as 19 Jan.

12. The Scala annals show nine *Aidas* shared by Raisa and Laura Cirino; however, Carlo Marinelli-Roscioni of Rome has provided me with very specific cast information showing Raisa singing all nine *Aidas*. A similar discrepancy exists in the run of *La Battaglia di Legnano*; the Scala annals show it being given five times, but Marinelli-Roscioni has six specific dates.

22 Feb	Francesca da Rimini	RR, Jacqueline Royer (Schiava), Toti Dal Monte (Biancofiore); Pertile, Danise. Marinuzzi.
26 Feb	Francesca da Rimini	Same as 22 Feb.
4 Mar	Francesca da Rimini	Same as 22 Feb.
8 Mar	Francesca da Rimini	Same as 22 Feb.

TEATRO COSTANZI, ROME
Emma Carelli, Director
Edoardo Vitale, Principal Conductor

Rome, Teatro Costanzi

23 Mar	Aida	RR, Casazza; Crimi, Rimini, Walter, Augusto Daddò. Vitale.
25 Mar	Aida	Same as 23 Mar.
28 Mar	Francesca da Rimini	RR, Giuseppina Zinetti (Schiava); Pertile, Rimini. Vitale.
31 Mar	Francesca da Rimini	Same as 28 Mar.
2 Apr	Aida	Same as 23 Mar except Gabriella Besanzoni for Casazza.
4 Apr	Francesca da Rimini	Same as 28 Mar.
14 Apr	Aida	Same as 23 Mar.

GRAN COMPAÑÍA LÍRICA ITALIANA
Faustina Da Rosa and Walter Mocchi, Directors
Giuseppe Barone, Music Director

Buenos Aires, Teatro Colón

28 May	La Battaglia di Legnano	RR; Crimi, Rimini, Mansueto.[13] Giuseppe Barone.
30 May	La Battaglia di Legnano	Same as 28 May.
1 Jun	La Battaglia di Legnano	Same as 28 May.
4 Jun	Aida	RR, Casazza; Crimi, Rimini, Mansueto, Dentale. Barone.
6 Jun	Aida	Same as 4 Jun.
7 Jun	La Battaglia di Legnano	Same as 28 May.

13. Some reference works give his name as Gaudio Mansueto, others as Mansueto Gaudio. In this chronology he will be listed as Mansueto.

DATE	PLACE	EVENT	CAST AND REMARKS
10 Jun 1916		*Aida*	Same as 4 June except Martinelli for Crimi.
17 Jun		*Aida*	Same as 4 June except Martinelli for Crimi.
23 Jun		*Un Ballo in Maschera*	RR, Giacomucci, Casazza; Martinelli, Rimini, Mansueto. Barone.
25 Jun		*Un Ballo in Maschera*	Same as 23 Jun.
8 Jul		*Gli Ugonotti* (*Les Huguenots* sung in Italian)	**RR: Valentina**, Esperanza Clasenti, Giuseppina Bertazzoli; Martinelli, Crabbé, Marcel Journet, Mansueto. Barone.
9 Jul		Gala	RR sings national anthem and arias. Also on program are Léon Lafitte, Angelo Scandiani, Journet, Crabbé, Dalla Rizza, Edoardo Di Giovanni (Edward Johnson), Mansueto, and Royer.
11 Jul	Cordobá	*Gli Ugonotti*	Same as 8 Jul.
12 Jul		*Aida*	Same as 4 Jun.
16 Jul	Buenos Aires, Teatro Colón	*Gli Ugonotti*	Same as 8 Jul.
17 Jul		*Aida*	RR, Royer; Martinelli, Rimini, Mansueto, Dentale. Barone.
19 Jul		*Gli Ugonotti*	Same as 8 Jul.
27 Jul		*Falstaff*	**RR: Alice Ford**, Ninon Vallin, Casazza, Adèle Roessinger; Ruffo (F), Tito Schipa, Crabbé. Barone.
29 Jul		*Falstaff*	Same as 27 Jul.
1 Aug		*Loreley*	**RR: Loreley**, Clasenti; Di Giovanni, Dentale. André Messager.
3 Aug (M)		*Falstaff*	Same as 27 Jul except Bertazzoli for Casazza.
3 Aug (E)		*Loreley*	Same as 1 Aug.
5 Aug		*Gli Ugonotti*	Same as 8 Jul.
6 Aug		Gala	*La Bohème*, Act III: RR; Schipa, Crabbé. *Isabeau*, Act III: Dalla Rizza; Di Giovanni. *La Traviata*, Act I: Maria Barrientos; Schipa. Ruffo sings Neapolitan songs.
7 Aug		*Gli Ugonotti*	Same as 8 Jul.
9 Aug		*Aida*	RR, Bertazzoli; Martinelli, Rimini, Journet, Dentale. Barone.

Date	Location / Production	Notes
10 Aug	*Falstaff*[14]	Same as 27 Jul except Bertazzoli for Casazza.
14 Aug	Montevideo, Teatro Solis	*Aida*	Same as 4 Jun.
18 Aug	*Falstaff*	Same as 27 Jul except Bertazzoli for Casazza.
19 Aug	*Gli Ugonotti*	Same as 8 Jul.
27 Aug	Gala (Red Cross benefit)	RR, Lafitte, Martinelli, Crabbé, and Ruffo. André Messager at the piano.
5 Sep	Rio de Janeiro, Teatro Municipal	*Aida*	Same as 4 Jun except Bertazzoli for Casazza.
11 Sep	*Falstaff*	Same as 27 Jul except Rimini for Ruffo.
15 Sep	*Gli Ugonotti*	Same as 8 Jul except Angelo Scandiani for Crabbé.
17 Sep	Gala[15]	*Aida*, Act III: RR, Crimi, Rimini. *Mefistofele*, Prologue: Journet. *Pagliacci*: Vallin; Crimi, Rimini.
23 Sep	São Paulo, Teatro Municipal	*La Battaglia di Legnano*	Same as 28 May.
26 Sep	*Gli Ugonotti*	Same as 8 Jul except Scandiani for Crabbé.
1 Oct	*Aida*	Same as 4 Jun except Bertazzoli for Casazza.
3 Oct	*Falstaff*	RR, Vallin, Bertazzoli; Rimini (F), Schipa, Scandiani. Barone.
7 Oct	*Mefistofele*	**RR: Margherita**, Bertazzoli; Crimi, Journet. Barone.

Fall 1916 | *Before returning to Chicago Raisa visits the New York photo studios of Herman Mishkin and Victor Georg, who take photographs that become famous.*

CHICAGO OPERA ASSOCIATION
Cleofonte Campanini, General Director

Date	Location / Production	Notes
13 Nov	Chicago, Auditorium	*Aida* (Opening Night)	RR, Claussen; Crimi, Rimini, James Goddard, Vittorio Arimondi. Campanini.
15 Nov	*Andrea Chénier*	**RR: Maddalena**, Crimi, Rimini. Campanini.
23 Nov	*Cavalleria Rusticana*	RR, Irene Pavloska; Crimi, Polese. Campanini. Followed by *Pagliacci*: Florence Easton; Muratore, Rimini, Louis Kreidler. Sturani.

14. The annals of the Colón do not list the 10 August *Falstaff*, but I own a copy of the program.

15. This Gala program was presented in honor of the Brazilian statesman Rui Barbosa.

DATE	PLACE	EVENT	CAST AND REMARKS
25 Nov 1916		Aida	Same as 13 Nov except Van Gordon for Claussen.
27 Nov		Andrea Chénier	Same as 15 Nov.
5 Dec		Andrea Chénier	Same as 15 Nov.
9 Dec		Cavalleria Rusticana	Same as 23 Nov.
14 Dec		Aida	Same as 13 Nov except Van Gordon for Claussen.
18 Dec		Falstaff	RR, Myrna Sharlow, Maria Claessens, Pavloska; Rimini (F), Juan Nadal, Polese. Campanini.
20 Dec		Cavalleria Rusticana	Same as 23 Nov.
26 Dec		Falstaff	Same as 18 Dec.
[1917]			
5 Jan		Francesca da Rimini	RR, Crimi, Rimini. Sturani.
13 Jan		Francesca da Rimini	Same as 5 Jan.
15 Jan		Francesca da Rimini	Same as 5 Jan.
17 Jan		Gli Ugonotti	RR, Jesse Christian (for Galli-Curci), Sharlow; Crimi, Alfred Maguenat, Journet, Arimondi. Campanini.
19 Jan		Gala	Le Vieil Aigle: **RR: Zina**; Dalmores, Maguenat, Désiré Defrère. Campanini. Francesca da Rimini, Act III; RR; Crimi, Rimini. Sturani. Grisélides, Act I: Garden; Maguenat, Journet. Campanini. Lucia, Mad Scene: Galli-Curci; Arimondi. Sturani.
21 Jan		Gala (Benefit for French and Italian war sufferers)	Francesca da Rimini, Act III: RR; Crimi, Rimini. Sturani. Roméo et Juliette, Balcony Scene: Galli-Curci; Muratore. Charlier. Thaïs, Act II, scene II: Garden; Dalmorès, Dufranne. Campanini. Il Barbiere di Siviglia (act ?): Galli-Curci; Nadal, Rimini, Trevisan, Arimondi. Campanini. Muratore sings "La Marseillaise."
Early 1917			

Raisa elects not to return to Europe under wartime conditions, forfeiting her opportunity to create Magda in La Rondine at Monte Carlo. Raisa and Rimini enjoy a long vacation at Asbury Park, New Jersey; sharing the same resort community are the Campaninis, the Zenatellos, and the Stracciaris.

? Apr   *Raisa and Rimini make their first recordings for Pathé Frères in New York City.*

MIGUEL SIGALDI COMPANY, MEXICO CITY
Giorgio Polacco, Musical Director

4 Sep	Mexico City, Teatro Arbeu	*Aida*	RR, Lillian Eubank; Leon Zinoviev, Rimini, Virgilio Lazzari. Polacco.
6 Sep		*Aida*	Same as 4 Sep.
9 Sep		*Aida*	Same as 4 Sep.
? Sep		*Aida*	Same as 4 Sep.
? Sep	Plaza El Toreo	*Aida*	Same as 4 Sep.
18 Sep	Teatro Arbeu	*Il Trovatore*	**RR: Leonora,** Claessens; Zinoviev, Polese, V. Lazzari. Polacco.
? Sep		*Aida*	Same as 4 Sep.
? Sep		*Il Trovatore*	Same as 18 Sep.
? Sep	Plaza El Toreo	*Aida*	Same as 4 Sep.
? Sep	Teatro Arbeu	*Il Trovatore*	Same as 18 Sep.
28 Sep		*Il Trovatore*	Same as 18 Sep.
30 Sep	Plaza El Toreo	*Il Trovatore*	Same as 18 Sep.
? Oct	Teatro Arbeu	*Aida*	Same as 4 Sep.
6 Oct		*L'Africana*	RR, Edith Mason; Zinoviev, Rimini, De Segurola, Lazzari. Polacco.
11 Oct		*Il Trovatore*	Same as 18 Sep except Maria Gay for Claessens.
12 Oct	Puebla, Mexico	*Aida*	Same as 4 Sep.
13 Oct		*Il Trovatore*	Same as 18 Sep.
17 Oct	Mexico City, Teatro Arbau	*L'Africana*	Same as 6 Sep.
18 Oct		*Serata d'onore*	RR in acts from *Aida, Il Trovatore,* and *L'Africana* with same casts, and *Gli Ugonotti,* Act III duet with V. Lazzari.
21 Oct	Plaza El Toreo	*Aida* [16]	Same as 4 Sep except Vicente Ballester for Rimini.

16. As compilers of chronologies know, "exact" dates from Mexico in this period are difficult to ascertain. Upon the conclusion of the season Raisa gave an interview to *Musical Courier* in which she stated that she sang twenty times in this Mexico season: eleven Aidas, seven Leonoras, and two Selikas. In a *Musical America* dispatch from Mexico dated 25 September 1917, it was indicated that Raisa had already sung Aida seven times and Leonora twice. The balance of the dates have been adjusted in accordance with this information; therefore, some of the dates used are approximate and may not hold up upon further research.

DATE	PLACE	EVENT	CAST AND REMARKS
		CHICAGO OPERA ASSOCIATION Cleofonte Campanini, General Director	
12 Nov 1917	Chicago, Auditorium	*Isabeau* (Pietro Mascagni), North American premiere (Opening Night)	**RR: Isabeau,** Carolina Lazzari, Sharlow; Crimi, Rimini, Arimondi. Campanini.
14 Nov		*Aida*	RR, Van Gordon; Zinoviev, Rimini, Goddard, Arimondi. Campanini.
17 Nov		*Isabeau*	Same as 12 Nov.
20 Nov		*Aida*	Same as 14 Nov.
26 Nov		*Gli Ugonotti*	RR, Christian, Sharlow; Crimi, Maguenat, Huberdeau, Arimondi. Arnoldo Conti.
4 Dec		*Gli Ugonotti*	Same as 26 Nov except Rodolfo Angelini-Fornari for Maguenat.
6 Dec		*Isabeau*	Same as 12 Nov.
9 Dec		*I Gioielli della Madonna*[17]	**RR: Maliella,** Luise Bérat; Crimi, Rimini. Charlier.
15 Dec		*I Gioielli della Madonna*	Same as 9 Dec.
17 Dec		*Concert	RR and Mischa Elman, violinist.
30 Dec		*Aida*	Same as 14 Nov except Sturani for Campanini.
[1918]			
2 Jan		*Isabeau*	Same as 12 Nov except Constantin Nicolay for Arimondi.
3 Jan		*I Gioielli della Madonna*	Same as 9 Dec.
16 Jan		*Francesca da Rimini*	RR, C. Lazzari; Crimi, Rimini. Sturani.

17. *I Gioielli della Madonna* was always advertised in Chicago as *Jewels of the Madonna.*

Date	Venue	Work	Details
18 Jan		Gala	Verdi: "Hymn of the Nations,"[18] RR. Campanini. *Aida*, Act III: RR; Crimi, Rimini. Campanini. *La Bohème*, Act III: Anna Fitziu, Sharlow; Nadal, Rimini. Sturani. *Thaïs*, Act II: Garden, Dalmorès, Dufranne. Charlier. *Pagliacci*, Prologue: Riccardo Stracciari. *Manon*, Act III: Vix; Maguenat, Huberdeau. Charlier. Vix sings "La Marseillaise."
24 Jan	New York City, Lexington Opera House	*I Gioielli della Madonna*	Same as 9 Dec except Giuseppe Gaudenzi for Crimi.
27 Feb	Hippodrome	Concert	Stars of the Chicago Opera: RR sings arias from *Il Trovatore*, Act IV, *I Vespri Siciliani*, and duet from *Gli Ugonotti* with Georges Baklanoff (Marcel).
1 Feb	Lexington Opera House	*Aida*	RR, Van Gordon; Lamont, Rimini, Nicolay, Arimondi. Sturani.
2 Feb		*Cavalleria Rusticana*	RR; Lamont, Rimini. Sturani. Followed by *Pagliacci*: Fitziu; Lamont, Stracciari, Defrère. Sturani.
7 Feb		*Cavalleria Rusticana*	Same as 2 Feb. Preceded by *Jongleur*: Vix; Dufranne, Defrère. Charlier.
13 Feb		*Isabeau*	Same as 12 Nov except Lamont for Crimi.
18 Feb	Boston, Opera House	*Aida*	Same as 1 Feb.
21 Feb		*Isabeau*	Same as 14 Nov except Lamont for Crimi.
23 Feb		*Cavalleria Rusticana*	Same as 2 Feb. Followed by *Pagliacci*, same as 2 Feb except Rimini for Stracciari.
27 Feb		*I Gioielli della Madonna*	Same as 9 Dec except George Hamlin for Crimi.
2 Mar		*Aida*	Same as 1 Feb.
18 Mar	Brooklyn, Academy of Music	Concert	
29 Mar	Philadelphia, Metropolitan Opera House	Concert	

18. The tenor showpiece "Hymn of the Nations" was given in a soprano edition. Although Verdi wrote it for the famous tenor Enrico Tamberlick, Covent Garden would not release him for the premiere in May 1862 at Her Majesty's Theatre and the solo part was sung by the great Hungarian–German soprano Therese Tietjens.

DATE	PLACE	EVENT	CAST AND REMARKS
31 Mar 1918	New York City, Hippodrome	Concert	Benefit for Naturalization League. With Nahan Franko's Symphony Orchestra.
2 Apr	Carnegie Hall	Concert	Auspices of Rubinstein Club.
5 Apr	Boston, Opera House	Concert	
7 Apr	New York City, Hippodrome	Concert[19]	
? Apr	Recording session, Aeolian-Vocalion Records, New York City		

GRAN COMPAÑÍA LÍRICA ITALIANA
Faustina Da Rosa and Walter Mocchi, Directors
Gino Marinuzzi, Music Director

DATE	PLACE	EVENT	CAST AND REMARKS
28 Jun	Buenos Aires, Teatro Colón	Aida	RR, Besanzoni; Pertile, Rimini, Mansueto, Dentale. Marinuzzi.
4 Jul		Aida	Same as 28 Jun.
5 Jul		Aida	Same as 28 Jun.
7 Jul		Falstaff	RR, Vallin, Matilde Blanco-Sadún; Rimini (F), Charles Hackett, Mariano Stabile. Marinuzzi.
9 Jul		Aida	Same as 28 Jun.
11 Jul		Falstaff	Same as 7 Jul.
14 Jul		Aida	Same as 28 Jun.
16 Jul		Norma	RR: Norma, Besanzoni; Catullo Maestri, Mansueto. Marinuzzi.
19 Jul		Norma	Same as 16 Jul.
22 Jul		Norma	Same as 16 Jul.
24 Jul		Norma	Same as 16 Jul.

19. In April and early May Raisa and Rimini "reportedly" gave some concerts. These were dates originally booked for Galli-Curci, but she was not able to fill them. Confirmation of this tour has not been found. Richard Aldrich in his Concert Life in New York suggests that Raisa, by taking these Galli-Curci dates, delayed her planned departure for South America by a month.

Date	Venue	Opera	Notes
28 Jul		*Norma*	Same as 16 Jul.
31 Jul		*Aida*	Same as 28 Jun.
2 Aug		*Don Giovanni*	RR, Spani, Vallin; Luigi Montesanto (DG), Hackett, Gaetano Azzolini, Mansueto. Marinuzzi.
3 Aug		*Aida*	Same as 28 Jun.
5 Aug		*Falstaff*	Same as 7 Jul.
7 Aug		*Norma*	Same as 16 Jul.
9 Aug		*Norma*	Same as 16 Jul.
16 Aug		*Norma*	Same as 16 Jul except Paul Franz for Maestri.
18 Aug		*Un Ballo in Maschera*	RR, Anita Giacomucci, Blanco-Sadun; Pertile, Rimini, Mansueto. Marinuzzi.
21 Aug		*Norma*	Same as 16 Jul except Franz for Maestri.
24 Aug		*Un Ballo in Maschera*	Same as 18 Aug.
26 Aug	Montevideo, Teatro Urquiza	*Norma*	Same as 16 Jul except Franz for Maestri.
1 Sep		*Aida*	Same as 28 Jun.
4 Sep		*Falstaff*	Same as 7 Jul.
6 Sep		*Norma*	Same as 16 Jul except Franz for Maestri.
8 Sep		*Un Ballo in Maschera*	Same as 18 Aug.
10 Sep		*Aida*	Same as 28 Jun.
23 Sep	Rio de Janeiro, Teatro Municipal	*Norma*	Same as 16 Jul except Franz for Maestri.
25 Sep		*Falstaff*	Same as 7 Jul.
28 Sep		*Un Ballo in Maschera*	Same as 18 Aug.
1 Oct[20]		*Norma*	Same as 16 Jul except Franz for Maestri.
4 Oct		*Aida*	Same as 28 Jun.

20. Raisa's manager, Jules Daiber, had booked an extensive concert tour (see *Musical America*, 1 August 1918). The tour was supposed to commence in New York 29 September and was to include concerts in Boston, Bangor, Portland, Philadelphia, Pittsburgh, Baltimore, Washington, Newark, Worcester, Lynn, Chicago, Detroit, and Dayton. It would appear that all or part of this tour was canceled because of the length of the South American season and the "extensive" travel time needed under wartime conditions to travel from Brazil to the east coast of the United States.

DATE	PLACE	EVENT	CAST AND REMARKS
8 Oct 1918		*Tosca*	**RR: Tosca**: Hackett, Montesanto. Vincenzo Bellezza.
10 Oct	São Paulo, Teatro Municipal	*Norma*	RR, Blanco-Sadún; Franz, Manusueto. Marinuzzi.
14 Oct		*Aida*	Same as 28 Jun.
17 Oct		*Tosca*	Same as 8 Oct except Pertile for Hackett.
? Oct	Recife	*Norma*[21]	RR, remaining cast unknown.

CHICAGO OPERA ASSOCIATION
Cleofonte Campanini, General Director

DATE	PLACE	EVENT	CAST AND REMARKS
20 Nov	Chicago, Auditorium	*Il Trovatore*	RR, Van Gordon; Dolci, Rimini, V. Lazzari. Sturani.
25 Nov		*Aida*	RR, Van Gordon; Lamont, Rimini, V. Lazzari, Arimondi. Polacco.
29 Nov		*Tosca*	RR; Dolci, Baklanoff, Trevisan. Polacco.
7 Dec		*La Gioconda*	**RR: Gioconda**, Van Gordon, C. Lazzari; Crimi, Rimini, V. Lazzari. Polacco.
10 Dec		*Tosca*	Same as 29 Nov.
12 Dec	Milwaukee, Pabst Theatre	*Tosca*	Same as 29 Nov except Campanini for Polacco.
14 Dec	Chicago, Auditorium	*Il Trovatore*	Same as 20 Nov except Kreidler for Rimini.
18 Dec		*Cavalleria Rusticana*	RR, Pavloska; Dolci, Maguenat. Polacco. Followed by *Pagliacci*: Fitziu; Lamont (for Muratore). Stracciari, Defrère. Sturani.
20 Dec		*Il Trovatore*	Same as 20 Nov except Lamont for Dolci.
24 Dec		*Cavalleria Rusticana*	Same as 18 Dec except Lamont for Dolci. *Pagliacci*, same as 18 Dec except John O'Sullivan for Lamont.
26 Dec	Medina Temple Auditorium	*Stabat Mater* (Rossini)	RR, Ruth Lutiger Gannon, Dolci, Journet. Campanini. RR has to encore the "Inflammatus"

21. The Recife *Norma* was cited in a 21 November 1918 *Musical Courier* summary of this South American tour. "She toured for four weeks in Brazil, appearing in São Paulo, Pernambuco [now known as Recife], and Rio de Janeiro." Subsequent research has not been able to confirm this performance.

Date	Venue	Opera	Cast / Notes
28 Dec	Chicago, Auditorium	*Aida*	Same as 25 Nov except Baklanoff for Rimini.
[1919]			
1 Jan		*La Gioconda*	Same as 7 Dec.
11 Jan	*Raisa undergoes emergency appendectomy.*		
13 Mar	Pittsburgh, Syria Mosque	*Il Trovatore*	Same as 20 Nov.
15 Mar	Detroit, Masonic Hall	*Cavalleria Rusticana*	Same as 18 Dec except Sturani for Polacco. Followed by *Pagliacci*: Fitziu; O'Sullivan, Stracciari. Campanini.
19 Mar		*Il Trovatore*	Same as 20 Nov.

TEMPORADA DE PRIMAVERA DE 1919, MEXICO CITY
Jose del Rivero's Company
Giorgio Polacco, Music Director

Date	Venue	Opera	Cast / Notes
19 Apr	Mexico City, Teatro Esperanza Iris	*Aida*	RR, Besanzoni, Dolci, Rimini, V. Lazzari. Polacco.
22 Apr		*Aida*	Same as 19 Apr.
? Apr		*Aida*	Same as 19 Apr.
27 Apr	Plaza El Toreo	*Aida*	Same as 19 Apr except Perini for Besanzoni.
? Apr	Teatro Esperanza Iris	*Aida*	Cast unknown.
1 May		*Gli Ugonotti*	RR, Mason; José Palet, Rimini, Mario Valle, V. Lazzari. Polacco.
6 May		*Gli Ugonotti*	Same as 1 May.
8 May		*Tosca*	RR, Dolci, Rimini. Polacco.
11 May	Plaza El Toreo	*Gli Ugonotti*	Same as 1 May.
15 May	Teatro Esperanza Iris	*Norma*	RR, Besanzoni; Dolci, V. Lazzari. Polacco.
? May		*Norma*	Same as 15 May except Perini for Besanzoni.
20 May		*Norma*	Same as 15 May.
23 May		*Serata d'honore*	RR in acts from *Aida, Gli Ugonotti,* and *Norma*.
29 May	Plaza el Toreo	*Norma*	Same as 15 May.

DATE	PLACE	EVENT	CAST AND REMARKS
? May 1919	Teatro Esperanza Iris	*Norma*	Same as 15 May.
5 Jun		*Norma*	Same as 15 May except Fausto Castellani for Dolci.
8 Jun	Plaza El Toreo	*Un Ballo in Maschera*	RR, Mason, Perini; Palet, Ruffo. Polacco.
13 Jun	Teatro Esperanza Iris	*La Gioconda*	RR, Besanzoni, Perini; Palet, Rimini, V. Lazzari. Polacco.
15 Jun	Plaza El Toreo	*La Gioconda*	Same as 13 Jun.
? Jun	Teatro Esperanza Iris	*Norma*[22]	Same as 15 May except Spadoni for Polacco.
10 Oct	Detroit	Concert	
	CHICAGO OPERA PRE-SEASON MIDWEST TOUR		
13 Oct	Milwaukee	*Aida*	RR, Eubank,[23] Dolci, Rimini, V. Lazzari, Arimondi. Teofilo De Angelis.
14 Oct		*Un Ballo in Maschera*	RR (for Destinnová), Sharlow, Eubank; Bonci, Baklanoff, Arimondi. De Angelis.
15 Oct	St. Paul, Auditorium	*Aida*	Same as 13 Oct.
17 Oct	Peoria	*Aida*	Same as 13 Oct.
20 Oct	Omaha, Auditorium	*Aida*	Same as 13 Oct.
22 Oct	Kansas City, Convention Hall	*Aida*	Same as 13 Oct.
24 Oct	Oklahoma City	*Aida*	Same as 13 Oct.
27 Oct	Fort Worth, Baptist Auditorium	*Aida*	Same as 13 Oct except Baklanoff for Rimini.
30 Oct	Houston, Auditorium	*Aida*	Same as 13 Oct.
1 Nov	Little Rock	*Aida*	Same as 13 Oct.
7 Nov	Dayton	*Concert	

22. As in the 1917 season in Mexico, some of the dates are necessarily approximations. I used several Mexican source books and coverage from *Musical America* and *Musical Courier* to plot this season. I am comfortable with the numbers of performances, the casts, and the venues, although there certainly may be errors. There were reported to be seven *Normas*.

23. Sophie Braslau was announced for this tour doing Amneris. She canceled because of illness and Lillian Eubank, an American mezzo-soprano from Texas, replaced her.

CHICAGO OPERA ASSOCIATION
Cleofonte Campanini, General Director

Date	Location / Event	Opera	Cast
18 Nov	Chicago, Auditorium	*La Nave*, North American premiere (Opening Night)	RR: **Basiliola**; Dolci, Rimini, Arimondi. Italo Montemezzi (composer, conductor, and supervisor).
29 Nov	Cincinnati	*Aida*	RR, Van Gordon; Dolci, Rimini, V. Lazzari, Arimondi. De Angelis.
30 Nov		*Concert	Same as 18 Nov.
1 Dec	Chicago, Auditorium	*La Nave*	
6 Dec		*Il Trittico* (Puccini)	RR: **Suor Angelica**, Van Gordon, Pavloska. *Gianni Schicchi*: Carlo Galeffi (GS); Evelyn Herbert, Claessens; Johnson, V. Lazzari, Arimondi. *Il Tabarro*: Dorothy Jardon, Claessens; Johnson, Galeffi. Marinuzzi.
10 Dec		*Tosca*	RR; Schipa, Rimini. Marinuzzi.
16 Dec		*Norma*	RR, Sharlow; Dolci, V. Lazzari, Mojica. Marinuzzi.
18 Dec		*Aida*	Same as 29 Nov.
19 Dec	*Campanini dies.*		
20 Dec	*Un Ballo in Maschera with RR is canceled.*	*Campanini funeral*	Members of company participate in muscial part of service. RR sings "Inflammatus" from *Stabat Mater*. Bonci sings "Ingemisco" from Verdi *Requiem*.
21 Dec			
22 Dec	*Gino Marinuzzi assumes music directorship of company.*		
22 Dec		*Il Trittico*	Same as 6 Dec.
26 Dec		*Un Ballo in Maschera*	RR, Macbeth, Claessens; Bonci, Rimini. De Angelis.
30 Dec		*Il Trittico*	Same as 6 Dec.
[1920]			
5 Jan		*Concert	

DATE	PLACE	EVENT	CAST AND REMARKS
7 Jan 1920			Norma is canceled, Hérodiade substituted. "The famous singer was indignant at the Juvenile Protective Association which threatened to prevent five-year-old Helen Berg from appearing in the piece. Raisa would not play Norma without the child."[24]
10 Jan		Tosca	RR; Dolci, Baklanoff. Marinuzzi.
12 Jan		Norma	Same as 16 Dec.
23 Jan		Falstaff	RR, Sharlow, Claessens, Pavloska; Rimini (F), Schipa, Defrère. Marinuzzi.
26 Jan			Opening night in New York was advertised to be Raisa in Norma. She has to cancel because of the flu.
3 Feb	New York City, Lexington Opera House	Norma	Same as 16 Dec.
6 Feb	Boston, Opera House	Falstaff	Same as 23 Jan.
8 Feb		*Concert	
11 Feb	New York City, Lexington Opera House	Il Trittico	Same as 6 Dec except Yvonne Gall for Jardon.
19 Feb		Norma	Same as 16 Dec.
21 Feb		Cavalleria Rusticana	RR; Dolci, Rimini. Marinuzzi. Followed by ballet Boudoir.
22 Feb	Hippodrome	Concert	Stars of Chicago Opera: RR and Bonci, Aida Tomb Scene.
25 Feb		La Gioconda	RR, Van Gordon, Claessens; Dolci, Rimini, V. Lazzari. Marinuzzi.
? Feb	Recording session, Vocalion Records, New York City		
28 Feb		Aida	Same as 29 Nov.
1 Mar	Boston, Opera House	La Gioconda	Same as 25 Feb.
4 Mar		Aida	Same as 29 Nov.

24. Clipping from 8 January issue of an unnamed Chicago newspaper.

Date	Venue	Work	Notes
7 Mar	Symphony Hall	Concert	Sunday afternoon concert with Chicago Opera orchestra and chorus under Marinuzzi; RR soloist.
9 Mar	Opera House	Il Trittico	Same as 6 Dec except Gall for Jardon.
13 Mar		Un Ballo in Maschera	Same as 26 Dec except Galeffi for Rimini.
? Mar	Recording session, Vocalion Records, New York City		
17 Mar	Pittsburgh, Syria Mosque	Un Ballo in Maschera	Same as 26 Dec.
18 Mar		Cavalleria Rusticana	Same as 21 Feb. Followed by Pagliacci: Fitziu; Lamont, Ruffo. Marinuzzi.
20 Mar	Cincinnati, Music Hall	Cavalleria Rusticana	Same as 21 Feb. Pagliacci, same as 18 Mar.
24 Mar	Detroit, Masonic Hall	Un Ballo in Maschera	Same as 26 Dec except Margery Maxwell for Macbeth.
27 Mar (M)	Cleveland, Auditorium	Cavalleria Rusticana	Same as 21 Feb except Defrère for Rimini. Pagliacci, same as 18 Mar.
27 Mar (E)		Tosca	Same as 10 Jan except Johnson for Dolci.
2 Apr	Boston, Opera House	Concert	
4 Apr	Chicago, Auditorium	Concert	
9 Apr	Newark, Mosque	Concert	
11 Apr	New York City, Hippodrome	Concert	
13 Apr	Baltimore, Lyric Theatre	Concert	
15 Apr	Washington, Auditorium	Concert	
18 Apr	Boston, Opera House	Concert	
21 Apr	Pittsburgh, Syria Mosque	Concert	
23 Apr	Philadelphia, Academy of Music	Concert	
25 Apr	New York City, Hippodrome	Concert	
28 Apr	St. Louis, Odeon	Concert	
2 May	Brooklyn, Academy of Music	Concert	
4 May	Spartanburg, S.C.	May Festival	Concert version of Aida: RR, Marguerite Fontrese; Lamont, Rimini, Charles Towbridge, Tittmann. Richard Hageman.

DATE	PLACE	EVENT	CAST AND REMARKS
8 May 1920	Charlotte, N.C.	May Festival	Concert: Sophie Braslau and Paul Althouse in addition to RR and Rimini.
11 May	Syracuse, N.Y.	May Festival	Concert.
14 May	Macon, Ga.	May Festival	Concert.
? May	Evanston, Ill., Northwestern Gymnasium	May Festival	Concert.
21 May	New York City, Hippodrome	Concert	Benefit: Bialystoker Relief Committee.
30 Sep	*Raisa's father, Herschel, stepmother, Chaya, and siblings Frieda and Aron arrive in New York, and Raisa sees her family for the first time in thirteen years.*		
2 Oct	Bangor, Maine, Auditorium	Music Festival	Concert; RR sings arias from *Norma, Trovatore* (Act IV), *I Vespri Siciliani,* and "Inflammatus" under William Rogers Chapman.
4 Oct	Portland, Maine, Exposition Building	Music Festival	Same as 2 Oct.
7 Oct	Canton, Ohio	Concert	
8 Oct	Columbus, Ohio, Memorial Hall	Concert	
15 Oct	Detroit, Massey Hall	Concert	
16 Oct	Duluth, Armory	Concert	
17 Oct	Chicago, Auditorium	Concert	
		CHICAGO OPERA PRE-SEASON MIDWEST TOUR	
18 Oct	Milwaukee, Pabst Theatre	*Cavalleria Rusticana*	RR, Riccardo Martin, Defrère. Followed by *Pagliacci:* Marcella Craft; Lamont, Ruffo, Mojica. Marinuzzi.
20 Oct	Springfield, Ill., State Arsenal	*Cavalleria Rusticana*	Same as 18 Oct except Pietro Cimini for Marinuzzi.
22 Oct	Des Moines	*Cavalleria Rusticana*	Same as 18 Oct except Cimini for Marinuzzi.
25 Oct	Sioux City, Iowa	*Cavalleria Rusticana*	Same as 18 Oct except Lamont for Martin.

Date	Venue	Work	Notes
27 Oct	Sioux Falls, S.D., Coliseum	Cavalleria Rusticana	Same as 18 Oct.
30 Oct	Saint Paul, Auditorium	Cavalleria Rusticana	Same as 18 Oct. *Pagliacci*: Sharlow; Lamont, Galeffi, Defrère, Mojica. Marinuzzi.
3 Nov	New York City, Waldorf Astoria	*Morning Musicale	
5 Nov	Biltmore Hotel	*Morning Musicale	RR substitutes for Caruso.
8 Nov	Memphis, Auditorium	*Concert	
10 Nov	*Raisa and Rimini marry in civil ceremony in Chicago.*		
13 Nov	Cleveland, Auditorium	*Concert	

CHICAGO OPERA ASSOCIATION
Gino Marinuzzi, Musical Director

Date	Venue	Work	Notes
18 Nov	Chicago, Auditorium	I Gioielli della Madonna	RR, Carmen Pascova; Lamont, Rimini. Cimini.
20 Nov		Tosca	RR; Joseph Hislop, Baklanoff. Marinuzzi.
22 Nov		Il Trovatore	RR, Van Gordon; Lamont, Galeffi, Nicolay. Cimini.
24 Nov		Andrea Chénier	RR, Johnson, Ruffo. Santini.
26 Nov		I Gioielli della Madonna	Same as 18 Nov.
29 Nov		Tosca	Same as 20 Nov.
30 Nov	Cincinnati	*Concert	
2 Dec	Chicago, Auditorium	Andrea Chénier	Same as 24 Nov.
3 Dec	Orchestra Hall	*Concert	Benefit for Andreas Dippel. Participants: RR, Ruffo, Galeffi, Gall, Schipa, Van Gordon, Craft, Baklanoff, Arimondi.
5 Dec	Auditorium	Aida	RR, Besanzoni, Hislop, Rimini, V. Lazzari, Dentale. Marinuzzi.
6 Dec		I Gioielli della Madonna	Same as 18 Nov.
11 Dec		Cavalleria Rusticana	RR, Lamont, Defrère. Marinuzzi. Followed by *Pagliacci*: Maxwell, Johnson. Conductor?
15 Dec		Falstaff	RR, Maxwell, Claessens, Pascova; Rimini (F), Schipa, Defrère. Marinuzzi.

DATE	PLACE	EVENT	CAST AND REMARKS
19 Dec 1920		Concert	First anniversary memorial for Campanini. RR again sings "Inflammatus."
24 Dec		*Lohengrin* (in English)	RR, Van Gordon; Johnson, Louis Kreidler, Edouard Cotreuil, Defrère. Marinuzzi.
29 Dec		*Otello*	RR; Charles Marshall, Ruffo, Mojica, Dentale. Cimini.
[1921]			
1 Jan		*I Gioielli della Madonna*	Same as 18 Nov.
6 Jan		*Lohengrin*	Same as 24 Dec.
15 Jan		*Lohengrin*	Same as 24 Dec.
16 Jan		*Otello*	Same as 29 Dec except Rimini for Ruffo.
? Jan	*Mary Garden assumes directorship of the Chicago Opera.*		
24 Jan	New York City, Manhattan Opera House	*Norma*	RR, Besanzoni; Lamont, V. Lazzari. Marinuzzi.
27 Jan		*I Gioielli della Madonna*	Same as 18 Nov.
1 Feb		*Otello*	Same as 29 Dec.
6 Feb	Boston, Opera House	*Concert	
8 Feb	New York City, Manhattan Opera House	*I Gioielli della Madonna*	Same as 18 Nov.
12 Feb		*Otello*	Same as 29 Dec.
? Feb	*Recording session, Vocalion Records, New York City*		
17 Feb		*Otello*	Same as 29 Dec.
19 Feb		*Cavalleria Rusticana*	RR; Martin, Rimini. Cimini. Followed by *Pagliacci*: Zeppilli; Johnson, Ruffo, Defrère. Cimini.
20 Feb	Hippodrome	*Concert	
22 Feb	Manhattan Opera House	*Tosca*	Same as 20 Nov.

Date	Venue	Opera	Notes
25 Feb		*Cavalleria Rusticana*	Same as 19 Feb except Defrère for Rimini. *Pagliacci*, same as 19 Feb.
? Mar	*Recording session, Vocalion Records, New York City*		
4 Mar	Baltimore, Lyric Theatre	*Otello*	Same as 29 Dec except Rimini for Ruffo.
9 Mar		*Otello*	Same as 29 Dec.
11 Mar	Pittsburgh, Syria Mosque	*Lohengrin*	Same as 24 Dec.
15 Mar	Cleveland, Auditorium	*Lohengrin*	Same as 24 Dec.
18 Mar	Cincinnati, Music Hall	*Lohengrin*	Same as 24 Dec.
24 Mar	Dallas, Fair Grounds	*Lohengrin*	Same as 24 Dec except Pascova for Van Gordon.
26 Mar		*Cavalleria Rusticana*	Same as 11 Dec. Followed by *Pagliacci*: Maxwell; Muratore, Rimini, Defrère. Polacco.
30 Mar	San Antonio	*Tosca*	RR; Lamont, Rimini. Polacco.
1 Apr	El Paso, Liberty Hall	*Tosca*	RR; Martin, Rimini. Cimini.
2 Apr	Los Angeles, Hippodrome	*Concert	
4 Apr	Auditorium	*Otello*	Same as 29 Dec except Rimini for Ruffo.
8 Apr		*Lohengrin*	Same as 24 Dec.
11 Apr	San Francisco, Lotta's Fountain	*Concert	Midday open-air concert.
11 Apr	Exposition Hall	*Otello*	RR; Marshall, Rimini. Polacco.
15 Apr		*Il Trovatore*	RR, Van Gordon; Lamont, Rimini, Nicolay. Cimini.
19 Apr		*Cavalleria Rusticana*	Same as 11 Dec. *Pagliacci*, same as 26 Mar.
21 Apr		*Lohengrin*	Same as 24 Dec.
23 Apr		*Tosca*	RR; Johnson, Rimini. Cimini.
26 Apr	Denver, Auditorium	*Otello*	Same as 29 Dec except Rimini for Ruffo.
28 Apr		*Lohengrin*	Same as 24 Dec.
2 May	Milwaukee	*Concert	
6 May	New York City, Hippodrome	*Concert	
9 May	Newark, Mosque	*Concert	

GRAN COMPAÑÍA LÍRICA ITALIANA
Walter Mocchi, Director
Gino Marinuzzi, Musical Director

DATE	PLACE	EVENT	CAST AND REMARKS
8 Jul 1921	Rio de Janeiro, Teatro Municipal	Aida	RR, Fanny Anitua: Antonio Cortis, Rimini, Cirino, Mario Pinheiro. Marinuzzi.
12 Jul		Aida	Same as 8 Jul.
15 Jul		Norma	RR, Anitua; Maestri, Cirino. Marinuzzi.
17 Jul		Aida	Same as 8 Jul.
20 Jul		Norma	Same as 15 Jul except Pinheiro for Cirino.
21 Jul	Cathedral	Requiem[25]	RR, ?; Cortis, Pinheiro.
24 Jul	Teatro Municipal	Tosca	RR; Cortis, Luigi Rossi-Morelli. Aldo Caneppa.
25 Jul		Gala	RR; members of company.
29 Jul		Lo Schiavo (in Italian)	**RR: Ilara**, dal Monte; Angelo Minghetti, Rimini, Pinheiro. Marinuzzi.
31 Jul		Lo Schiavo	Same as 29 Jul.
3 Aug		Lo Schiavo	Same as 29 Jul.
4 Aug		Gala	RR sings "Inflammatus" and grand aria from Lo Schiavo; Beniamino Gigli, Minghetti, Madeleine Bugg, José Segura-Tallien, Cirino, Tamiki Miura, and Rimini offer operatic selections. Leonid Massine dances.
7 Aug	São Paulo, Teatro Municipal	Aida	Same as 8 Jul.
13 Aug		Tosca	Same as 24 Jul.
19 Aug		Lo Schiavo	Same as 29 Jul.
? Aug		Lo Schiavo[26]	Same as 29 Jul.

25. The *Requiem* is in memory of Paulo Barseto, founder of the newspaper *A Pátira*. This was presumably the Verdi *Requiem*, mezzo and conductor unknown.

26. The Giuseppe Pugliese biography of Toti Dal Monte has in this period a performance of *Lo Schiavo* with Raisa in Bahia. However, Bahia does not fit geographically, as it is considerably north of Rio and the tour was moving south to Argentina. Tom Kaufman, the authority on South American tours, seriously doubts that this performance took place.

Date	Location	Opera	Notes
27 Aug	Buenos Aires, Teatro Coliseo	*Aida*	RR, Perini; Cortis, Rimini, Pinheiro, Dentale. Marinuzzi.
31 Aug		*Aida*	Same as 27 Aug.
4 Sep		*Tosca*	Same as 24 Jul except Gigli for Cortis.
12 Sep		*Norma*	Same as 15 Jul except Besanzoni for Anitua.
14 Sep		*Norma*	Same as 15 Jul except Besanzoni for Anitua.
17, 25 Sep	*Advertized Normas canceled because of Raisa's illness.*		
28 Sep		*Norma*	RR, Perini; Maestri, Pinheiro. Marinuzzi.
30 Sep		*Norma*	Same as 28 Sep.
3 Oct	Rosario	*Norma*	Same as 28 Sep.
5 Oct	Buenos Aires, Teatro Cervantes	*Concert*	Benefit: Hospital Israelita, Raisa wing.
9 Oct	Teatro Coliseo	*Norma*	Same as 28 Sep except Besanzoni for Perini.
12 Oct	Montevideo, Teatro Urquiz	*Norma*	Same as 28 Sep except Besanzoni for Perini.
5 Nov	Dayton, Memorial Hall	*Concert*	
? Nov	Baltimore, Lyric Theatre	*Concert*	
? Nov	Charles City, Iowa	*Concert*	
10 Nov	Lincoln, Neb., Auditorium	*Concert*	
12 Nov	Toledo, Coliseum	*Concert*	

CHICAGO OPERA ASSOCIATION
Mary Garden, Directa

Date	Location	Opera	Notes
15 Nov	Chicago, Auditorium	*Tosca*	RR (for Lina Cavalieri); Tino Pattiera, Baklanoff. Angelo Ferrari.
19 Nov		*Aida*	RR, Eleanor Schlusshauer-Reynolds; Pattiera, Rimini, V. Lazzari, Cotreuil. Ferrari.
24 Nov		*Tannhäuser*	**RR: Elisabeth**, Van Gordon, Jeanne Dusseau; Richard Schubert, Joseph Schwarz, James Wolf. Ferrari.
30 Nov		*Tannhäuser*	Same as 24 Nov.
3 Dec		*Otello*	RR; Marshall, Rimini, Mojica, V. Lazzari. Cimini.
6 Dec		*Tannhäuser*	Same as 24 Nov.

DATE	PLACE	EVENT	CAST AND REMARKS
8 Dec 1921		*Tosca*	Same as 15 Nov.
10 Dec		*Aida*	Same as 19 Nov except Van Gordon for Reynolds.
12 Dec		*Tannhäuser*	Same as 24 Nov.
14 Dec		*Otello*	Same as 3 Dec.
17 Dec		*Tosca (for Monna Vanna)*	Same as 15 Nov.
21 Dec		*Aida*	Same as 19 Nov except Van Gordon for Reynolds.
24 Dec		*Tosca*	Same as 15 Nov.
27 Dec		*I Gioielli della Madonna*	RR, Claessens; Lamont, Rimini. Cimini.
[1922]			
2 Jan		*I Gioielli della Madonna*	Same as 27 Dec.
7 Jan	Chicago, Auditorium	*Tannhäuser*	Same as 24 Nov.
? Jan		*Concert	
19 Jan	Newark, Mosque	*La Fanciulla del West*	**RR: Minnie,** Ulysses Lappas, Rimini, Paul Payan. Polacco.
22 Jan	New York City, Manhattan Opera House	*Concert	
26 Jan		*La Fanciulla del West*	Same as 19 Jan.
29 Jan	Hippodrome	*Concert	With Cleveland Orchestra.
3 Feb	Manhattan Opera House	*I Gioielli della Madonna*	Same as 27 Dec.
8 Feb		*Tannhäuser*	Same as 24 Nov.
11 Feb		*La Fanciulla del West*	Same as 19 Jan.
13 Feb		*Tannhäuser*	Same as 24 Nov.
15 Feb		*I Gioielli della Madonna*	Same as 27 Dec.
17 Feb	Biltmore Hotel	*Morning Musicale	
18 Feb	Manhattan Opera House	*Aida*	Same as 19 Nov.
22 Feb		*Otello*	Same as 3 Dec.

Date	Location	Work	Notes
27 Feb	Philadelphia, Metropolitan Opera House	*Tannhäuser*	Same as 24 Nov.
4 Mar	Baltimore, Lyric Theatre	*I Gioielli della Madonna*	Same as 27 Dec.
7 Mar	Baltimore, Lyric Theatre	*Tannhäuser*	RR, Van Gordon, Maxwell; Martin, Schwarz, Wolf. Cimini.
11 Mar	Pittsburgh, Syria Mosque	*Aida*	RR, Van Gordon; Johnson, Rimini, V. Lazzari, Cotreuil. Cimini.
12 Mar	Chicago, Auditorium	*Lohengrin*	RR, Van Gordon; Johnson, Baklanoff, Cotreuil, Defrère. Polacco.
14 Mar	Milwaukee, Auditorium	*Tannhäuser*	Same as 7 Mar except Johnson for Martin.
16 Mar	Ann Arbor	*Concert	
18 Mar	St. Paul, Auditorium	*Tannhäuser*	Same as 7 Mar except Johnson for Martin.
23 Mar	Portland, Ore., Auditorium	*Lohengrin*	Same as 12 Mar.
25 Mar		*Aida*	Same as 11 Mar except Lamont for Johnson.
27 Mar	San Francisco, Exposition Hall	*Aida*	Same as 11 Mar.
28 Mar	Lotta's Fountain	*Concert	Repeat of successful 1921 noontime outdoor concert.
30 Mar	Exposition Hall	*Tannhäuser*	Same as 7 Mar except Johnson for Martin.
31 Mar		*Lohengrin* (for *Jongleur*— Mary Garden ill)	Same as 12 Mar.
1 Apr		*I Gioielli della Madonna*	Same as 27 Dec.
2 Apr	Lotta's Fountain	*Concert	As on 28 Mar.
4 Apr	Exposition Hall	*Tannhäuser*	Same as 7 Mar.
8 Apr		*La Fanciulla del West*	RR; Johnson, Rimini, Payan. Alexander Smallens.
11 Apr	Los Angeles, Philharmonic Auditorium	*I Gioielli della Madonna*	Same as 27 Dec.
12 Apr	Pershing Square	*Concert	Same as 28 Mar.
14 Apr	Philharmonic Auditorium	*Tannhäuser*	RR, Van Gordon, Maxwell; Johnson, Schwarz, Cotreuil, Cimini.
17 Apr	Denver, Denver Post Bldg.	Concert	Broadcast on radio only in the western United States.
20 Apr	Auditorium	*Tannhäuser*	Same as 14 Apr.
22 Apr	Wichita, Forum	*Aida*	Same as 11 Mar except Lamont for Johnson.
26 Apr	Grand Rapids, Armory	Concert	

DATE	PLACE	EVENT	CAST AND REMARKS
? Apr 1922	Kansas City, Schubert Theatre	Concert	
30 Apr	Chicago, Auditorium	Concert	
? May	Baltimore, Lyric Theatre	Concert	
? May	Harrisburg, Orpheum Theatre	Concert	
5 May	Toronto, Massey Hall	Concert	
7 May	New York City, Hippodrome	Concert	Benefit: Hebrew Orphan's Home.
? May	St. Paul, Auditorium	Concert	
22 May	Virginia, Minn.	Concert	
24 Oct	Denver, Auditorium	Concert	
26 Oct	St. Joseph, Mo., Auditorium	Concert	
29 Oct	Cleveland	Concert	
30 Oct	Pittsburgh, Syria Mosque	Concert	
1 Nov	Toledo, Coliseum	Concert	
3 Nov	Springfield, Ohio	Concert	
5 Nov	New York City, Century Theatre	Concert	

CHICAGO CIVIC OPERA COMPANY
Samuel Insull, President
Giorgio Polacco, Principal Conductor

13 Nov	Chicago, Auditorium Broadcast[27]	*Aida* (Opening Night)	RR, Ina Bourskaya; Marshall, Formichi, V. Lazzari, Cotreuil, Polacco.

27. *Radio Digest*, 11 November, reported: "Every opera suited to Radiophony will be broadcast by KYW, veteran class B (400 meter) station of the Westinghouse Company. KYW it will be remembered broadcast the Chicago Opera last season."

Date	Opera	Cast
18 Nov	*I Gioielli della Madonna*	RR, Claessens; Lamont, Rimini, Cimini.
20 Nov	*Tosca*	RR; Crimi, Formichi. Ettore Panizza.
22 Nov	*Il Trovatore*	RR, Louise Homer; Crimi, Rimini. Polacco.
28 Nov	*Aida*	Same as 13 Nov.
2 Dec	*I Gioielli della Madonna*	Same as 18 Nov.
5 Dec	*La Fanciulla del West*	RR; Crimi, Rimini. Panizza.
	Claudia Muzio makes her Chicago Civic Opera debut in Aida.	
7 Dec	*Il Trovatore*	Same as 22 Nov.
8 Dec	*I Gioielli della Madonna*	Same as 18 Nov.
14 Dec	*Il Trovatore*	Same as 22 Nov except Van Gordon for Homer.
23 Dec	*Il Trovatore*	**RR: Rachel**, Mason; Marshall, Minghetti, V. Lazzari. Panizza.
31 Dec	*La Juive (in Italian)*[28]	

[1923]

Date	Opera	Cast
4 Jan	*La Juive*	Same as 31 Dec.
6 Jan	*La Forza del Destino*	**RR: Leonora**, Pavloska; Crimi, Rimini, V. Lazzari. Polacco.
16 Jan	*La Forza del Destino*	Same as 6 Jan.
19 Jan	*Gala*	*Aida*, Act III: RR, Marshall, Formichi. Panizza. *Pagliacci*, Act I: Mary McCormic; Lamont, Rimini. Richard Hageman. *L'Amore dei Tre Re*, Act I, scene I: Garden; Crimi, Baklanoff. Polacco. *Mefistofele*, Act IV: Mason; Minghetti, Ivan Steschenko. Cimini. *Die Walkire*, Act III, scene 3: Van Gordon; Baklanoff. Polacco.

Boston, Opera House

Date	Opera	Cast
20 Jan	*La Juive*	Same as 31 Dec.
27 Jan	*Il Trovatore*	Same as 22 Nov except Formichi for Rimini.
3 Feb	*I Gioielli della Madonna*	Same as 18 Nov.

Washington, Poli's Theatre

Date	Opera	Cast
5 Feb	*Aida*	Same as 13 Nov except Van Gordon for Bourskaya.

Pittsburgh, Syria Mosque

Date	Opera	Cast
8 Feb	*I Gioielli della Madonna*	Same as 18 Nov.

28. *La Juive* was always in Raisa's Chicago Civic Opera career sung in Italian; however, it was always billed and advertised not as *L'Ebrea*, but as *The Jewess*.

DATE	PLACE	EVENT	CAST AND REMARKS
10 Feb 1923		*Cavalleria Rusticana*	RR; Lamont, Rimini. Cimini. Followed by *Pagliacci*: Muzio, Marshall, Formichi, Defrere. Cimini.
? Mar	*Recording session, Vocalion Records, New York City*		
? Apr	*Recording session, Vocalion Records, New York City*		
8 Apr	New York City, Hippodrome	Concert	Benefit: Jewish Teacher's Seminary.
12 May	Chicago, Auditorium	Concert	Benefit: Jewish Drive.
? May	New York City, Carnegie Hall	Concert	
? May	Akron, Armory	Concert	
26 Oct	Shamokin, Pa., Majestic Theatre	Concert	
30 Oct	Atlanta, Armory	Concert	
1 Nov	Memphis, Auditorium	Concert	
4 Nov	Cleveland, Auditorium	Concert	
5 Nov	Detroit	Concert	

CHICAGO CIVIC OPERA COMPANY
Samuel Insull, President
Giorgio Polacco, Principal Conductor

DATE	PLACE	EVENT	CAST AND REMARKS
13 Nov	Chicago, Auditorium	*La Juive*	RR, Macbeth; Marshall, Minghetti, V. Lazzari. Panizza.
17 Nov		*Il Trovatore*	RR, Van Gordon; Crimi, Rimini, V. Lazzari. Cimini.
21 Nov		*La Juive*	Same as 13 Nov.
23 Nov		*L'Africana*	RR, Macbeth; Marshall, Formichi, Alexander Kipnis, V. Lazzari. Panizza.
28 Nov		*Aida*	RR, Homer; Marshall, Formichi, V. Lazzari, Cotreuil. Polacco.
1 Dec		*L'Africana*	Same as 23 Nov.

Date	Location	Opera	Cast/Notes
4 Dec		*Aida*	Same as 28 Nov.
10 Dec		*La Juive*	Same as 13 Nov.
13 Dec		*Otello*	RR, Marshall, Rimini, Mojica, Kipnis. Panizza.
15 Dec		*Cavalleria Rusticana*	RR; Pavloska, Crimi, Rimini, Cimini. Preceded by *Snowbird* (Theodore Stearns): Maxwell; Lamont, Cotreuil. *Maestro di Cappella* (Paer): Mabel Sherwood; Trevisan. Isaac Van Grove.
17 Dec	Detroit, Masonic Hall	*L'Africana*	Same as 23 Nov.
19 Dec	Chicago Auditorium	*Concert	
22 Dec		*Otello*	Same as 13 Dec.
29 Dec		*La Juive*	RR, Lucille Westen; Marshall, Minghetti, Kipnis. Panizza.
[1924]			
2 Jan		*Otello*	Same as 13 Dec except Schwarz for Rimini.
10 Jan		*Cavalleria Rusticana*	Same as 15 Dec except Alfred Piccaver for Crimi. Followed by *Pagliacci*: Claire Dux; Fernand Ansseau, Formichi, Defrère. Panizza.
16 Jan		*Il Trovatore*	Same as 17 Nov except Lamont for Crimi.
25 Jan		Gala[29]	
28 Jan	Boston, Opera House	*L'Africana*	Same as 23 Nov except Westen for Macbeth.
9 Feb		*Otello*	Same as 13 Dec.
11 Feb	Cleveland, Auditorium	*La Juive*	Same as 13 Nov except Mason for Macbeth.
14 Feb		*Cavalleria Rusticana*	RR; Lamont, Defrère. Cimini. Followed by *Pagliacci*: Muzio, Marshall, Rimini, Defrère. Panizza.
16 Feb	Pittsburgh, Syria Mosque	*La Juive*	Same as 13 Nov except Westen for Macbeth.
20 Feb	Detroit, Masonic Auditorium	*La Juive*	Same as 13 Nov except Westen for Macbeth.
22 Feb	Chattanooga, Memorial Auditorium	*La Juive*	Same as 13 Nov except Westen for Macbeth.

---

29. Details of this gala were impossible to ascertain. The *Chicago Tribune* in several articles about the event concentrated solely on the society aspect, with no details of the acts of the operas given. Raisa, Muzio, and Garden were part of this gala.

DATE	PLACE	EVENT	CAST AND REMARKS
27 Feb 1924	Houston, Auditorium	*La Juive*	Same as 13 Nov except Westen for Macbeth.
29 Feb	Dallas, Auditorium	*La Juive*	Same as 13 Nov except Westen for Macbeth.
5 Mar	Los Angeles, Philharmonic Auditorium	*La Juive*	Same as 13 Nov except Westen for Macbeth.
8 Mar	San Francisco, Casino Theater	*La Juive*	Same as 13 Nov except Westen for Macbeth.
12 Mar	Portland, Ore., Auditorium	*La Juive*	Same as 13 Nov except Westen for Macbeth.
14 Mar	Seattle, Arena	*La Juive*	Same as 13 Nov except Westen for Macbeth.
17 Mar	Salt Lake City, Tabernacle	Gala	*Aida*, Act III: RR; Lamont, Rimini. Polacco. *Otello*, Act II, Finale: Marshall, Baklanoff. Panizza. *Jongleur de Notre Dame*, Act II: Garden; Defrère, Kipnis. Polacco. *Mefistofele*, Act III: Mason; Minghetti, V. Lazzari. Polacco.
18 Mar	Denver, Auditorium	*La Juive*	Same as 13 Nov except Westen for Macbeth.

TEATRO ALLA SCALA, MILAN
Arturo Toscanini, Director

DATE	PLACE	EVENT	CAST AND REMARKS
1 May	Milan, La Scala	*Nerone* (Arrigo Boito), world premiere	**RR: Asteria,** Luisa Bertana; Pertile, Galeffi, Journet, Ezio Pinza. Arturo Toscanini.
4 May		*Nerone*	Same as 1 May.
6 May		*Nerone*	Same as 1 May.
8 May		*Nerone*	Same as 1 May.
10 May		*Nerone*	Same as 1 May.
13 May		*Nerone*	Same as 1 May except Benvenuto Franci for Galeffi.
15 May		*Nerone*	Same as 1 May except Franci for Galeffi.
18 May		*Nerone*	Same as 1 May except Franci for Galeffi.
20 May		*Nerone*	Same as 1 May except Franci for Galeffi.
7 Oct	Pittsburgh, Syria Mosque	Concert	

Date	Venue	Event	Cast
? Oct	New York City, Ritz Carlton Hotel Ballroom	Morning Musicale	
18 Oct	Carnegie Hall	Concert	
20 Oct	Denver, Auditorium	Concert	
25 Oct	Pittsburgh, Syria Mosque	Concert	
30 Oct	Dallas	Concert	

Date	Venue	Opera	Cast
5 Nov	Chicago, Auditorium	La Gioconda (Opening Night)	RR, Perini, Kathryn Meisle; Cortis, Formichi, Kipnis. Polacco.
8 Nov		Aida	RR, Augusta Lenska; Marshall, Formichi, V. Lazzari, Kipnis. Moranzoni.
11 Nov		Tannhäuser	RR, Van Gordon, Gladys Swarthout; Lamont, Schwarz, Kipnis. Henry Weber.
15 Nov		La Gioconda	Same as 5 Nov.
16 Nov		Cavalleria Rusticana	RR; Lamont, Defrère. Cimini. Followed by *Pagliacci*: McCormic; Ansseau, Formichi, Douglas Stanbury, Mojica. Moranzoni.
23 Nov		Aida	Same as 8 Nov.
25 Nov		Cavalleria Rusticana	Same as 16 Nov except Piccaver for Lamont.
30 Nov		La Gioconda	Same as 5 Nov.
4 Dec		La Juive	RR, Macbeth; Marshall, Romeo Boscacci, V. Lazzari. Cimini.
13 Dec		I Gioielli della Madonna	RR, Claessens, Swarthout; Lamont, Rimini. Cimini.
14 Dec		*Concert	RR, Cantor Mordechai Herschmann, Kipnis.
15 Dec		Aida	Same as 8 Nov.
20 Dec		La Juive	Same as 4 Dec.
26 Dec		Otello	RR, Marshall, Schwarz, Mojica, Kipnis. Moranzoni.

DATE	PLACE	EVENT	CAST AND REMARKS
[1925]			
1 Jan		I Gioielli della Madonna	Same as 13 Dec.
3 Jan		La Gioconda	Same as 5 Nov.
14 Jan		Otello	Same as 26 Dec.
18 Jan		Aida	Same as 8 Nov?
23 Jan		Gala	Gioconda, Act IV: RR, Van Gordon; Cortis, Formichi. Moranzoni. Monna Vanna, Act II, Scene II: Garden; Ansseau. Polacco. La Traviata, Act III: Muzio; Schipa, William Beck. Cimini. Roméo et Juliette, Act I: Mason; Hackett, Defrère, Formichi. Polacco.
26 Jan	Boston, Opera House	Aida	Same as 8 Nov except Van Gordon for Lenska.
7 Feb		I Gioielli della Madonna	Same as 13 Dec.
9 Feb	Washington, Auditorium	Tannhäuser	Same as 11 Nov except Cotreuil for Kipnis.
14 Feb		La Gioconda[30]	RR, Van Gordon, Lenska; Cortis, Rimini, Kipnis. Polacco.
17 Feb	Pittsburgh, Syria Mosque	Tannhäuser	Same as 11 Nov.
19 Feb	Cleveland, Auditorium	La Gioconda	Same as 14 Feb except V. Lazzari for Kipnis.
24 Feb	Chattanooga, Auditorium	Tannhäuser	Same as 11 Nov except Cotreuil for Kipnis.
27 Feb	Memphis, Auditorium	La Gioconda	RR, Lenska, Perini; Cortis, Rimini, V. Lazzari. Polacco.
2 Mar	Dallas, Fair Park Auditorium	La Gioconda	RR, Perini, Lenska; Cortis, Rimini, Kipnis. Polacco.
4 Mar	Tulsa, Convention Hall	La Gioconda	RR, Lenska, Perini; Cortis, Rimini, Kipnis. Polacco.
6 Mar	St. Louis, Odeon Theatre	La Gioconda	Same as 4 Mar.
12 Mar	Cincinnati, Music Hall	La Gioconda	RR, Van Gordon, Lenska; Cortis, Rimini, V. Lazzari. Polacco.
14 Mar	Milwaukee, Pabst Theatre	La Gioconda	Same as 12 Mar?

30. On this tour three mezzo-sopranos (Van Gordon, Lenska, and Perini) alternated roles (Laura and La Cieca); hence the multiple listings. The Laura is always listed first and La Cieca second.

TEATRO ALLA SCALA, MILAN
Arturo Toscanini, Director

Milan, La Scala

13 Apr	*Nerone*	RR, Bertana; Pertile, Franci, Journet. Toscanini.
16 Apr	*Nerone*	Same as 13 Apr.
19 Apr	*Nerone*	Same as 13 Apr.
24 Apr	*Nerone*	Same as 13 Apr.
30 Apr	*Il Trovatore*	RR, Anitua; Pertile, Franci, Fernando Autori. Toscanini.
2 May	*Il Trovatore*	Same as 30 Apr.
4 May	*Il Trovatore*	Same as 30 Apr.
6 May	*Il Trovatore*	Same as 30 Apr.
12 May	*Falstaff*	RR, Ines Maria Ferraris, Casazza; Rimini (F), Alessio De Paolis, Leone Paci. Toscanini.
15 May	*Falstaff*	Same as 12 May.

AMERICAN-ITALIAN-FRENCH GRAND OPERA COMPANY, PARIS
Paolo Longone, Directeur Général

Paris, Théâtre de la Gaîté-Lyrique

23 May	*Il Trovatore*	RR, Casazza; Pedro Lafuente, Montesanto, Didur. Moranzoni.
26 May	*Il Trovatore*	Same as 23 May.
1 Jun	*Falstaff*	RR, Queena Mario, Casazza; Rimini (F), Hackett, Defrère, Didur. Panizza.

RAVINIA FESTIVAL
Louis Eckstein, Director
Gennaro Papi, Music Director

Highland Park, Pavilion

30 Jun	*Aida*	RR, Bourskaya; Martinelli, Danise, Léon Rothier, Louis D'Angelo. Gennaro Papi.
3 Jul	*Madama Butterfly*	**RR: Cio-Cio-San**, Bourskaya; Mario Chamlee, Mario Basiola. Papi.
5 Jul	*Aida*	Same as 30 Jun.

DATE	PLACE	EVENT	CAST AND REMARKS
10 Jul 1925		Cavalleria Rusticana	RR; Chamlee, Rimini. Papi. Followed by *Pagliacci*: Marie Sundelius; Martinelli, Danise, Defrère. Papi.
12 Jul		Il Trovatore	RR, Bourskaya; Martinelli, Danise, Lazzari. Papi.
16 Jul		Madama Butterfly	Same as 3 Jul.
21 Jul		Cavalleria Rusticana	Same as 10 Jul.
23 Jul		Il Trovatore	Same as 12 Jul except Rimini for Danise.
25 Jul		La Juive[31]	RR, Macbeth; Martinelli, Armand Tokatyan, Rothier. Louis Hasselmans.
1 Aug		Fedora	**RR: Fedora**, Maxwell; Martinelli, Danise. Papi.
2 Aug			*After the Fedora Raisa cancels 5 August Madama Butterfly and 8 August Ballo in Maschera owing to her father's death in New York City on 2 August. She and Rimini go to New York for the funeral and she then takes a one-week shivah (mourning) period.*
11 Aug		La Juive	Same as 25 Jul.
14 Aug		Tosca	RR; Chamlee, Danise. Papi.
16 Aug		Madama Butterfly	Same as 3 Jul.
19 Aug		Fedora	Same as 1 Aug.
22 Aug		Un Ballo in Maschera	RR, Macbeth, Bourskaya; Martinelli, Danise. Papi.
25 Aug		Aida	Same as 30 Jun.
27 Aug		Tosca	Same as 14 Aug.
2 Sept		I Gioielli della Madonna, Act II	RR, Chamlee, Rimini. Papi.
5 Sep		Tosca	Same as 14 Aug.
7 Sep		Gala	*Madama Butterfly*, Act I: RR; Martinelli, Rimini. *Manon*, Act III, scene 2: Lucrezia Bori; Martinelli. *Don Pasquale*, Acts II and III: Bori; Schipa, Rimini. Papi.

31. Raisa sang Rachel in Italian; the rest of the cast sang in French.

LOS ANGELES GRAND OPERA ASSOCIATION
Richard Hageman, General Musical Director

Date	Venue	Opera	Cast
29 Sep	Los Angeles, Shrine Auditorium	*Aida*	RR, Meisle; Lappas, Rimini, Cotreuil. Richard Hageman.
3 Oct		*Cavalleria Rusticana*	RR; Hackett, Ballester. Hageman. Preceded by *La Navarraise*: Alice Gentle.

CHICAGO CIVIC OPERA COMPANY
Samuel Insull, President
Giorgio Polacco, Principal Conductor

Date	Venue	Opera	Cast
3 Nov	Chicago, Auditorium	*Der Rosenkavalier* (Opening Night)	RR, Olga Forrai, Mason; Kipnis, Beck, Mojica. Polacco.
7 Nov		*Un Ballo in Maschera*	RR, Van Gordon, Clara Shear; Marshall, Robert Steel. Polacco.
10 Nov		*Aida*	RR, Van Gordon; Marshall, Formichi, V. Lazzari, Kipnis. Polacco.
13 Nov		*Der Rosenkavalier*	Same as 3 Nov.
15 Nov		*Il Trovatore*	RR, Lenska; Cortis, Richard Bonelli, V. Lazzari. Weber.
18 Nov		*Un Ballo in Maschera*	Same as 7 Nov.
20 Nov	Ft. Wayne, Ind.	*Aida*	Same as 10 Nov.
28 Nov	Chicago, Auditorium	*Der Rosenkavalier*	Same as 3 Nov except Cortis for Mojica.
29 Nov		*Madama Butterfly*	RR, Pavloska; Hackett, Rimini. Polacco.
2 Dec		*Tosca*	RR; Hackett, Baklanoff. Moranzoni.
6 Dec		*Der Rosenkavalier*	RR, Forrai, Mason; Kipnis, Howard Preston, Theodore Ritch. Polacco.
10 Dec		*Madama Butterfly*	Same as 29 Nov.
12 Dec		*Falstaff*	RR, Mason, Claessens, Pavloska; Rimini (F), Hackett, Steel. Polacco.
14 Dec		*Un Ballo in Maschera*	Same as 7 Nov except Lenska for Van Gordon.
19 Dec	Detroit	*Concert	
20 Dec	Chicago, Auditorium	*Aida*	Same as 10 Nov except Lenska for Van Gordon.

DATE	PLACE	EVENT	CAST AND REMARKS
26 Dec 1925		*A Light from Saint Agnes* (W. Franke Harling), world premiere	**RR: Toinette;** Lamont, Baklanoff. Harling. Followed by *Pagliacci*: Muzio; Ansseau, Formichi, Defrère. Moranzoni.
30 Dec		*Aida*	Same as 10 Nov.
[1926]			
7 Jan		*Tosca*	Same as 2 Dec except Cortis for Hackett.
13 Jan		*Falstaff*	Same as 12 Dec.
15 Jan		*La Juive*	RR, Mason; Marshall, Mojica, Kipnis. Weber.
17 Jan		*Madama Butterfly*	Same as 29 Nov.
22 Jan		Gala	*Un Ballo in Maschera*, Act II: RR; Marshall, Steel. Polacco. *Andrea Chénier*, Act III: Muzio; Cortis, Formichi. Polacco. *Roméo et Juliette*, Act II: Garden; Ansseau. Polacco. *La Bohème*, Act I: Mason; Cortis, Rimini, Lazzari. Moranzoni.
24 Jan		*Concert	
28 Jan	Boston, Opera House	*Der Rosenkavalier*	Same as 3 Nov.
30 Jan		*Un Ballo in Maschera*	Same as 7 Nov except Ruffo for Steel.
31 Jan	*On this short visit to New York Raisa and Rimini meet with Toscanini at the Astor Hotel, where they see the Turandot score for the first time. There is a short run-through with the maestro.*		
31 Jan	New York City, Mecca Temple	*Concert	
1 Feb	Boston, Opera House	*Falstaff*	Same as 12 Dec.
9 Feb	Washington, Auditorium	*Tosca*	RR; Cortis, Rimini. Moranzoni.
11 Feb	Baltimore, Lyric Theatre	*Un Ballo in Maschera*	Same as 7 Nov except Bonelli for Steel.
16 Feb	Cleveland, Keith's Palace Theatre	*Madama Butterfly*	Same as 29 Nov except Lamont for Hackett.
19 Feb		*Otello*	RR, Marshall, Ruffo, Mojica, Kipnis. Moranzoni.

Date	City / Venue	Opera	Notes
22 Feb	Buffalo, Consistory	*Aida*	Same as 10 Nov except Rimini for Formichi.
25 Feb	Cincinnati, Memorial Auditorium	*Der Rosenkavalier*	RR, Forrai, Mason; Kipnis, Preston, Cortis. Polacco.
26 Feb	Chattanooga, Memorial Auditorium	*Aida*	Same as 10 Nov except Bonelli for Formichi.
1 Mar	Birmingham, Municipal Auditorium	*Aida*	Same as 10 Nov except Rimini for Formichi.
4 Mar	Memphis, Municipal Auditorium	*Aida*	Same as 10 Nov except Rimini for Formichi.
8 Mar	Miami, Coliseum	*Aida*	Same as 10 Nov except Rimini for Formichi.
12 Mar		*Otello*	Same as 19 Feb except Rimini for Ruffo.

TEATRO ALLA SCALA, MILAN
Arturo Toscanini, Director

Date	City / Venue	Opera	Notes
31 Mar	Milan, La Scala	*Nerone*	RR, Bertana; Pertile, Franci, Journet. Toscanini.
2 Apr		*Nerone*	Same as 31 Mar.
6 Apr		*Nerone*	Same as 31 Mar.
10 Apr		*Nerone*	Same as 31 Mar.
25 Apr		*Turandot* (Giacomo Puccini), world premiere	**RR: Turandot**, Maria Zamboni; Miguel Fleta, Rimini (Ping), Carlo Walter. Toscanini. 25 April premiere did not include the Franco Alfano ending.

Toscanini withdraws from Turandot citing nervous exhaustion.

Date	City / Venue	Opera	Notes
27 Apr		*Turandot*	Same as 25 Apr.
29 Apr		*Turandot*	Same as 25 Apr.
30 Apr			
1 May		*Falstaff*	RR, Ferraris, Casazza; Rimini (F), Piero Menescaldi, Ernesto Badini. Panizza.
4 May		*Falstaff*	Same as 1 May.
6 May		*Falstaff*	Same as 1 May.
8 May		*Turandot*	RR, Zamboni; Franco Lo Giudice, Rimini, Walter. Panizza.

DATE	PLACE	EVENT	CAST AND REMARKS
11 May 1926		*Turandot*	Same as 8 May.
13 May		*Turandot*	Same as 8 May.
15 May		*Turandot*	Same as 8 May.
18 May		*Turandot*	Same as 8 May.
19 May		*Falstaff*	RR, Ines Alfani-Tellini, Casazza; Rimini (F), Menescaldi, Paci. Panizza.

LOS ANGELES GRAND OPERA ASSOCIATION
Richard Hageman, General Muscial Director

6 Oct	Los Angeles, Shrine Auditorium	*Tosca*	RR; Cortis, Baklanoff. Hageman.
9 Oct		*Il Trovatore*	RR, Homer; Aroldo Lindi, Rimini, V. Lazzari. Gaetano Merola.
14 Oct		*Madama Butterfly*	RR, Meisle; Paul Althouse, Bonelli. Hageman.
16 Oct		*Aida*	RR, Meisle; Lindi, Rimini, V. Lazzari. Hageman.
? Oct	Fresno	Concert	
? Oct	San Francisco	Concert	
? Oct	Seattle	Concert	
? Oct	Vancouver	Concert	
? Oct	Salt Lake City	Concert	
? Nov	Kalamazoo	Concert[32]	

CHICAGO CIVIC OPERA COMPANY
Samuel Insull, President
Giorgio Polacco, Principal Conductor

32. These concerts were listed in a 23 October 1926 *Musical America* Annual, where concert managers list some of the current and future dates of their clients. In this case the listing was submitted by Raisa's manager, R. E. Johnson. This concert tour has been only partially confirmed.

Date	Venue	Opera	Cast
9 Nov	Chicago, Auditorium	*I Gioielli della Madonna*	RR, Lenska, Anna Hamlin (Stella); Lamont, Rimini. Moranzoni.
16 Nov		*Aida*	RR, Van Gordon; Marshall, Formichi, V. Lazzari, Kipnis. Polacco.
19 Nov		*La Juive*	RR, Eidé Norena; Marshall, Mojica, Kipnis. Weber.
22 Nov	Indianapolis, Murat Theatre	*Concert	
24 Nov	South Bend	*Concert	
26 Nov	Milwaukee, Pabst Theatre	*Aida*	Same as 16 Nov except Lenska for Van Gordon.
28 Nov	Chicago, Auditorium	*I Gioielli della Madonna*	Same as 9 Nov.
1 Dec		*La Juive*	Same as 19 Nov except Mason for Norena.
3 Dec		*Cavalleria Rusticana*	RR; Lindi, Defrère. Moranzoni. Followed by *Pagliacci*: Norena; Ansseau, Formichi, Defrère, Mojica. Weber.
9 Dec		*I Gioielli della Madonna*	Same as 9 Nov.
13 Dec		*La Juive*	Same as 19 Nov.
25 Dec		*La Juive*	Same as 19 Nov.
31 Dec		*Don Giovanni*	RR, Louise Loring, Mason; Vanni-Marcoux (DG), Schipa, V. Lazzari, Kipnis, Trevisan. Polacco.
[1927]			
6 Jan		*Der Rosenkavalier*	RR, Elsa Alsen, Mason; Kipnis, Polese, Ritch. Polacco.
10 Jan		*I Gioielli della Madonna*	Same as 9 Nov.
13 Jan		*Don Giovanni*	Same as 31 Dec.
15 Jan		*Tosca*	RR; Ansseau, Vanni-Marcoux. Moranzoni.
16 Jan		*La Juive*	Same as 19 Nov except Macbeth for Norena.
24 Jan		*Don Giovanni*	Same as 31 Dec.
25 Jan		*Concert	
26 Jan		*Der Rosenkavalier*	Same as 6 Jan.
28 Jan		Gala	*Tosca*, Act II: RR: Cortis, Vanni-Marcoux. Polacco. *Martha*, Act II: Mason; Cortis, V. Lazzari, Trevisan. Moranzoni. *Il Trovatore*, Act IV: Muzio, Lenska; Lamont, Bonelli. Weber.
29 Jan		*Un Ballo in Maschera*	RR, Shear, Lenska; Marshall, Bonelli, Antonio Sabino.

DATE	PLACE	EVENT	CAST AND REMARKS
30 Jan 1927		*Concert	Benefit: Bialystok society.
2 Feb	Boston, Opera House	I Gioielli della Madonna	Same as 9 Nov.
10 Feb		Don Giovanni	RR, Loring, Mason; Vanni-Marcoux (DG), Hackett, Pavel Ludikar, Kipnis, Trevisan. Polacco.
14 Feb	Baltimore, Lyric Theatre	Aida	RR, Van Gordon; Cortis, Rimini, V. Lazzari, Kipnis. Polacco.
16 Feb	Washington, Poli's Theatre	Un Ballo in Maschera	Same as 29 Jan.
19 Feb	Pittsburgh, Syria Mosque	Aida	Same as 16 Nov except Rimini for Formichi.
21 Feb	Buffalo, Lafayette Theatre	Il Trovatore	RR, Van Gordon; Cortis, Rimini, V. Lazzari. Moranzoni.
26 Feb	Chattanooga, Soldiers & Sailors Auditorium	Un Ballo in Maschera	Same as 29 Jan.
28 Feb	Birmingham, Municipal Auditorium	Il Trovatore	Same as 21 Feb except Bonelli for Rimini.
4 Mar	Jackson, Municipal Auditorium	Cavalleria Rusticana	Same as 3 Dec except Cortis for Lindi. Followed by Pagliacci: Mason; Marshall, Rimini, Defrère. Polacco.
6 Mar	Houston, Municipal Auditorium	Aida	RR, Van Gordon; Marshall, Bonelli, V. Lazzari, Cotreuil. Polacco.
7 Mar	San Antonio, Municipal Auditorium	Aida	Same as 16 Nov except Rimini for Formichi.
11 Mar	Dallas, Fairgrounds	I Gioielli della Madonna	Same as 9 Nov except Cortis for Lamont.
14 Mar	Tulsa, Convention Hall	Aida	RR, Lenska; Marshall, Rimini, V. Lazzari, Cotreuil. Polacco.
16 Mar	Joplin, Mo., Memorial Hall	Aida	Same as 14 Mar except Van Gordon for Lenska.
17 Mar	Wichita, The Forum	Cavalleria Rusticana	Same as 3 Dec except Cortis for Lindi. Pagliacci same as 4 Mar.
19 Mar	Detroit, Masonic Auditorium	I Gioielli della Madonna	Same as 9 Nov except Cortis for Lamont.
20 Mar		Aida	Same as 6 Mar.
22 Mar	Akron, Keith-Albee Theater	Il Trovatore	Same as 21 Feb except Lenska for Van Gordon.
27 Mar	Cleveland	Concert	

Date	Location	Type	Notes
6 Apr			RR and Rimini record arias and duets for Brunswick in New York.
10 Apr	New York City, Carnegie Hall	Concert	
? Apr	Madison Square Garden	Concert	
? Apr	Akron, Jewish Center	Concert	
18 Apr	Cincinnati, Music Hall	Concert	
20 Apr			RR and Rimini record arias and duets for Brunswick in New York.
? Apr	Louisville, Women's Club	Concert	
22 Sep	Venice, Piazza S. Marco	Concert	Open-air concert; RR sings arias from *Norma* and *Aida*, duets with Rimini from *La Gioconda* and *Il Trovatore*. Benefit: Italian Aviation League
28 Oct	Ann Arbor, Hill Auditorium	Concert	

CHICAGO CIVIC OPERA COMPANY
Samuel Insull, President; Giorgio Polacco, Principal Conductor

Date	Location	Opera	Cast
6 Nov	Chicago, Auditorium	*Aida*	RR, Van Gordon; Marshall, Formichi, Kipnis, Chase Baromeo. Polacco.
11 Nov		*La Gioconda*	RR, Van Gordon, Lenska; Marshall, Formichi, Baromeo. Polacco.
14 Nov		*Il Trovatore*	RR, Lenska; Cortis, Bonelli, Baromeo. Weber.
22 Nov		*Un Ballo in Maschera*	RR, Lenska, A. Hamlin; Marshall, Bonelli. Sabino.
24 Nov	**Broadcast**	*La Gioconda*	Same as 11 Nov.
26 Nov		*Falstaff*	RR, Mason, Claessens, Pavloska; Rimini (F), Cortis, Polese. Polacco.
30 Nov		*I Gioielli della Madonna*	RR, Lenska, Lamont, Rimini. Moranzoni.
2 Dec	Milwaukee, Pabst Theatre	*I Gioielli della Madonna*	Same as 30 Nov.
10 Dec	Chicago, Auditorium	*I Gioielli della Madonna*	Same as 30 Nov.
17 Dec		*Un Ballo in Maschera*	Same as 22 Nov.
26 Dec		*La Gioconda*	Same as 11 Nov except Lorna Doone Jackson for Van Gordon.
31 Dec	**Broadcast**	*Die Fledermaus* (in English)	**RR: Rosalinde**, Pavloska, Mojica (Orlofsky), Hackett, Lamont, Rimini, V. Lazzari. Weber. Toti Dal Monte sings "Carnival of Venice" in Act II Party Scene (New Year's Eve only).

DATE	PLACE	EVENT	CAST AND REMARKS
[1928]			
9 Jan		*Die Fledermaus*	Same as 31 Dec.
11 Jan		*Falstaff*	Same as 26 Nov.
15 Jan		*I Gioielli della Madonna*	Same as 30 Nov except Cortis for Lamont.
17 Jan		*La Gioconda*	RR, Lenska, Jackson; Marshall, Formichi, Baromeo. Polacco.
19 Jan		*Die Fledermaus*	Same as 31 Dec.
22 Jan		*Concert	First Rosa Raisa Scholarship Fund Benefit.
25 Jan		*Il Trovatore*	Same as 14 Nov except Lamont for Cortis.
26 Jan		*Aida*	RR (for Muzio), Lenska; Marshall, Montesanto, V. Lazzari, Baromeo. Polacco.
27 Jan		Gala	*Aida,* Act III: RR; Marshall, Rimini. Moranzoni. *Loreley,* Act I: Muzio; Cortis, Montesanto. Sabino. *Pagliacci,* Act I: Norena; Ansseau, Bonelli. Weber. Ballet: *Spanish Caprice.*
30 Jan	Boston, Opera House	*La Gioconda*	Same as 11 Nov.
7 Feb		*I Gioielli della Madonna*	Same as 30 Nov except Cortis for Lamont.
13 Feb	Rochester, N.Y. **Broadcast**	*Concert	Family Party Hour, WCCO.
14 Feb	Akron, Keith-Albee Palace Theater	*Aida*[33]	Same as 6 Nov.
15 Feb	Detroit **Broadcast**	*Concert	General Motors Hour.
16 Feb	Masonic Auditorium	*La Gioconda*	Same as 11 Nov.
18 Feb		*Il Trovatore*	Same as 14 Nov.

33. Muzio at this point cancels for the remainder of the tour; Marie Rappold and Myrna Sharlow are brought in to take some of the pressure off Raisa, who will still sing seventeen times in the next six weeks in fifteen different cities.

Date	City, Venue	Opera	Notes
20 Feb	Columbus, Auditorium	*Aida*	Same as 6 Nov except Rimini for Formichi.
24 Feb	Chattanooga, Soldiers & Sailors Auditorium	*Cavalleria Rusticana*	RR; Hackett, Rimini. Polacco. Followed by *Pagliacci*: Mason; Marshall, Bonelli, Defrère. Weber.
25 Feb	Memphis, Municipal Auditorium	*I Gioielli della Madonna*	Same as 30 Nov except Cortis for Lamont.
27 Feb	Tulsa, Convention Hall	*Il Trovatore*	Same as 14 Nov except Rimini for Bonelli.
29 Feb	Wichita Falls, Municipal Auditorium	*Aida*	Same as 6 Nov except Rimini for Formichi.
2 Mar	San Antonio, Municipal Auditorium	*La Gioconda*	Same as 11 Nov except Rimini for Formichi.
7 Mar	Los Angeles, Shrine Auditorium	*La Gioconda*	Same as 11 Nov.
10 Mar	Oakland, Auditorium	*Aida*	Same as 6 Nov.
15 Mar	Sacramento, Memorial Auditorium	*La Gioconda*	Same as 11 Nov.
17 Mar	Seattle, Fifth Ave. Theater	*Cavalleria Rusticana*	Same as 24 Feb except Defrère for Rimini.
19 Mar	Portland, Ore., Auditorium	*La Gioconda*	Same as 11 Nov except Rimini for Formichi.
22 Mar	Denver, Auditorium	*Aida*	Same as 6 Nov.
27 Mar	Lincoln, Neb., University Coliseum	*Aida*	Same as 6 Nov.
29 Mar	Minneapolis, Auditorium	*Il Trovatore*	Same as 14 Nov except Rimini for Bonelli.
30 Mar		*Aida*	RR, Van Gordon; Marshall, Rimini, V. Lazzari, Baromeo. Polacco.

Fall 1928 *Raisa, under doctor's orders, cancels the 1928–1929 season. She recovers from illness and returns to Chicago for the last part of the final season in the Auditorium.*

CHICAGO CIVIC OPERA COMPANY
Samuel Insull, President
Giorgio Polacco, Principal Conductor

Date	City, Venue	Opera	Notes
31 Dec	Chicago, Auditorium	*Norma*	RR, Coe Glade; Marshall, V. Lazzari. Polacco.

DATE	PLACE	EVENT	CAST AND REMARKS
[1929]			
4 Jan	Milwaukee	*Cavalleria Rusticana*	RR; Cortis, Defrère. Moranzoni. Followed by *Pagliacci*: Marion Claire; Lappas, Bonelli, Barre Hill, Mojica. Weber.
12 Jan	Chicago, Auditorium	*Tosca*	RR; Hackett, Vanni-Marcoux. Moranzoni.
14 Jan		*Don Giovanni*	RR, Hilda Burke, Mason; Vanni-Marcoux (DG), Hackett, Lazzari, Kipnis. Polacco.
17 Jan		*Norma*	Same as 31 Jan.
23 Jan		*Aida*	RR, Van Gordon; Marshall, Bonelli, V. Lazzari, Baromeo. Polacco.
26 Jan		*Cavalleria Rusticana*[34]	RR; Lamont, Montesanto. Moranzoni. Preceded by *Judith* (Honegger): Garden, Burke; Formichi, Cotreuil, Mojica. Polacco.
30 Jan	Boston, Opera House	*Aida*	Same as 23 Jan except Kipnis for Lazzari.
? Feb	*Raisa and Rimini record arias and duets for Brunswick in New York.*		
17 Feb	Detroit, Masonic Auditorium	*Norma*	Same as 31 Dec.
22 Feb	Birmingham, Municipal Auditorium	*Norma*	Same as 31 Dec.
25 Feb	Jackson, Municipal Auditorium	*Norma*	Same as 31 Dec.
2 Mar	San Antonio, Municipal Auditorium	*Norma*	Same as 31 Dec.
8 Mar	Los Angeles, Philharmonic Auditorium	*Norma*	Same as 31 Dec.

34. Although she performed in *The Dybbuk* there in 1936 with the Detroit Opera, the 26 January *Cavalleria* is Raisa's last "operatic" performance on the stage of the Auditorium with the Chicago Civic Opera.

12 Mar	Fresno, High School Auditorium	*Norma*	Same as 31 Dec.
16 Mar	Oakland, Auditorium	*Norma*	Same as 31 Dec.
? Apr	Vienna	Concert	
? Apr	Berlin	Concert	
? Apr	Genoa	Concert[35]	

TEATRO SAN CARLO, NAPLES
Edoardo Vitale, Musical Director

25 Apr	Naples, Teatro San Carlo	*Norma*	RR, Gianna Pederzini; Isidoro Fagoaga, Tancredi Pasero. Vitale.
28 Apr		*Norma*	Same as 25 Apr.
30 Apr		*Norma*	Same as 25 Apr.
3 May		*Norma*	Same as 25 Apr except Constantino Percy for Pasero.

TEATRO COLÓN, BUENOS AIRES
Faustina Da Rosa, Concesionario
Hector Panizza, Musical Director

29 May	Buenos Aires, Teatro Colón	*Turandot*	RR, Natalie De Sanctis; Georges Thill, Walter. Panizza.
3 Jun		*Turandot*	Same as 29 May except Zoraida Carucci for De Sanctis.
11 Jun		*Norma*	RR, Bertana; Pedro Mirassou, Pasero. Franco Capuana.
13 Jun		*Norma*	Same as 11 Jun.
16 Jun		*Norma*	Same as 11 Jun.
20 Jun		*Norma*	Same as 11 Jun.
27 Jun 1929		*Il Trovatore*	RR, Bertana; Vicente Sampere, Apollo Granforte, Pasero. Panizza.
29 Jun		*Norma*	Same as 11 Jun.
10 Jul		*Norma*	Same as 11 Jun except Giorgio Lanskoy for Pasero.

35. The concerts in Vienna, Berlin, and Genoa are unconfirmed. There is a reference to these concerts in a 1931 newspaper article, "How Raisa Gambled Her Life and a Fortune to Have a Baby," by Meyer Zolotareff in an unnamed Chicago newspaper. The article, which details Raisa's activities over the preceding three years, is very specific about these concerts happening; however, it does not indicate whether they took place in 1928 or 1929. I am very uncertain as to whether these concerts ever happened at all, as I have never seen any other references to them.

DATE	PLACE	EVENT	CAST AND REMARKS
27 Jul 1929		Aida	RR, Rosette Anday; Mirassou, Rimini, Lanskoy, Walter. Angelo Questa.
1 Aug		Norma	Same as 11 Jun except Lanskoy for Pasero.
2 Aug			Pregnancy complications rule out planned participation in Buenos Aires premiere of Respighi's La Campana Sommersa.
7 Aug	Teatro de la Opera	Aida	RR, Anday; Sampere, Rimini, Journet, Lanskoy. Questa.
13 Aug		Concert	Benefit: Hospital Israelita, Raisa wing.
17 Aug	Rosario, Teatro Opéra	Norma	RR, Bertana; Mirassou, Lanskoy. Questa.

CHICAGO CIVIC OPERA COMPANY
Samuel Insull, President
Giorgio Polacco, Principal Conductor

DATE	PLACE	EVENT	CAST AND REMARKS
1 Nov	Oak Park, Ill.	*Concert	
4 Nov	Chicago, Civic Opera	Aida (Opening Night)[36] **broadcast**	RR, Van Gordon; Marshall, Formichi, V. Lazzari, Baromeo. Polacco.
10 Nov		Norma	RR, Glade; Marshall, Baromeo. Emil Cooper.
14 Nov		Falstaff	RR, Alice Mock, Claessens, Pavloska; Rimini (F), Cortis, Defrère. Polacco.
16 Nov	**broadcast**	Norma	Same as 10 Nov.
19 Nov		Tosca	RR; Hackett, Vanni-Marcoux. Moranzoni.
25 Nov		Falstaff	Same as 14 Nov.
30 Nov		Tosca	Same as 19 Nov.
1 Dec	Auditorium	*Concert	Benefit: Little Company of Mary Hospital.

36. The new Civic Opera House was now the venue of the Chicago Civic Opera. Raisa was selected to inaugurate the new theater.

Date	Location	Opera	Cast
7 Dec	Civic Opera **broadcast**	*Aida*	Same as 4 Nov except Giovanni Inghilleri for Formichi.
9 Dec		*La Juive*	RR, Mock; Marshall, Ritch, Kipnis. Cooper.
11 Dec		*Falstaff*	Same as 14 Nov.
17 Dec		*La Juive*	Same as 9 Dec except Baromeo for Kipnis.
22 Dec		*Aida*	Same as 4 Nov.
28 Dec		*Norma*	Same as 10 Nov.
31 Dec		*Conchita*	**RR: Conchita**, Thelma Votipka (Dolores); Cortis, Hill. Moranzoni.
[1930]			
4 Jan		*Norma*	Same as 10 Nov.
8 Jan		*Conchita*	Same as 31 Dec.
16 Jan		*Conchita*	Same as 31 Dec.
18 Jan	**broadcast**	*La Juive*	Same as 9 Dec.
24 Jan		*La Gioconda*	RR, Glade, Ada Paggi; Marshall, Formichi, Baromeo. Cooper.
27 Jan		*La Gioconda*	Same as 24 Jan except Van Gordon for Glade.
4 Feb	Boston, Opera House	*Aida*	Same as 4 Nov.
7 Feb	New York City, Biltmore Hotel	*Morning Musicale	
8 Feb	Washington, Constitution Hall	*Concert	
12 Feb	Boston, Opera House	*Tannhäuser*	RR, Frida Leider (V); Theodor Strack, Bonelli, Kipnis. Polacco.
21 Feb	Detroit, Masonic Auditorium	*Tannhäuser*	Same as 12 Feb except Maria Olczewska for Leider.
28 Feb	Louisville, Memorial Auditorium	*Tannhäuser*	RR, Glade; Marshall, Bonelli, Baromeo. Cooper.
4 Mar	Memphis, Municipal Auditorium	*Norma*	Same as 10 Nov.

DATE	PLACE	EVENT	CAST AND REMARKS
13 Mar 1930	Dallas, Fair Grounds	*Tannhäuser*	Same as 28 Feb.
15 Mar	San Antonio, Municipal Auditorium	*Tannhäuser*	Same as 28 Feb except Olczewska for Glade.
21 Mar	Minneapolis, Auditorium	*Il Trovatore*	RR, Olczewska; Marshall, Bonelli, Baromeo. Cooper.
29 Mar	Kansas City, Convention Hall	*La Gioconda*	Same as 24 Jan.
? Apr	Charleston, S.C.	Concert	
6 Apr	Chicago, Auditorium	*Concert	Benefit: Rosa Raisa Scholarship Fund.
30 May	*Raisa returns to Bialystok for the first time since 1906–1907 for a private visit.*		
21 Oct	Pittsburgh, Syria Mosque	Concert	Benefit: Montefiore Hospital

CHICAGO CIVIC OPERA COMPANY
Samuel Insull, President

DATE	PLACE	EVENT	CAST AND REMARKS
30 Oct	Chicago, Civic Opera	*I Gioielli della Madonna*	RR, Claessens, Jennie Tourel (Young Mother); Cortis, Rimini. Moranzoni.
3 Nov		*Norma*	RR, Glade; Marshall, Baromeo. Cooper.
8 Nov	**broadcast**	*I Gioielli della Madonna*	Same as 30 Oct except Paggi for Claessens.
12 Nov		*Norma*	Same as 3 Nov.
15 Nov		*Un Ballo in Maschera*	RR, Van Gordon, Mock; Marshall, John Charles Thomas, Salvatore Baccaloni (Tom). Cooper.
18 Nov		*I Gioielli della Madonna*	Same as 30 Oct except Paggi for Claessens.
27 Nov		*Un Ballo in Maschera*	Same as 15 Nov except Bonelli for Thomas.
29 Nov	**broadcast**	*Un Ballo in Maschera*	Same as 15 Nov except Bonelli for Thomas.
3 Dec		*I Gioielli della Madonna*	Same as 30 Oct.
9 Dec		*Un Ballo in Maschera*	Same as 15 Nov except Bonelli for Thomas.

Date	Venue	Work	Cast / Notes
20 Dec		*Cavalleria Rusticana*	RR; Cortis, Defrère. Moranzoni. Followed by *Pagliacci*: Burke; Marshall, Formichi, Defrère. Frank St. Leger.
[1931]			
14 Jan		*Cavalleria Rusticana*	Same as 20 Dec except Robert Ringling for Defrère. Followed by *Pagliacci*: Burke, Marshall, Bonelli, Mario Fiorella. St. Leger.
17 Jan	Chicago, Ashland Auditorium	*Concert	
21 Jan	Pittsburgh, Syria Mosque	*Concert	Benefit: Hadassah (Women's Zionist Organization of America).
Jan			*Under doctor's orders, Raisa retires from the stage awaiting birth of her daughter. Rosa Giulietta Frieda Rimini is born 7 July 1931.*

CHICAGO CIVIC OPERA COMPANY
Samuel Insull, President

Date	Venue	Work	Cast / Notes
21 Dec	Chicago, Civic Opera	*La Juive*	RR, Leola Turner; Marshall, Ritch, Baromeo. Cooper.
30 Dec		*La Juive*	Same as 21 Dec.
[1932]			
2 Jan		*Cavalleria Rusticana*	RR; Cortis, Augusto Beuf. Isaac Van Grove. Followed by *Pagliacci*: Muzio, Marshall, Victor Damiani, Defrère. St. Leger.
7 Jan		*La Gioconda*	RR, Van Gordon, Sonia Sharnova; Cortis, Formichi, Baromeo. Cooper.
9 Jan		*La Juive*	Same as 21 Dec.
12 Jan	**broadcast**	*Cavalleria Rusticana*	Same as 2 Jan. *Pagliacci*, same as 2 Jan except Formichi for Damiani.
16 Jan		*La Gioconda*	Same as 7 Jan except Marshall for Cortis.
25 Jan		*La Gioconda*[37]	Same as 7 Jan except Marshall for Cortis.
1 Feb	Denver, Auditorium	Concert	

37. This performance marks the end of Raisa's career with the Chicago Civic Opera. She does not go on the tour this season. The company ceases operations 13 February after the two-week season in Boston.

DATE	PLACE	EVENT	CAST AND REMARKS
			TEATRO REALE, ROME
			(Formerly Teatro Costanzi)
9 Mar 1932	Rome, Teatro Reale	*Norma*	RR, Ebe Stignani; Dolci, Giacomo Vaghi. Marinuzzi.
12 Mar		*Norma*	Same as 9 Mar.
15 Mar		*Norma*	Same as 9 Mar.
20 Mar		*Norma*	Same as 9 Mar.
26 Mar		*Norma*	Same as 9 Mar.
1 Apr		*Norma*	Same as 9 Mar.
7 Apr	Teatro Argentina	Concert	RR, Pertile, Vaghi.
? Aug	Venice, Piazza San Marco	Concert	Benefit: Fascist Aid Organization.
			TEATRO VITTORIO EMANUELE, RIMINI
			Umberto Berettoni, Music Director
31 Aug	Rimini, Teatro Vittorio Emanuele	*Tosca*	RR; Gigli, Rimini. Umberto Berettoni.
2 Sep		*Tosca*	Same as 31 Aug.
			TEATRO ALLA SCALA, MILAN
[1933]			
19 Jan	Milan, La Scala	*Una Partita* (Riccardo Zandonai), world premiere	**RR: Manuela;** Nino Piccaluga, Piero Biasini. Sergio Failoni (Zandonai supervising). Followed by *Gianni Schicchi:* Maria Dragoni, Rimini (GS); Piero Pauli. Failoni.
? Jan		*Una Partita*	Same as 19 Jan.
? Jan		*Una Partita*	Same as 19 Jan.
			TEATRO CARLO FELICE, GENOA
			Gaetano Bavagnoli, Musical Director

30 Jan	Genoa, Teatro Carlo Felice	Tosca	RR; Alessandro Ziliani, Rimini. Marinuzzi.
2 Feb		Tosca	Same as 30 Jan.
5 Feb		Tosca	Same as 30 Jan.
8 Feb		Tosca	Same as 30 Jan.
12 Feb		Tosca	Same as 30 Jan.

MAGGIO MUSICALE FIORENTINO (Inaugural Season)
Vittorio Gui, Musical Director

| 14 May | Florence, Teatro Comunale | Falstaff | RR, Mason, Casazza; Rimini (F), Dino Borgioli, Badini. Victor De Sabata. |
| 16 May | | Falstaff | Same as 14 May. |

ROYAL OPERA–COVENT GARDEN, LONDON
Charles Moor, Acting Managing Director

24 May	London, Covent Garden	Tosca	RR; Minghetti, Formichi. Antonio Votto.
29 May		Tosca	Same as 24 May[38]
29–30 Jun	*Raisa makes her last commercial recordings with La Scala Orchestra under Franco Ghione at the Milan Conservatorium.*		

ARENA DI VERONA
Antonio Votto, Musical Director

| 29 Jul | Verona, Arena | Gli Ugonotti | RR, Adelaide Saraceni, Pederzini; Giacomo Lauri-Volpi, Rimini, Pasero, Umberto Di Lelio. Votto. |
| 3 Aug | | Gli Ugonotti | Same as 29 Jul. |

38. Harold Rosenthal, in *Two Centuries of Opera at Covent Garden*, states that Raisa sang only one performance, the other being sung by Olga de Foras; however, I own a copy of the 29 May program with no substitution information indicated. The Covent Garden archives believe Raisa sang the 29 May *Tosca*. Rosenthal is probably correct, as he is specific about the name of the replacement even though the chronology in his book shows Raisa sang Tosca twice.

DATE	PLACE	EVENT	CAST AND REMARKS
6 Aug 1933		*Gli Ugonotti*	Same as 29 Jul.
10 Aug		*Gli Ugonotti*	Same as 29 Jul.
14 Aug		*Gli Ugonotti*	Same as 29 Jul.
	Berlin, Städtische Oper		STÄDTISCHE OPER, BERLIN Artists from La Scala, Milan[39] Ettore Panizza, Musical Director
13 Oct		*Tosca*	RR, Gigli, Formichi. Panizza. Hitler, Goebbels, and Hess attend.
15 Oct		*Tosca*	Same as 13 Oct.
	Verona, Teatro Nuovo		TEATRO NUOVO, VERONA
20 Oct		*Tosca*	RR, Carlo Merino, Rimini. Conductor unknown.
? Oct		*Tosca*	Same as 20 Oct.
	Treviso, Teatro Comunale		TEATRO COMUNALE, TREVISO Giacomo Armani, Music Director
4 Nov		*La Gioconda*	RR, Albertina Damonte, Rosita Salgary; Alessandro Granda, Basiola, V. Lazzari. Giacomo Armani.
5 Nov		*La Gioconda*	Same as 4 Nov.
11 Nov		*La Gioconda*	Same as 4 Nov.
	Chicago, Civic Opera		CHICAGO GRAND OPERA COMPANY[40] Paul Longone, General Manager
30 Dec		*Aida*	RR, Eleanor La Mance (Mrs. Longone); John Pane-Gasser, Claudio Frigerio, Baromeo, Norman Cordon. Papi.

39. This was not an official tour by La Scala; it was billed as "Artists from La Scala."
40. Chicago Grand Opera is a new company organized by Paul (Paolo) Longone.

[1934]

Date	Venue	Opera	Cast
1 Jan		*Tosca*	RR; Dimitri Onofrei, Amato. Papi.
3 Jan		*Cavalleria Rusticana*	RR; Chamlee, Defrère. Papi. Followed by *Pagliacci*: Burke; Lindi, Frigerio, Frederick Jencks. Papi.
10 Jan		*Turandot*, Chicago premiere	RR, Marion Claire; Lindi, Baromeo. Papi.
13 Jan		*Il Trovatore*	RR, La Mance; Lindi, Carlo Morelli. Papi. Followed by ballet *Bolero*.
16 Jan		*Turandot*	Same as 10 Jan except Pane-Gasser for Lindi.
20 Jan		*La Gioconda*	RR, La Mance, Paggi; Pane-Gasser, Morelli, Cordon. Papi.
23 Jan		Gala	*Aida*, Acts I and II: RR, Glade (for Sigrid Onegin); Pane-Gasser, Morelli, Baromeo, Mark Love. Papi. *Pagliacci*, Prologue: Morelli. Leo Kopp. *La Gioconda*, Act III, scene II: Barbara Darlys, La Mance, Paggi; Pane-Gasser, Morelli, Amund Sjovik. Papi. *Lucia*, Fountain Scene: Mildred Gerber. Kopp.
25 Jan		*Il Trovatore*	Same as 13 Jan.
27 Jan		*Turandot*	Same as 10 Jan.

NEW BOSTON OPERA COMPANY
Tomasso Nazzaro, General Manager

Date	Venue	Opera	Cast
6 Feb	Boston, Opera House	*Aida*	RR, Dreda Aves; Lindi, Mario Valle, Harold Kravitt. Cesare Sodero.

TEATRO GENTILE, FABRIANO

Date	Venue	Opera	Cast
? Jun	Fabriano, Teatro Gentile	*La Gioconda*[41]	RR, Damonte; Ettore Parmeggiani, Rimini, V. Lazzari. Armani.
? Jun		*La Gioconda*	Same as above.
? Jun		*La Gioconda*	Same as above.

41. The Fabriano *Giocondas* were in commemoration of the 100th anniversary of Ponchielli's birth.

DATE	PLACE	EVENT	CAST AND REMARKS
			CASINO, VICHY
15 Jul 1934	Vichy, Casino	*Tosca*	RR; Ziliani, Formichi. Francesco Salfi.
26 Aug		*Tosca*	RR; Lauri-Volpi, Domenico Viglione-Borghese. Salfi.
			TEATRO DE LA ZARZUELA, MADRID
			Giuseppe Podestà, conductor
[1935]			
14 Apr	Madrid, Teatro Zarzuela	*Tosca*	RR; Granda, Rimini. Giuseppe Podestà.[42]
			TEATRO LA FENICE, VENICE
			Franco Capuana, Director
20 Apr	Venice, Teatro la Fenice	*Norma*	RR, Nini Giani; Antonio Melandri; José Santiago-Font. Capuana.
23 Apr		*Norma*	Same as 20 Apr.
25 Apr		*Norma*	Same as 20 Apr.
			CHICAGO CITY OPERA
			Paul Longone, General Director
9 Nov	Chicago, Civic Opera	*Cavalleria Rusticana*	RR; Tokatyan, Joseph Royer. Papi. Preceded by Ballet: *Gold Standard* (Ibert), with Ruth Page. Rudolph Ganz.
20 Nov		*Turandot*	RR, Claire; Tokatyan, Cordon. Papi.
22 Nov		*Aida*	RR, La Mance; Pane-Gasser, Morelli, Baromeo. Papi.
27 Nov		*Aida*	RR, La Mance; Pane-Gasser, Jean Fardulli, V. Lazzari. Papi.

42. This was a gala in honor of the fourth anniversary of the Spanish Republic; President Alcalá Zamora was in attendance. At the end of the opera, several singers from the company sang operatic and zarzuela arias.

Date	Place	Work	Cast / Notes
2 Dec		La Fiamma (Ottorino Respighi), North American premiere	RR: **Silvana**, La Mance, Sharnova; Joseph Bentonelli, Morelli, Cordon. Hageman.
7 Dec	Auditorium	La Fiamma	Same as 2 Dec.
22 Dec	Auditorium	Concert	Benefit for Jewish refugees from Germany. RR and Mischa Mischakoff, violinist. Auspices: Jewish Labor Committee.
[1936]			
24 Jan	Detroit	Concert	
? Feb	Cleveland	Concert	

DETROIT CIVIC OPERA
The Arts of Musical Russia

Date	Place	Work	Cast / Notes
6 May	Detroit, Masonic Hall	The Dybbuk (Il Dibuk) (Lodovico Rocca), North American premiere (in English)	RR: **Leah**; Frederick Jagel, Nino Riusi, Royer. Ghione.
7 May	Chicago, Auditorium	The Dybbuk[43]	Same as 6 May.
9 May	Chicago, Auditorium	The Dybbuk	Same as 6 May.
13 May	New York City, Carnegie Hall	The Dybbuk	Same as 6 May.
15 May		The Dybbuk	Same as 6 May.
16 May		The Dybbuk	Same as 6 May.

CHICAGO CITY OPERA
Paul Longone, General Director

Date	Place	Work	Cast / Notes
31 Oct	Chicago, Civic Opera	La Fiamma (Opening Night)	RR, La Mance, Sharnova; Bentonelli, Ruisi. Weber.
6 Nov		La Fiamma	Same as 31 Oct.

43. In this concentrated run of *The Dybbuk*, Jeanne Palmer (Soudeikine) sang Leah in the performances on the alternate days: 7 May (matinee), 8 May, 14 May, and 16 May (matinee).

DATE	PLACE	EVENT	CAST AND REMARKS
13 Nov 1936		*Cavalleria Rusticana*	RR; Tokatyan, Rimini. Moranzoni. Preceded by *Gianni Schicchi*: Burke; Raymond Middleton (GS); Bentonelli. Moranzoni.
2 Dec		*La Juive*	RR, Vivian Della Chiesa; Martinelli, William Martin, Baromeo. Weber.
20 Dec	Auditorium	Concert	
[1937]			
? Feb	Detroit, Masonic Hall	Concert	
7 Mar	Chicago, Auditorium	Concert	
? Mar	Civic Opera	Concert	Auspices: International Workers' Order.
3 Apr	New York City, Madison Square Garden	Concert	Celebration of the fifteenth anniversary of the Yiddish-language newspaper *Morgen Freiheit* (left wing); RR sings arias from *I Vespri Siciliani* and *Pique Dame*, Tchaikovsky's "Be It a Bright Day," and Yiddish and Russian songs, accompanied by Carol Longone.
27 Oct	Chicago, Orchestra Hall	Concert	Benefit: Prothose Memorial Cancer Hospital.
		CHICAGO CITY OPERA Paul Longone, General Director	
25 Nov	Chicago, Civic Opera	*Cavalleria Rusticana*	RR; Kenneth Sakos, Defrère. Moranzoni. Followed by *Pagliacci*: Burke; José Luccioni, Morelli. Angelo Cannarutto.
4 Dec		*La Juive*	RR, della Chiesa; Martinelli, Martin, Baromeo. Kopp. Raisa's last stage performance.
[1938]			
4 Jul	Soldier Field	Fourth of July	RR sings national anthem.
9 Jul	Grant Park	Free open-air concert	RR sings arias from *Il Trovatore, I Vespri Siciliani, La Traviata,* and *Norma.*

Summer   *Raisa and Rimini open a voice studio in the Congress Hotel; they later move to 920 Michigan Avenue.*

[1943]

? Apr   New York City, Madison Square Garden   Rally-Concert   Sponsored by left-wing groups urging United States to open a second front in Europe to take pressure off USSR.

Concert Repertoire

Listed here are the arias, duets with Rimini, and songs that Raisa sang in her concerts. I have found the programs of many of Raisa's concerts over the years and I have tabulated the selections below. Unless the encores were reported in the newspapers, these songs and arias are not known to me. Her Russian and Yiddish folk songs were generally encore pieces and are mostly unidentified; therefore this listing is very incomplete in those categories. Paul Hume told me:

> I heard Raisa only once in concert. She was not the broad artist in the concert field that, say, Muzio was, but a Raisa concert was something special because, in addition to some fine Lieder, and great arias, she would always end with a group of Russian and Yiddish folk songs. I remember the night I heard her in a concert, it was the Sunday night before Christmas, 1936, in the old Auditorium Theater. For one encore she sang "Night," a Russian folk song she recorded on a tan-label 10-inch Vocalion, with a ravishing ppp high G, reached by swooping up to it from an octave below. But the final encore scared me out of my mind. She began singing this very rhythmic Yiddish song, and it had such a pronounced beat that the audience began clapping in unison rhythm and I, in the gallery, thought the place would fall down. She was a thing of fire at least 75 percent of the time she was singing.

Most of Raisa's concerts were with Rimini. In almost all the programs that I examined Raisa sang at least two-thirds of program and Rimini never more than one-third. The printed concert programs of that era reveal only half the picture of a concert, as the encores were often numerous.

It is more difficult to trace Raisa's American concert career than those of many other artists because she often sang in venues that were not reported in the mainstream music publications from which I obtained most of the information presented here. Concerts and benefits before Jewish organizations and in support of Jewish causes were not often reported in *Musical America, Musical Courier,* and *Musical Leader.* The listing here was compiled from reports of concerts that were reviewed after the fact or concerts that were announced and probably took place. I have not personally seen all the reviews, although I have seen many. In the 1920s it was often reported upon their return from Italy in the autumn that Raisa and Rimini would give a certain number of concerts (in the range of ten to twenty), but there was little or no reportage of these events. Having studied the American concert careers of many artists in this period, I became aware of a pattern of frequently reporting concert activity early in a performer's career because of its news value. Once the artist was well established in the concert field, however, detailed reporting often ceased. There was no consistent formula for reporting concert activity in the various cities that sent periodic reports to the national music magazines; oftentimes the researcher seeking such information is engaging in a "needle in a haystack" effort.

ARIAS

I Vespri Siciliani: "Bolero"; *Norma:* "Casta Diva"; *Cavalleria Rusticana:* "Voi lo sapete"; *Aida:* "Ritorna vincitor, "O patria mia"; *Il Trovatore:* "Tacea la notte placida"; "D'amor sull'ali rosee"; *Le Nozze di Figaro:* "Voi che sapete"; "De vieni, non tardar"; *William Tell:* "Selva opaca"; *Tosca:* "Vissi d'arte"; *La Juive:* "Il va venir"; *Pique Dame (Queen of Spades):* Lisa's aria; *L'Enfant Prodigue:* "Air de Lia"; *Ernani:* "Ernani! Ernani, involami"; *Don Giovanni:* "Or sai chi l'onore," "No mi dir"; *Andrea Chénier:* "La mamma morta"; *Semiramide:* "Bel raggio"; *Stabat Mater:* "Inflammatus"; *La Gioconda:* "Suicidio"; *Lohengrin:* "Elsa's Traum"; *Tannhäuser:* "Dich teure Halle"; *La Forza del Destino:* "Pace, pace, mio Dio"; *Snegurotchka:* "Song of the Shepherd Lehl"; *La Traviata:* "Ah fors' è lui / Sempre libera"; *Otello:* "Ave Maria"; *La Wally:* "Ebben"; *Jeanne d'Arc:* "Adieu, Forrêts"; *Le Cid:* "Pleurez mes yeux!"

DUETS WITH RIMINI

Il Trovatore: "Mira d'acerbe lagrime"; *Don Giovanni:* "Là cí darem la mano"; *Il Flauto Magico* (Zauberflöte): "La dove prende"; *Luisa Miller:* Luisa / Miller duet; *Hamlet:* "Doute de la lumière"; *Don Pasquale:* "Pronta io son / Vado corro";

Thaïs: "Te souvient-il du lumineux voyage"; *Mignon*: "Légères hirondelles"; *Cavalleria Rusticana*: "Turiddu mi tolse l'onore"; *La Favorita*: Leonora/Alfonso duet; "Les Rameaux" and "Crucifixus" (J. B. Faure); "Guarda che bianca luna" (Campana); "Nina" (Gierca); "Squelle soari" (Denza); "Pastorale" (Saint-Saëns); "La Nina Barcarola" (Campana).

Songs: *Arie Anticche*

"Se tu m'ami" (Pergolesi); "Le Violette" (Scarlatti); "Pur dicesti" (Lotti); "Per la Gloria" (Pergolesi); "Danza Fanciulla" (Durante); "Chi vuol la Zingherella" (Paisiello); "Oh del mio dolce ardor" (Gluck); "Ah mai non cessate" (Donaudy); "Ave Maria" (Cherubini); "Stornello" (Giuranna); "Clorinda."

Lieder

"Du Bist wie eine Blume" (Schumann); "Ständchen" (Strauss); "Widmung" (Schumann); "Träume" (Wagner); "Wiegenlied" (Brahms); "Spring" (Beethoven). Raisa usually sang Lieder in Italian translations.

French Songs

"Jeunes Filletes" (arr. Weckerlin); "Dans le printemps" (Garat); "Plaisir d'amour" (Martini); "Un doux lien" (DelBrook); "Tes yeux" (Rabey); "Hymne au soleil" (Georges); "Chanson Norvégienne" (Foudrain).

Chestnuts

"Ave Maria" (Bach-Gounod and Schubert); "El Arriero" (Nogero); "Home Sweet Home" (Bishop); "La Paloma" (Yradier); "Addio" (Tosti); "O sole mio" (di Capua).

American / English Art Songs

"Shepherd" (Purcell); "Twilight Dreams" (Silberta); "When I Go Alone" (Buzzi-Peccia); "Star of Yours" (Rogers); "The Great Awakening" (Kramer); "At the Well" (Hageman); "Missing You" (Caldwell); "Into the Light" (LaForge); "Me Company Along" (Hageman); "All for You" (Martin); "Robin, Robin, Sing Me a Song" (Spross); "April Weather" (Rogers); "Danza" (Chadwick); "Do Not Go My Love" (Hageman); "Ashes of Roses" (Woodman); "Happiness" (Hageman); "Just You" (Burleigh); "Southern Song" (Landon Ronald); "Hills" (LaForge); "Ma Curly Headed Baby" (Clutsam); "Iris" (Wolf); "By a Lonely Forest Pathway" (Griffes); "The Years at the Spring" (Beach), "Pale Moon" (Logan); "Keys of Heaven" (Dunhill); "My Love Is a Muleteer"; "When Song Is Sweet"; "Ecstasy."

RUSSIAN ART SONGS

"Kakneholnu" (Rachmaninoff); "Berceuse" (Gretchaninoff); "Gude Veta" (Gretchaninoff); "None but the Lonely Heart" (Tchaikovsky); "Autumn" (Arensky); "Little Star" (Mussorgsky); "Tears" (Rachmaninoff); "Be It a Bright Day" (Tchaikovsky); "O Cease thy Singing Maiden Fair" (Rachmaninoff); "Matuschka" (Golubushka); "Kaknie Boino" (Rachmaninoff); "Sabily" (Oppelia); "Witeresek" (Cherinavsky).

RUSSIAN FOLK SONGS

"Bayuschki Bayo"—lullaby; "Volga Boatman"; "Natchizka"; "Night"; "Kalinka."

YIDDISH SONGS

"Eili, Eili";[1] "Oisen" (Arensky); "Rachem" (Manna-Zucca); "Voron" (Rubleva); "Yorzheit" (Silberta); "Oi Tate"; "The Rabbi's Invocation" (Saminsky), "Oyf'n Pripetshik"; "A Kind on Eleim."

1. "Eili, Eili" was the most frequently requested and performed of Raisa's concert encores. The Vocalion recordings identify "Eili, Eili" as a "Traditional Hebrew Melody," but it has a more specific history. The beloved song first appeared in a late nineteenth-century Yiddish-language operetta, *Rauchel*, by Isaac Halevy Hurvitz. In an important scene a young girl is stoned to death in a marketplace, and she sings "My God, My God, Why Hast Thou Forsaken Me?" The young artist who played this scene had difficulty learning the play's complex dialogue. On very short notice the great Yiddish Theater actor Boris Tomashevsky (grandfather of Michael Tilson Thomas) supplied the half-Hebrew, half-Yiddish text, based on the Twenty-second Psalm, verse 2, and Jacob Sandler, the chorus master of *Rauchel*, composed the famous melody. "Eili, Eili" became so popular among the Yiddish-speaking immigrants in America that it virtually became their anthem. The song traveled to Europe, where it also became popular. The composer Joseph Bonime, who worked in both the popular and classical music fields, arranged the song for Raisa's voice in 1917.

[286]

Discography

It is almost impossible to date most of Raisa's recordings, especially the all-important Vocalion recordings, with precision; in most cases the best that can be hoped for is a good approximation. It is known that the Pathé recordings were made in New York in April 1917, as there were reports of this session in *Musical Courier*. The Vocalion hill and dales were recorded in 1918; this is based on advertising in the trade magazines. The Vocalion lateral recordings were probably made in New York in at least seven sessions from 1920 to 1923: the first tracks in February 1920, and more in February 1921. On November 4, 1922, Gennaro Papi of the Metropolitan Opera asked for permission, as per his contract, to make recordings with the Aeolian-Vocalion orchestra; these presumably include the ones he made with Raisa. He is also listed as the conductor on the labels of the 1923 Vocalions.

The Country Music Foundation of Nashville, Tennessee, now holds the recording logs of the old Vocalion and Brunswick companies. This is not as unusual as it may seem at first glance, since both Vocalion and Brunswick were primarily popular and dance labels. The Foundation could not determine the dates for the Raisa Vocalion recordings, even after I supplied them with the matrix numbers. It seems "the ledgers for this company appear to have been destroyed long ago."[1] On close inspection, it becomes apparent that Vocalion's matrix numbering system was not the industry standard. Recent research by Peter Chaplin of Scotland has established the months, if not the exact dates, of the Vocalion records based on a reconstruction of the company's numbering scheme. Advertisements for the duets recorded by Raisa and Rimini for Brunswick were found in late 1927, 1928, and 1929. With the release of Ross Laird's encyclopedic four-volume

---

1. Email to me from the Brunswick-Vocalion expert Ross Laird, 12 May 2001.

Brunswick Records in 2001 we can now date them accurately. The four sides Raisa recorded for Voce del Padrone were made on June 29 and June 30, 1933.

In this discography I give the title of the opera, the title of the selection, and the name of the composer. Then I give the matrix number, then the published number that appears on the original published recording. The Pathés are listed with two record numbers, the second representing the number on the record when they were issued as two-sided recordings. There is no consistent matrix number system on the Pathés. For the Vocalion lateral records, when a third number is listed it represents the number on the record when the record was issued in two-sided format. All selections are sung in Italian, unless otherwise noted.

Pathé Frères—Paper-Label Discs, Vertical Cut
New York, April 1917

1. *Andrea Chénier*: La mamma morta (Giordano)
   (66077) 60062
2. *Aida*: O patria mia (Verdi)
   (66086) 60070
3. *L'Africana*: In grembo a me (Meyerbeer)
   (66087) 60055
4. *Aida*: Ritorna vincitor (Verdi)
   (66128) 60054
5. *Norma*: Casta Diva (Bellini)
   (66149) 60055
6. "Capelli d'oro"; Stornello (Oddone)
   (66223) 60062
7. *Il Trovatore*: D'amor sull'ali rosee (Verdi)
   (66257) 60070
8. *Cavalleria Rusticana*: Voi lo sapete (Mascagni)
   (matrix number unknown) 60054

Aeolian-Vocalion (Recordings), Vertical Cut
New York, 1918

9. "Oif'n pripetshik" [By the fireplace] (Yiddish)
   (A579) unpublished
10. *Cavalleria Rusticana*: Voi lo sapete (Mascagni)
    (A667) 30010
11. *Cavalleria Rusticana*: Voi lo sapete (Mascagni)
    (A668) 30010
12. *Il Trovatore*: Timor di me . . . D'amor sull'ali rosee (Verdi)
    (A669) 54007
13. "Eili, Eili" (Traditional, arr. Joseph Bonime) (Yiddish)
    (A692) 30011
14. *La Gioconda*: Suicidio (Ponchielli)
    (1855) 54027

Vocalion Recordings, Lateral Cut
New York, February 1920 – April 1923

15. "Eili, Eili" (Traditional, arr. Joseph Bonime) (Yiddish)
    February 1920
    (5504) 30101
16. "Eili, Eili" (Traditional, arr. Joseph Bonime) (Yiddish)
    February 1920
    (5505) 30101
17. *Norma*: Casta Diva (Bellini)
    February 1920
    (5508) 55001
18. *I Vespri Siciliani*: Mercè, dilette amiche (Bolero) (Verdi)
    March 1920
    (5781) 30115 (60047)
19. *I Vespri Siciliani*: Mercè, dilette amiche (Bolero) (Verdi)
    March 1920
    (5782) 30115 (60047)

20. *Don Giovanni*: Là ci darem la mano (Mozart)
    with Giacomo Rimini, March 1920
    (5810) 30108 (60019) UK 3015 3100
21. *Don Giovanni*: Là ci darem la mano (Mozart)
    with Giacomo Rimini, March 1920
    (5811) 30108 (60019) UK 3015 3100
22. *Il Trovatore*: Miserere (Verdi)
    with Giulio Crimi, March 1920
    (5813) 55007
23. *La Gioconda*: Suicidio (Ponchielli)
    March 1920
    (5850) B70034
24. "Kalinka" (Folk song) (Russian)
    February 1921
    (7033) 30160 (60036)
25. "Night" (Folk song) (Russian)
    February 1921
    (7039) 30165 (60036)
26. "None but the Lonely Heart" (Tchaikovsky) (Russian)
    February 1921
    (7093) 30134
27. *Otello*: Ave Maria (Verdi)
    February 1921
    (7098) 52007 (B70018)
28. *Aida*: La fatal pietra (Verdi)
    with Giulio Crimi, February 1921
    (7104) 52023
29. *Aida*: O terra addio (Verdi)
    with Giulio Crimi, February 1921
    (7106) 52043 (A70034)
30. "Le Crucifix" (Jean-Baptiste Faure) (French)
    with Giacomo Rimini, March 1921
    (7143) 52031 (A70032)

31. *La Forza del Destino*: Pace, pace, mio Dio (Verdi)
    March 1921
    (7163) 52013 (A70018)
32. *La Forza del Destino*: Pace, pace, mio Dio (Verdi)
    March 1921
    (7164) 52013 (A70018)
33. *Tosca*: Vissi d'arte (Puccini)
    February 1922
    (8636) 30155 (60047)
34. *Tosca*: Vissi d'arte (Puccini)
    February 1922
    (8637) 30155 (60047)
35. *Cavalleria Rusticana*: Voi lo sapete (Mascagni)
    March 1923
    (10984) 52048 (A70031)
36. "La paloma" (Yradier) (Spanish)
    March 1923
    (10996) 52051 (B70031) UK 0201 0199
37. *Aida*: Ritorna vincitor (Verdi)
    March 1923
    (11011) A70007
38. *Aida*: O patria mia (Verdi)
    March 1923
    (11035) B70007
39. *Il Trovatore*: Miserere (Verdi)
    with Armand Tokatyan, April 1923
    (11189) 55010 (B70032) UK 0201 0198
40. *Il Trovatore*: Mira d'acerbe lagrime (Verdi)
    with Giacomo Rimini, April 1923
    (11095) (A70039) UK 0221
41. *Mefistofele*: L'altra notte (Boito)
    (11157) (A70036) UK 0221
42. *Madama Butterfly*: Un bel dì vedremo (Puccini)
    April 1923
    (11190) (B70036)

43. *Ernani*: Sorta è la notte . . . Ernani! Ernani, involami (Verdi)
April 1923
(11192) (B70039)

Brunswick Records
New York, 1927 and 1929

44. *Die Zauberflöte*: La dove prende (Mozart)
with Giacomo Rimini, 6 April 1927
(E22277-78) unpublished
45. *Il Trovatore*: Tacea la notte placida (Verdi)
6 April 1927
(E22279-0-1) unpublished
assigned cat. no. 15132 but not released
46. *Die Zauberflöte*: La dove prende (Mozart)
with Giacomo Rimini, April 1927
(E22446-1) 15131 15135
47. *Don Giovanni*: Là ci darem la mano (Mozart)
with Giacomo Rimini, 20 April 1927
(E22547) 15131 15135
48. *Cavalleria Rusticana*: Voi lo sapete (Mascagni)
20 April 1927
(E22548-1) 15174 15132
49. *Ernani*: Ernani! Ernani, involami (Verdi)
April 1927
(E22449-3) 15174 A7710
50. *Cavalleria Rusticana:* Turiddu mi tolse l'onore (Mascagni)
with Giacomo Rimini, February 1929
(XE29230-3) 90004
51. *Il Trovatore:* Mira d'acerbe lagrime (Verdi)
with Giacomo Rimini, February 1929
(XE29231-3) 90004

52. *Norma:* Ah, bello a me ritorna (Bellini)
February 1929[2]
(XE29236) unpublished

Voce del Padrone
Milan, 29 and 30 June 1933[3]

53. *Tosca:* Vissi d'arte (Puccini)
(2M 1442-2) DB2122 Victor 14400B
54. *Cavalleria Rusticana:* Voi lo sapete (Mascagni)
(2M 1443-1) DB2123
55. *La Gioconda:* Suicidio (Ponchielli)
(2M 1445-2) DB2122
56. *Andrea Chénier:* La mamma morta (Giordano)
(2M 1446-2) DB2123 Victor 14400A

2. At this recording session the Brunswick logs show matrix numbers E29233
and E29234 as untitled. It is reasonable to assume that these were takes of
"Casta Diva," which would have been the logical sequence and the "Side A"
of a twelve-inch *Norma* record. The log shows E29235 as Rimini in the "Sere-
nade" from *I Gioiella della Madonna*.
3. Correct dating of 29 and 30 June is courtesy of Alan Kelly, the world authority on HMV recordings. Email from Larry Lustig to author, 3 August 2001.

THE RECORDINGS

The first time I heard any of Rosa Raisa's recordings I was mystified as to what the fuss was about. Yes, the voice was beautiful, the singing correct, even spectacular at times; but I just didn't "get it." This is a common reaction; one must live with Raisa's recordings, listen to them repeatedly, to discover the gems in the quarry. Obviously I have found the effort worthwhile. Among the fifty-four surviving 78-rpm sides there are indisputable failures, but there are also performances that are among the very best. Although records don't lie, it is equally true that records don't tell the whole story, especially with powerful, high voices.

From Raisa's best recordings we can ascertain certain things. We can hear the dark crimson beauty and individuality of her voice, its distinctive richness and its melancholy, as well as the ease of its upper register. Typically, the great singers have a unique sound, and Raisa certainly does not sound like anyone else who comes to mind. We can hear how she shaped music in the confines of the early recording studio, where she breathes, her sense of musical logic and legato. There is often something almost formal about her musical statements. Stinson felt she was not overly personal in her singing, that there often was a detachment in her almost instrumental treatment of the musical line. If one follows the score, for instance, as she sings her 1923 "O patria mia," one is struck by the consummate perfection of her legato, with the occasional grace notes and turns all in place. But it is a legato of many hammered strokes, all on the breath, each note individually struck but flowing one note into the next in an inevitable musical arch. Her vocal placement too was quite different from, say, Ponselle's or Rethberg's in the same selection. One is struck by the very different organization of their voices. Both Ponselle and Rethberg have more classically top-to-bottom homogenous voices. Ponselle's is anchored toward the middle and bottom, and Rethberg's is still more uniform, but of a smaller cast. Raisa's voice tends to flame as it goes above the staff with an incredible ease and her less rich-sounding middle register is anchored to a very large chest voice. Ward Marston seems to have found in his remasters the correct meshing of the registers. The middle now seems fuller and less detached from the rest of the voice.[4]

From the recordings one can form a reasonable idea of the timbre of Raisa's voice. For example, she recorded the *Cavalleria Rusticana* aria "Voi lo sapete" six times in five different recording ambiances: 1) in 1917, for Pathé, using the hill and dale (vertical cut) process; 2) twice in 1918, for Aeolian-Vocalion, using the hill and dale (vertical cut) process; 3) in 1923, for Vocalion, using the lateral cut process; 4) in 1927, for Brunswick, using the electrical process; and 5) in 1933, for Voce del Padrone (His Master's Voice), using the electrical process. The different combinations of recording process, equipment used, studio size, orchestra size, and placement of singer in relation to horn or microphone result in five quite distinct representations of Raisa's voice. Except for a few minor differences, the performances, which span some sixteen years, are identical in phrasing and interpretation. The Vocalion verticals seem to my ears the most resplendent example of her voice, the Pathé the least satisfactory, the Vocalion lateral the most detached. In the Brunswick electrical her voice sounds thin, and in the HMV electrical her voice, while at its most beautiful, seems troubled. In all versions of the *Cavalleria* aria she dips vehemently into chest voice at "me l'ha rapito" in the middle section and at "io piango" at the end of the aria; it is best managed on the Vocalion lateral, but it is the most gripping on the Vocalion verticals and the HMV electrical.

Raisa always contended that her volume was never captured on recordings. She wrote to me, "For example, all your collection of my recordings I don't have—because I would listen to them and then break them into pieces—they never showed the volume of my voice—just a faint remembrance of how I sounded on the stage."[5] One can agree that the volume heard is not in accordance with her legend and contemporary accounts, but one does hear a very large voice handled with

4. Ward Marston's masterly compilation, "Rosa Raisa, The Complete Recordings," Marston 53001-2 (three CDs).

5. Raisa, letter to author, 23 March 1962.

ease. It is the sheer freedom of her voice, the total lack of strain or effort, that suggests the overwhelming power that is part of the Raisa myth. Could it be that in front of either the acoustic horn or the electric microphone she felt "spooked" and never really let out her tremendous top voice, or that she backed away lest she blast? The B-flats at the end of the *Madama Butterfly* aria are fairly astounding for both focus and ease. In the *Mefistofele* aria the high notes have an ease and width that suggest the kind of power so often spoken of in contemporary critiques. It is interesting that the *Butterfly* and *Mefistofele* come out of the April 1923 recording session. In all the duets with Rimini he seems to make the larger sounds. Yet almost all the reviews I have examined indicate that his was a light and dry voice; therefore, we must assume that in the duets he was placed far closer to the horn or microphone in the hope that this placement might achieve proper balance. But this gives his voice more ping and immediacy, while Raisa's voice in the duets tends to sound diffused and distant. It is also clear from the reviews cited that her vocal peak was around 1922–1926; although still indicative of a great singer, her 1929 and 1933 recordings show some loss of the plush and velvet. One does hear some of the burnished gold of her voice on the 1933 HMVs.

All of the Pathé vertical-cut recordings present problems, but we should not dismiss them. They were recorded in April 1917 in New York, about the time Raisa was to have honored Puccini's wish to create Magda in *La Rondine* at Monte Carlo but was forced by the war to stay in the United States. It is clear that they were recorded in a daylong marathon, with probably no allowance for retakes (to the best of my knowledge none have survived). Most are three- to three-and-a-half-minute reductions of pieces that ideally require four to five minutes to be as complete as is "musically" possible. Obviously in her first recording session Raisa "let out" her voice, but the dead acoustics of the room in which the recordings were made blunted the results. This assertion is literally "on record," as less than a year later Raisa recorded both the *Cavalleria* and the *Trovatore* arias for Vocalion using *their* superior hill and dale process, with totally different results. The bottled-up Pathé sound is replaced by vocal splendor—perhaps not the power and richness of her legend, but sufficient to make the contrast clear. The extra minute available on the Vocalions improves on the abbreviated nature of the Pathés. On the 1917 "D'amor sull'ali rosee" (66070) only her ability to achieve the high notes and snap out trills is evident in what is otherwise a perfunctory run-through of this elegiac song. The Vocalion (54007) with the recitative included reveals some of the rapture as well as the striking high notes (a piano D-flat, for instance) with clean ornamentation. The "Voi lo sapete" (60054) is even more indicative of Pathé's deficits; the interpretation in both versions is identical, yet the results are not even comparable. The Vocalion *Cavalleria* aria (30010—takes A667 and A668) is one of Raisa's very best; freed from any constraints, she is able to produce a cascade of voice, a superb line, and palpable emotion.

The *Andrea Chénier* "La mamma morta" (60062), the first number she made, should be contrasted with the 1933 electrical version (DB 2123), from her final recording sessions. The three-minute Pathé is vocally interesting, but pales next to the electrical take even though Raisa does not appear to have been in her best voice for the latter version. The earlier one is a neutral traversal of the notes; the latter is a rich personal statement, with declamatory bite and feats of vocal power, as well as studied restraint when called for by the music and text. The *L'Africana* (60055) "In grembo a me" is one of the few successful sides from this session, with easy, soft high notes and clean trills. The two *Aida* arias should have been much better, for by the time these recordings were made Raisa had made a big name for herself as the Ethiopian princess. The "Ritorna vincitor" (60054), without the declamatory opening section, starts with the passage "*e l'amor mio,*" not often included on 78-rpm versions if the piece is recorded from the first measures because of the length of the aria. The "O patria mia" (60070) reveals a splendid high C, but the ascent to that note is so wayward that it negates any pleasure at her having achieved that supreme note.

"Casta Diva" (60055) is intriguing, if only for the fact that, at the time of the recording, *Norma* was not yet in her active stage repertoire. This should be her showcase recording, but this abridgment gives only one verse of the cavatina and a reduced allegro. By placing her voice in the dead middle to achieve a beautiful and rolling sound, she limits her ability to reach brilliant high A's and the B-flat with ease. The cadenza and trill are remarkable but intonation problems reduce the enjoyment. The allegro is properly brisk and has remarkable coloratura from such an abundant voice, but the high C at the end is not taken, as it appears she is out of breath. One wonders why it was approved, and indeed whether there even was an approval process. In the 1920 Vocalion version of the cavatina (55001), she initially places her voice higher and thereby fails to make the opening phrases as imposing as they may have been, but the high A's and B-flats ring out with extraordinary ease; the cadenza and trill are better still, although awkward intonation at the resolution of the trill is slightly troublesome. In the 1929 version of the allegro (XE 29236), sung with great exuberance and skillful, seemingly spontaneous, and inspired ornamentation, she achieves one of the great high C's on record. I submit that this previously unpublished recording goes a long way in explaining what Raisa was about as a vocalist. To be sure, it is very exhibitionistic, but a spirit of sheer greatness permeates this recording. It is clear that in 1929, after Raisa had achieved a great success in Chicago upon her return to the stage after a long absence, Brunswick recorded both cavatina and allegro with the intention of rivaling the Ponselle version on Victor. Only the allegro has survived, and that was never published until the Marston compilation. A debt of gratitude is owed Richard Bebb for making this unpublished recording available via Ward Marston's compilation. One can only hope that sometime in the future the aria proper will be unearthed. This is yet another of the many "might-have-beens" that plague the Raisa recording career. It is evident from her three recordings of the aria that Raisa was a singer with a wide-ranging voice who frequently adjusted her placement to better encompass music with tessitura considerations.

In the first session for Pathé Raisa recorded only one song, the stornello "Capelli d'oro" (60062) by Oddone. She navigates the simple song dipping in and out of her luxurious chest register, but her reading is not as charming as Salome Kruszelnicka's Fonotipia recording of this modest number.

Raisa recorded only four selections for Vocalion using their hill and dale process in 1918. The *Trovatore* and *Cavalleria* I discussed above in comparison to the poorer Pathé versions. The *Gioconda* "Suicide" aria (54027) has the virtue of revealing the thrust of Raisa's voice at full tilt. This rendition has ungainly register breaks but is otherwise vocalized with great ease and serves as her blueprint for the even finer 1933 electrical rendering, with its sepulchral chest tones and well-taken high notes. The "Eili, Eili" (30011) was a Raisa encore piece throughout her career, and after retirement she often sang it in private to the delight of her friends and co-religionists. Simply put, this song, so treasured by her generation of eastern European Jewish immigrants scarred by the horrors of pogroms, is a plea to God for understanding. He is asked why He has countenanced the Jews' wanderings and sufferings despite their having kept the faith. The song ends with the Hebrew credo, "Shema Yisroel." Raisa sings this simple song in a heartfelt and affectionate way. It stands alone, even compared to several cantorial renditions and the smooth and cultured singing of Nina Koshetz. The cello-like beauty of the young Raisa voice and her loving way with her own Yiddish language is unique. It is strange that this version, recorded in 1918 and sung by a twenty-five-year-old singer, should be markedly superior to the 1920 versions (30101, takes 5504 and 5505), which are glossier but by comparison superficial.

Since the above paragraph was written, a previously unpublished recording, in test pressing form, has surfaced. "Oif'n pripetshik" (matrix #A579) is now known to have been the earliest of Raisa's Vocalion verticals, and it is a major find. It is a simple Yiddish song, freely translated as "By the fireplace." I am told that it is a sweet song about a rabbi teaching his young charges the aleph, beths (abc's). Raisa employs not her operatic voice, but rather a subdued and affectionate coloring. Although the song rests mostly in the lower middle part of her voice, she dips into her chest voice without the grinding one hears on some of her operatic pieces. The high note at the end is an F-sharp. This song, along with the "Eili, Eili," conjures up what the encore portion of a Raisa concert must have been like. Since the song is virtually perfect in the test pressing, one wonders why it was not released; its appearance kindles hope anew that additional unpublished material will surface in the future.

In early 1920 Raisa contracted with Vocalion to be the featured artist in their new classical catalogue. Vocalion was primarily a popular and dance music label, and its signing of major opera stars marked a serious effort to move "upscale." Raisa had annual sessions with Vocalion from 1920 through 1923, in New York; for the last two of these sessions Vocalion hired Gennaro Papi of the Metropolitan Opera to conduct the Aeolian Orchestra for the recordings. The first two issues were the "Casta Diva" and "Eili, Eili," which came out on Vocalion's premium-priced blue label; the relative merits of these were discussed above. This "Casta Diva" is an interesting collection of vocal feats integrated into Bellini's sublime melody. Raisa catches the reverent spirit of the aria and exhibits the easiest and largest high notes, sings "quella pace, che regnar" an octave up to a high B-flat, still maintaining a pianissimo tone, a variation attributed to the first Norma, Giuditta Pasta, then dazzles with an incredible cadenza and finishes with a full-voiced trill. Presumably the cadenza and trill were the ones taught her by Barbara Marchisio, about which she elaborated when discussing her first Normas in 1918, at the Teatro Colón in Buenos Aires. This performing authenticity also applies to the cadenzas in the *Trovatore* recordings discussed earlier. As such, students of nineteenth-century performing practices should take note, as Marchisio was involved with her sister, Carlotta, in many *Norma* and *Trovatore* performances in the early history of those operas. Yet, with all the showy and difficult exploits performed, the incidents of glottal catches, nasality, and awkward breathing are perhaps more numerous than one might wish, and match some of the criticisms of her Norma. Again, the uneven character of this recording leads one to wonder exactly what the Raisa Norma was like in performance. An interesting consideration is that when someone years later told her that Raisa in her recordings placed a trill at the end of the aria, Ponselle was aghast. Ponselle felt that a trill, an ornamental device, should never be used in the "Casta Diva"; however, both Patti and Sembrich on their recordings of the aria (sung essentially as *vocalises*) sing the same trill. Clearly this was a sanctioned nineteenth-century practice. Some modern singers have reinstated this trill. Surely Raisa sang the trill the three times Ponselle heard her Norma (1920, 1921, and 1929).

The "Bolero" from *I Vespri Siciliani* (30115, takes 5781 and 5782) is one of Raisa's flashiest recordings and is the most revealing of her technical prowess. The bravura is breathtaking. Its brilliance and format make it easier to imagine as a dazzling encore at a concert than as part of the flow of the complete opera; for that one goes to Maria Callas or Renata Scotto. For a more modern audience it's akin to Victoria de los Angeles singing the "Seguidilla" or Leontyne Price singing "Summertime" in a concert setting. Raisa simply astonishes with her armory of trills and runs, and even touches a secure high C-sharp for a brief second. She manages full-voiced trills and slow trills, fluid runs and staccato runs. For the lowest note she dips into chest voice insouciantly. Marston uncovered two takes of this aria, seemingly identical but with a two-second difference in running time. Over the years many have praised this recording for its virtuosity, while others have found it to be aggressive and artistically shallow. Ponselle's much-acclaimed and similarly spirited early Columbia rendition, which EMI's Walter Legge thought to be of historic merit, is tame by comparison.

The popular "Là ci darem la mano" (30108, takes 5810 and 5811) from *Don Giovanni* was a Raisa-Rimini encore duet throughout their careers. It has very little to do with Mozart and a lot to do with their personalities. Rimini maintains a firm line and Raisa in the background does not use her dramatic soprano voice, instead adopting a seductive and well-modulated understated quality. She can't resist inserting a high note at the end, but this mezzo-piano A-flat is pulled out effortlessly. This is essentially a souvenir of a period when this duet, sung like a popular tune, appealed to less "sophisticated" audiences than those who enjoy it now. Mozart at that time was not the icon he has since become in our age, when musical scholarship and authentic performing practices are the rule.

The *Trovatore* "Miserere" (55007) with the tenor Giulio Crimi is an impassioned statement of this grand scene. Raisa's phrasing expresses the proper emotional turbulence and Crimi is in fine voice. Raisa inserts an optional high C at the end, but this note is not as striking as it might have been, since this abbreviated version cuts the preceding phrases that build to that note, thereby robbing the high C of its context. On the remake of the duet a few years later with Armand Tokatyan (55010) the same note is more remarkable.

The *Gioconda* "Suicide Aria" (B70034) is one of Raisa's least impressive records from this period. It seems merely a perfunctory run-through without her usual passion, and at times the voice even drops out of focus. It is mostly smooth, but hardly the statement one expects from so dramatic a performer, especially since Vincent Sheean thought that her "Suicidio" was so hair-raising he could remember it vividly almost forty years later.

The Russian song "Kalinka" (30160) is a warhorse that Russian singers have performed from time immemorial. Raisa's version is one of the best examples of her mastery of vocal art. Note how she is able to play with her voice, even in the middle register, swelling and diminishing her tones with total control. The song has a nice lilt and rhythm. "Night" (30165) displays more facets of Raisa's vocal control. The long line sung with moderate power is sustained throughout the range of her voice. She ends with a triple-piano G. The Tchaikovsky favorite, "None but the Lonely Heart"—or, as indicated on the label, "Ye Who Have Yearned Alone" (30134)—is sung with tortured emotion. Nasality intrudes at the beginning, but Raisa rises to a ringing climax. This is one of the better versions on record. These three are all we have recorded of Raisa's large Russian repertoire. The frequently programmed Rachmaninoff songs and the *Pique Dame* aria are yet more "might-have-beens."

The *Otello* "Ave Maria" (52007) is a curious effort. Desdemona was one of Raisa's more frequently performed roles at the time this recording was made. It has a prayerful quality that is touching, and it is mostly well vocalized, yet it just doesn't succeed as it should. The lower chest voice declamation is properly understated, the transition to head voice deftly accomplished, and the concluding high A-flat well taken, but the whole is strangely not greater than the sum of its parts.

The *Aida* tomb scene, consisting of two separate recordings—"La fatal pietra" and "O terra addio" (52023 and 52043)—made in 1921 with Giulio Crimi, is one of the better acoustic versions. Raisa for her part sings with sculpted accuracy and stays in the background, with Crimi closer to the recording horn. She rises to the high A's and B-flats with superb ease, taking many of them pianissimo. One feels the reserves of power there to be called for. It is almost but not quite in the Ponselle/Martinelli class.

Faure's "Le Crucifix" (52031) was a somewhat strange title for the Riminis to record in 1921. True, it was one of the standard soprano-baritone duets of the song literature and very much programmed at the time the recording was made. (On occasion the couple even sang Faure's "Les Rameaux" in their concerts.) Rimini, who is nearer to the horn, sings his part with flowing tone, and Raisa delivers her lines with security and boldness. She rises to a very easy high B-flat with no evident strain.

"Pace, pace, mio Dio" from *La Forza del Destino* (52013, takes 7163 and 7164) has to be one of Raisa's best but least appreciated recordings. She sings the sweeping aria with enormous reserve and proper feeling. The turns and grace notes hold no terrors for her. Although the Vocalion lateral recording process does not reveal her vocal velvet as the verticals do, one senses that one is hearing only about 60 percent of what a better-engineered recording would disclose, even a 1921 recording. She floats the piano B-flat "invan la pace" with an ease that needs no setting up to reach; the tone is pure, beautiful, and the crest of a vocal arch. It was common in recorded versions at that time to omit the final "maledizione" and that is regrettable, for they would surely play into Raisa's strength. The second version is a half-minute shorter, and the piano B-flat, although quite fine, is not the marvel of the earlier take.

Before Marston's "Rosa Raisa, The Complete Recordings," the 1922 "Vissi d'arte" from *Tosca* (30155, takes 8636 and 8637) had never before been available on either LP or CD. It is one of the discoveries that make the "Complete Raisa" such an achievement. It is so easily vocalized and so correct in its phrasing. The high B-flat is not the huge tone one expects; it is rather a soft but firm note that is almost suspended in air. The two versions vary in sentiment, but in most respects they are identical, only two seconds different in length. As dramatic realizations, though, these are not comparable to the 1933 electrical.

The history of Raisa's "Vissi d'arte" contains a puzzle. It seems Vocalion, when they needed to reissue one of her recordings, pulled the alternative take from the shelf and assigned it the same number. I was surprised after having collected Raisa's 78-rpm recordings for more than thirty years to discover five issued alternative takes. In almost all instances the substitutes are so close to the first that I had never noticed. It is also very difficult to find matrix numbers on the Vocalions, as they are pressed beneath the label, and one has to turn the record under strong light, and feel the label, to know that a matrix number is present at all.

If one needs confirmation that the Vocalion laterals are not in the league of the verticals, the *Cavalleria Rusticana* aria should be evidence beyond doubt. Listening to the lateral (52048), recorded five years after the vertical-cut version (30010), one could swear one was listening to a different voice; the velvet and the overtones simply are not there. As a reading of the aria, it is similar to the other five versions; worthy of note is that Raisa manages the middle-section dip into chest voice more deftly. Uncharacteristically, she does not sustain the high A at the end with her usual security.

For the popular Spanish song "La paloma" we are able to compare Raisa's 1923 studio recording (52051) with the existing 1926–1927 electrical Vitaphone film soundtrack. In 1923 she sings the song with classical vocal production and exhibits graces and turns that could be the envy of the lightest soprano. In the film she is very outgoing, and when in the middle of the song she dips into her chest voice, she breaks into a big smile. It is clear she wanted to highlight this effect. The Vocalion is a lovely rendition—perhaps a bit too operatic, for it lacks the simplicity of the Galli-Curci. To my ear the voice is firmer on the record than on the film soundtrack.

The two big *Aida* arias, "Ritorna vincitor" (A70007) and "O patria mia" (B70007), never issued single-sided, are vastly better than the 1917 Pathés. But as with the *Cavalleria* aria discussed above, here again the plush and overtones of the voice are missing. One wonders how the voice would sound in the Vocalion vertical process that gives it a more three-dimensional aura. However, accepting the sound and the recording ambiance given, these two renderings tell us a great deal about Raisa. The "Ritorna" is vocally firm and expansive in the first section and properly introspective in the last, with many well-taken soft high notes. The "Nile" aria is beautifully phrased with firm legato and soaring line. The high C is not as remarkable as one expects, given her reputation for this feat. She ascends to the note beautifully, but to my ear she presses rather than floats the note. The feeling is inescapable that she wanted this most exposed high C to be even better than it is. Sung piano, the two high A's in the concluding section are exquisite.

The 1923 "Miserere" from *Il Trovatore*, with the young Armand Tokatyan (55010), is superior to the version with Crimi recorded three years earlier. The voice isn't as imposing in the opening phrases, mostly in the middle range, but it is superbly produced. The optional high C is simply radiant as a feat of pure vocal ease. With Rimini she sings her first recording of the Act IV duet, "Mira d'acerbe lagrime" (A70039), a duet they recorded for the 1926–1927 Vitaphone film, and in 1929 electrically for Brunswick. Rimini is properly robust as Di Luna, and Raisa is obviously comfortable in this musical style. The difficult coloratura ripples as if it were the easiest thing in the world. She ends the duet with a well-taken, utterly free high C.

The *Mefistofele* "L'altra notte" (A70036) is the one recording many commentators feel best captures the Raisa voice and style of legend, as her voice here does sound very large. This dramatic performance is remarkably sung with perfect high notes and the real trills as indicated in the score. Raisa manages the shifts from head to chest voice with faultless control. The power of the high voice almost breaks through the sonic din of the Vocalion process. Others have been warmer and simpler in this aria, but this is without question Raisa's recorded masterpiece.

The "Un bel dì" from *Madama Butterfly* (B70036) is an aria one does not normally associate with the powerhouse voice of Raisa, but she had a very successful run of the opera in 1925 and 1926. As the reviews quoted indicate, in her interpretation she kept the voice light, and let it ring out only in the most dramatic passages, such as "per non morir." She caps the aria with two splendid high B-flats, firm, solid, never wavering. One can almost project from this what her *Turandot* high-lying phrases might have sounded like.

The "Ernani! Ernani, involami" (B70039) is one of Raisa's less familiar recordings. It is curious that she gives the recitative but not the cabaletta. It seems that if four and a half minutes were available she would have done better to omit the recitative and conclude with a rousing ending, even if abridged, as does Ponselle. For in the aria proper we get a momentary view of how deftly she moves the voice through the highs and lows with grace and ease. The high C's that top the runs are cleanly taken. This is one of her very best efforts on record.

The two Mozart duets, "Là ci darem la mano" from *Don Giovanni* and "La dove prende" from *The Magic Flute* (15131, 15135), are essentially run-throughs showing no special affinity for Mozart style as presently understood. They are given as *vocalises*, and as such they are acceptable but not distinguished. Raisa in the *Magic Flute* duet rises to easy B-flats in the upward runs. Again, these are essentially souvenirs of Raisa and Rimini's concert encores, nothing more.

The extremely rare ten-inch Brunswick of the *Cavalleria Rusticana* and *Ernani* arias (15132, 15174) is mysterious, as it was issued only in the German and Swiss markets—not one of the Riminis' venues. As with the previously discussed Brunswicks, the voice sounds lean and even tinny. The *Cavalleria* is her fifth published take of this aria and the performance and phrasing are similar to the others. It is, however, much less remarkable. The *Ernani* is so truncated that one can't really tell very much; however, Raisa does manage the runs and the high C's very easily. We are fortunate to have this recording, but only because of its rarity; it is not particularly revealing and does not fill in any gaps in the Raisa recording puzzle.

The rare *Cavalleria Rusticana* Santuzza-Alfio duet "Turiddu mi tolse l'onore" (90004) is a strange choice for her all-too-few Brunswick recordings, but we are grateful to have any scene not often recorded. The long phrases of this verismo music are phrased as smoothly as bel canto. The highest lines are not as comfortable as one expects, and she does stroke the glottis as the line dips low. Strangely, she does not end the duet with the optional high note.

The second studio recording of "Mira d'acerbe lagrime" (90004) finds Raisa in good voice, although Brunswick's dead acoustics make the voice seem thin. The coloratura hurdles are dispatched with her accustomed ease, but uncharacteristically she eschews the optional high C at the end. This more orthodox reading probably duplicates the way she must have sung it for Toscanini at La Scala four years earlier. Rimini gives his usual strong performance.

The same cannot be said for the Brunswick *Norma*, "Ah, bello a me ritorna," cited above in discussing her earlier *Norma* recordings. This has to be considered an important document. True, as in the six previously discussed Brunswicks, the voice does not have the body one expects, but the sheer glory of the singing tells us much about the famous Raisa Norma. The *Gramophone* magazine critic John Steane was taken with this performance: "Outstanding is the single previously unpublished item, the cabaletta 'Ah! Bello a me ritorna' from *Norma*, recorded by Brunswick in [February] 1929. A superb demonstration of vocal mastery, it seems totally unaware of difficulties. The semiquaver passagework, the bold intervals, the matching of rhythmic energy with lyric grace, all are mastered with apparent ease; and having the whole record to itself (rather than sharing with the 'Casta Diva' as on the earlier Pathé version), the piece can be given complete, with the luxury of the second verse skillfully embellished."

It is now known that this recording was made within weeks of her return to the Chicago stage on New Year's Eve 1928. The exuberance, along with the technical display and even the suspicion of occasional wavering from pitch, matches the reviews cited of that occasion.

The four verismo arias recorded in Milan for Voce del Padrone in June 1933 have to be considered the products of Raisa's most successful recording session. Even though she is not in her very best vocal trim, and the engineers reportedly had difficulty with microphone placement, the voice has a crimson beauty seldom heard from Raisa or anyone else. All four titles repeat earlier versions made when she was in more youthful and firmer voice, but these unrushed readings have the stamp of her genius. The *Tosca* (DB2122), *Cavalleria Rusticana* (DB2123), *Gioconda* (DB2122), and *Andrea Chénier* (DB2123) can be considered near definitive readings. The "perchè's" of Tosca, the "l'amai's" of Santuzza, the "dentro l'avel" of Gioconda, and the "voce piena d'armonia" of Maddalena have rarely been done better, in my estimation. Certainly there are occasional lapses from pitch, there are fissures in the tone, the highest notes have for the first time a suspicion of a beat all too common with singers past their best days, but her authority and mastery make these flaws seem beside the point. Raisa's vocal power can be sensed behind the limitations of the recording process. There is a note in the Voce del Padrone company's logs that there were problems with Raisa's "bad" microphone technique in this June 29 session, strongly suggesting "blasting." This confirms the longstanding rumors that at this session her voice was too big and that she had to be placed in the middle of the orchestra.[6]

The Vitaphone soundtracks and films add yet another dimension to her output. One hopes that the planned Getty Foundation–underwritten "Vitaphone Project," using the best originals and computer-enhanced methods, will better reveal these lip-synched cinema shorts. One also hopes that the apparently lost 1927–1928 "Eili, Eili" and Tosti's "Addio" will yet be unearthed. These numbers were reviewed in the musical journals of the time when they were shown in movie

6. Email from Peter Chaplin to Larry Lustig of *Record Collector*, 1 June 2001.

houses around the country. Of all the performers I have seen in the Vitaphone operatic shorts, Raisa is one of the least skillful at lip-synching.

The *Trovatore* duet with Rimini is complete with the recitative and middle section that had been omitted in the abridged studio recordings of this scene by Vocalion and Brunswick. Seeing an eight-minute version allows us some understanding of performance practices of an earlier time. Rimini is immobile, standing stage front bellowing out his lines; in comparison, Raisa looks small in the background. The recitative and middle sections are well done. Unlike her two studio recordings, Raisa is a bit untidy with the downward staccato runs toward the end, and she allows herself an extra second to prepare for the stunning concluding high C, thus making the effect somewhat provincial.

The two songs, "La paloma" and "Plaisir d'amour," have many good points. Both are too operatic and "public" for the intimate sentiments involved. Raisa views these songs as opportunities to show off—her fiorature in "La paloma" and her trill in "Plaisir d'amour." These priorities make for some ungraceful phrasing. The voice sounds considerably larger than in her commercial recordings, and her unmistakable timbre is evident, but there is a frustrating lack of focus and tonal centering in the two songs. These rare audiovisual glimpses add only a little to what we already know about Raisa.

Although Raisa very much disliked her recordings because they did not show off her vocal power, I feel there is enough there to tell us some things about her as an artist and musician. Trained by Barbara Marchisio in the mid-nineteenth-century school of singing, she very often exhibits the graces and skills attributed to that school. As a modern singer she is very comfortable with veristic expression and is often able to integrate her emotional delivery with the classicism of the old school. It is our loss that she recorded such a limited repertoire and that the sound engineers of her recording labels were not able to find a way to let her perform in the studio as she must have performed on the stage, without constraints. I think we can probably determine the basic sound, if not the scope, of her instrument. It is a shame that

neither she nor her recording companies attempted the "Inflammatus," the great second-act scene from *Turandot*, her big scenes from
La Juive, Lisa's grand aria from *Pique Dame*, the poker scene from *La
Fanciulla del West*, the great arias from *Don Giovanni*, *Lohengrin*,
and *Tannhäuser*, or even the sparkling duet from *Don Pasquale* and
the dramatic one from *Luisa Miller* that were such rousing specialties
in her concerts with Rimini. Even in the operas that are represented
in her solo recordings, there are duets and trios from *Aida*, *Norma*,
La Gioconda, *Il Trovatore*, and *Andrea Chénier* that cry for represen-
tation but will unfortunately never be heard. In the five recording
ambiances used plus the Vitaphone soundtracks there are enough
similarities to assure us that we are getting the blueprint if not the
final product of her amazing voice. I am hopeful that in the years to
come there will be occasional discoveries of unissued recordings that
will help fill in the puzzle further, if not complete it.

Notes

1. Licia Albanese told me in 1995 that her teacher Giuseppina Baldassare-Tedeschi had said that in her day Rosa Raisa was a "name among names" in the glamorous world of Italian opera.

2. Unlike that of some artists, Raisa's age is never in question. Since she made her operatic debut in 1913 at age twenty, there is no question that her birth year was 1893. There is some discrepancy whether she was born on May 23 or May 30. I have seen both her naturalization certificate and her passport, and her given birth date is May 30, 1893.

3. *Universal Jewish Encyclopedia* (New York: Funk and Wagnalls, 1938).

4. Raisa's nephew Professor Louis Stein, the son of her full sister, Sonya, recalled being told his maternal grandmother's maiden name was Constantinovsky; however, on the new tombstone Raisa commissioned for her in 1930, her maiden name, as transliterated from the Hebrew-Yiddish, is Krasnatawsky. Presumably this was copied from the original 1899 tombstone.

5. I received two different drafts of the unpublished autobiography and miscellaneous pages in Raisa's hand from both Raisa's daughter, Giulietta ("Jolly"), and her granddaughter, Suzanne Homme. The latter draft already contained some of Mary Watkins Cushing's rewrites. All excerpts from these sources, considered Raisa's memoirs, will be marked at the beginning with a ✄ and end with a ✄.

6. *Encyclopedia Judaica*, vol. 13 (Jerusalem: Keter Publishing House Jerusalem Ltd., 1971), 698.

7. Ibid. Although this encyclopedia places the number of dead at seventy-five, and I deem Raisa's youthful memory faulty, in the memoir she relates that when she visited the Jewish cemetery in 1930 she saw the monument for the nine hundred dead of the 1906 pogrom. Perhaps this pogrom was more massive than is currently thought.

8. Goldie Stone, *My Caravan of Years, an Autobiography* (New York: Bloch Publishing Company, 1945), 190. Bloch at that time was the leading publisher of Judaica in the United States. The book is a memoir of a grateful immigrant intoxicated with American democracy and its embrace of peoples from all ethnic groups. Stone devotes a whole chapter to her unique connection with

Rosa Raisa, with whom she forged a sort of mother-daughter relationship. In 1945 Raisa sent copies of this book to her nephews and nieces.

9. Gorky wrote the first important biography of Chaliapin.

10. When Raisa wrote her memoir in 1962–1963 she often used very Catholic phrases and constructions, even when describing her very Jewish early life. See chapter 13.

11. Raisa says in the memoir that she sang the "Ave Maria" from *Otello* in the church; I believe that is unlikely, as the *Otello* selection is a full operatic aria and is rarely sung as a "song." This is an instance where Raisa's memory probably tricked her. It is more likely that she sang the Schubert or Bach-Gounod "Ave Maria" on that occasion.

12. *Musical America*, 8 November 1924, 4. The article is titled, "Rosa Raisa to create role of 'Turandot.'" The informative feature article is cast as a fairy tale, covering Raisa's early life and a career that was to be capped the following year with the *Turandot* creation. For various reasons the premiere was put off until 1926 (see chapter 8).

13. In some interviews over the years Raisa stated that she sang "Casta Diva" at her graduation, and in others she stated that she sang "Bel raggio." It is possible she sang both. In any event, it was the first time she ever sang with an orchestra.

14. In most interviews over the years, and in her memoir, the very important Campanini audition is reported to have taken place in spring 1913. However, *Musical America* (7 December 1912, 14) published this report: "Already engaged for the [centennial] season in Parma are Giovanni Martinelli . . . and Raisa Burstein, a new soprano whose laurels thus far have been won on the concert stage, especially in Rome at the Augusteum. The Verdi Centenary will frame her début in Parma."

15. Personal communication, courtesy of Gaspare Nello Vetro of Parma. He has authored a set of books about the brothers Campanini, the tenor Italo and the conductor Cleofonte, and Arturo Toscanini, all from Parma.

16. *Orfeo* magazine, 22 September 1913. This quote was published in Michael Scott's *The Record of Singing*, vol. 2 (New York: Holmes and Meyer Publishers, 1979), 71.

CHAPTER TWO

1. Edward C. Moore, *Forty Years of Opera in Chicago* (New York: Horace Liveright, 1930), 126.

2. From clipping files in the New York Public Library, Lincoln Center, Perform-

ing Arts Division. Byline Clarence Eddy, in an unidentified Chicago newspaper.

3. Stone, *My Caravan of Years*, 189.

4. *Musical Leader*, May 1914.

5. Byron Hegel, unnamed Philadelphia newspaper; clipping files of the New York Public Library, Performing Arts Division.

CHAPTER THREE

1. From Raisa's memoir.

2. This is the opera *Fedra* that was to be linked so closely to Rosa Ponselle a decade later. Romani was to become Ponselle's lover.

3. Giacomo Lauri-Volpi, *Voci Parallele* (1955; Bologna: Edizioni Bongiovanni, 1977), 72. Lauri-Volpi sets up parallels between many of the great singers of the past. He analyzes Raisa and compares her to Cecilia Gagliardi, an important early twentieth-century Italian dramatic soprano who unfortunately made no recordings. He sets up Rosa Ponselle with Maria Caniglia, Maria Jeritza with Giuseppina Cobelli, etc.

4. The considerable research of Charles Jahant and Thomas Kaufman was put at my disposal. From their massive data I identified the Aidas who appeared in Buenos Aires from 1905 to 1915. These Aidas appeared with the opera companies that played the major opera houses: Teatro de la Opéra, the "new" Colón, and the Coliseo. The indefatigable Tom Kaufman has produced well-documented chronologies (most still unpublished) of Italian opera in South and Central America.

5. Toscanini conducted seven performances of *Falstaff* with Rimini as Falstaff and Maria Farnetti, Ines Maria Ferraris, Virginia Guerrini, Tito Schipa, and Ernesto Badini. In all, Toscanini conducted forty-two performances in this season at the Dal Verme, with singers such as Muzio, Caruso (in two *Pagliaccis*), Rosina Storchio, Ester Mazzoleni, Bonci, and Riccardo Stracciari as the big stars.

6. After 1933 Raisa slowly wound down her career because of her maternal duties. Rimini continued working in Italy up until 1936. In 1936 he was the impresario of the Stagione Lirica Carnevale at Parma's Teatro Regio.

7. In our day, when stage directors rehearse operas down to the most minute detail, the idea of planting one's foot on a specific step to a specific bar of music does not seem so strange. Ricordi's detailed stage directions and Raisa's "mini-rebellion" at his power would be unlikely today. Raisa was clearly anticipating a future in which it would no longer be Bellini's *Norma*, but Luca Ronconi's *Norma*, for instance.

8. There are two contemporary accounts of this very important backstage greeting and meeting. *The Musical Leader* for October 1916 published a long article titled "The Youngest Prima Donna," and *The Music News* (Chicago), also October 1916, published an article titled "The Brilliant Career of Rosa Raisa." These articles summarize Raisa's two years away from the United States performing in Italy and South America.

9. A 1917 advertisement in *Musical America* quotes an unnamed reviewer: "Aida brought once more to us the privilege of being alternately moved to tears and thrown into transports of enthusiasm. Rosa Raisa again celebrated a real triumph. Her divine voice and marvelous singing, Toscanini did well to call her the 'Tamagno of dramatic sopranos.'" In other essays I have written about Raisa, I have paraphrased this quote as "female Tamagno," which I feel captures the essence of Toscanini's reported opinion.

CHAPTER FOUR

1. Robert Tuggle, *The Golden Age of Opera* (New York: Holt, Rinehart and Winston, 1983), 143.

2. From Raisa's memoir.

3. It is doubtful the Rudolfo in *La Bohème* was McCormack; more likely it was Bassi in the earlier season or Crimi in the later one.

4. From Raisa's memoir.

5. A search of documents and contract files at the Metropolitan Opera Archives yielded no signed or unsigned contracts. This does not exclude the possibility that Raisa and Met management discussed her engagement by the Metropolitan Opera. Not every discussion or possible invitation is documented in a form that has been preserved. Raisa in many interviews over the years alludes to various contract offers by the Met, especially early in her career. There is no reason to believe that this is not true.

6. Fray José Francisco de Guadalupe Mojica, O.F.M., *I, a Sinner* (Chicago: Franciscan Herald Press, 1963), 192. Mojica describes Rimini at this time as "Raisa's sweetheart."

7. Richard Aldrich, *Concert Life in New York, 1902–1923* (New York: G. P. Putnam's Sons, 1941), 563.

CHAPTER FIVE

1. The prospectus of the 1919–1920 Chicago Opera season quotes: "Maestro Mocchi, director of the Teatro Colón, says that in all his operatic experience of many years her performance in *Norma* is the greatest he has ever heard."

2. Moore, *Forty Years of Opera in Chicago*, 190.

3. This review from the *Chicago Journal* was reproduced in an advertisement Raisa placed in *Musical Courier*. In those days artists very often after a big success published a collection of reviews to drive home the point. In reading these valuable citations one has to notice which important critics' reviews are not included, and one often has to read between the lines to determine if the alleged success was really that great a success. Ponselle, Rethberg, and Muzio frequently published their favorable critiques. Artists of the caliber of Caruso and Flagstad rarely felt the need to publish their good reviews.

4. Vincent Sheean, *First and Last Love* (New York: Random House, 1956), 43, 47.

5. Vincent Sheean to author, 6 April 1962.

6. Samuel Rosenblatt, *Yossele Rosenblatt: The Story of His Life as Told by His Son* (New York: Farrar, Straus and Young, 1954), 143 – 44.

7. The Seligman quote is from Mary Jane Matz's article, "First Ladies of the Puccini Premieres: Geraldine Farrar," *Opera News*, 3 February 1962, 25.

8. *Chicago Tribune*, 20 December 1919, 1.

9. Moore, *Forty Years of Opera in Chicago*, 200 – 201.

CHAPTER SIX

1. The Ganna Walska incident is placed here in this chronological narrative, but it took place in the 1920 – 1921 season. Garden assumed directorship at the end of that season in Chicago, held that position during the 1921 part of the national tour, and was the director for the entire 1921 – 1922 season.

2. Ronald Davis, *Opera in Chicago* (New York: Appleton-Century, 1966), 131.

3. Mary Garden and Louis Biancolli, *Mary Garden's Story* (New York: Simon and Schuster, 1951), 171.

4. Undated Sunday article penned soon after the *Norma* performance. It was customary for a critic of Henderson's stature to write essays about performance practices and style, citing performance history to make points.

5. *Brooklyn Eagle*, undated, but also a Sunday piece written after the repeat on February 19.

6. James A. Drake, *Rosa Ponselle: A Centenary Biography* (Portland, Ore.: Amadeus Press, 1997), 186.

7. "Ponselle was confident about these recollections, despite the inconsistencies some of them revealed. She was certain, for instance, that Titta Ruffo and Rosa Raisa had been in the small audience of artists whom Gatti-Casazza had assembled to hear her." Drake, *Centenary Biography*, 34. Robert Tuggle, the Metropolitan Opera archivist, is certain this never happened.

8. Rosa Ponselle and James A. Drake, *Ponselle: A Singer's Life* (New York: Doubleday, 1982), 79–80.

9. James A. Drake, "Ponselle Reminisces," *High Fidelity*, April 1977. In her 1982 biography Ponselle relates that after she and Romano Romani heard Raisa in a New York Hippodrome concert in early 1918, Romani told her that he thought her better than Raisa. Ponselle then states, "Like Emmy Destinn and Claudia Muzio, Raisa was something of a goddess to me and I refused to believe that I was in her league as a soprano. (To this day, despite what opera historians have written, I still tend to dismiss it.)"

10. There was extensive coverage of Rafaella's claims in the Chicago newspapers. As Rimini died without a will, the courts had to decide the relative size of the shares of his estate. Rafaella was awarded one-third; Raisa and her daughter (with Rimini), Jolly, were awarded one-third each. The villa in San Floriano, the couple's chief asset, was already in Raisa's name.

11. From an advertisement in the *Musical Digest*, 19 November 1921. Raisa indicates that she turned down Toscanini for *Norma* and *La Wally*, and Rimini the inaugural *Falstaff* of Toscanini's new Scala regime. The December 1921 dates the conductor offered conflicted with the couple's Chicago commitments.

12. Toscanini had conducted *Norma* in South America and Turin in the 1890s, but never in the twentieth century, when he was acknowledged the pre-eminent conductor, especially of Italian opera.

13. Front page of the *San Francisco Examiner*, 12 April 1921, half-page photo of the 20,000-strong crowd listening to this concert; Raisa sang "Vissi d'arte," "Tacea la notte placida," and "I Love You, California," by Silverwood and Frankenstein (which has since become the official state song).

14. *San Francisco Call*, 13 April 1921, 1.

15. *New York Tribune*, 6 March 1921.

16. Mary Garden was quoted as saying that Rosa Raisa was one of her "worst problems" because she "was ruining her splendid voice by singing not wisely, but too well."

17. Robert Baxter, "Of Songs and Singers," *Opera News*, 9 April 1983, 62. I wrote to Arrau for clarification as to whether he was referring to the Teatro Colón (1918 or 1929) or the Teatro Coliseo (1921) performance. Arrau asked his manager and press representative, Friede F. Rothe, to write me. From that letter, dated 12 July 1984: "It was in 1921 that he heard Raisa at the Teatro Colón. He remembers it well because he was playing his first concerts as a young artist; six recitals at the Teatro Cervantes which was then a beautiful

new concert hall. He was 18 years old, old enough to remember a marvelous soprano who was also beautiful." However, if it was 1921, it was the Coliseo.

18. Letter from A. Pollastra to Gatti-Casazza, 30 July 1921. Metropolitan Opera archives.

19. "Mephisto's Musings," *Musical America,* 7 May 1921: "Both Titta Ruffo and Rosa Raisa have passed the $2,000 mark, which has also in her new contract been passed by Farrar (at the Metropolitan Opera). Muratore, they say, has gone up to $2,800 with the Chicago company, where he is indispensable, for without him Mary Garden would not be able to give the performances that she does, and as she is now the boss, the rest follows." "Mephisto's Musings" was a weekly opinion-gossip column.

20. I was amazed to discover, in going through old newspaper archives researching this book, that the arrival of the Chicago Opera in major cities such as Los Angeles, San Francisco, Seattle, and Houston was front-page news. Mary Garden was a particular favorite of reporters because she produced good and often provocative quotes, occasionally even stirring controversy. She had opinions on a vast array of subjects, from her favorite color of men's eyes to current political events.

21. Henry T. Finck, *My Adventures in the Golden Age of Music* (New York and London: Funk and Wagnalls, 1926), 369.

22. From the mid-1940s to the early 1960s the shoe was on the other foot. The caustic Cassidy regularly wrote scathingly of the Metropolitan Opera on its spring visits to Chicago. She found either some (not all) of the presentations mediocre or the artists not of the highest quality, often comparing the offerings and the artists to her fond remembrances of the old Chicago Opera. After the Lyric Opera of Chicago became well established in the late 1950s, for financial and other reasons the Met stopped visiting Chicago after 1962.

CHAPTER SEVEN

1. Charles Jahant, "Muzio Onstage," *Saturday Review of Literature,* 28 December 1957.

2. See salary information for 1931–1932 in chapter 11.

3. Although Aida and Norma are Raisa's two most famous roles at the Chicago Opera, one could reasonably name Maliella and Rachel as the roles in which she had no competition.

4. A full year before, in the *Musical Courier,* 16 March 1922, there was an advertisement: "Announcement Extraordinary! International Tours, Ltd. Frederic Shipman, Manager, has secured for 30 concerts in Australia (June, July, August 1923) for Rosa Raisa and Giacomo Rimini."

5. In a December 1922 interview with *Musical Courier*, regarding her summer plans, Raisa told the magazine that after her trip to Italy in June, "I will go to Germany to study Isolde with Lilli Lehmann and therefore will sing 'Tristan und Isolde' next season"—another of the many "might have beens."

6. *Musical Courier*, 27 May 1924, 38.

CHAPTER EIGHT

1. Raisa, interview by Studs Terkel, WFMT Radio Chicago, November 1959; edited version on Marston, *Rosa Raisa: The Complete Recordings* (53001-2), disc 3, band 15: Raisa's account of her selection for Asteria.

2. In May 1924 the *Musical Leader* published some background material on *Nerone*. The report quotes a 14 December 1912 letter Caruso wrote to his European manager, Emil Ledner, about Boito's interest in Caruso appearing in *Nerone* if Boito could ever complete the opera.

3. Mussolini and Toscanini were already feuding over political matters, and Mussolini would not set foot inside La Scala at this time.

4. *Musical Courier*, 24 April 1924, 21.

5. Raisa, interview by Ben Grauer, "Toscanini: The Man behind the Myth," NBC Radio, taped in New York in 1963 and broadcast in 1964; Raisa, interview by Terkel, November 1959; Raisa, intermission interview by John Gutman, Metropolitan Opera broadcast of *Turandot*, 24 February 1962.

6. Telegram from Scandiani to Johnson, 7 October 1924. A photocopy of the telegram was published in *Musical Courier* in early May 1926, when the Raisa/Jeritza controversy was in the press. Ben H. Atwell, who was connected to the Chicago Opera publicity office, released the telegram to the periodical, writing: "We have sought (and still wish) to avoid being drawn into a vapid and vulgar controversy over the intentions of the great master who is now dead—especially when these intentions were so clearly defined by himself in life and executed by his trustees. The continued bombardment of questions on the subject from representatives of both local and out-of-town newspapers constrains us to make public such documentary evidence as exists in our files and to beg to be excused from useless discussion of what is now history."

7. Harvey Sachs, *Toscanini* (Philadelphia: J. B. Lippincott Co., 1978), 178.

8. Gutman and Grauer interviews. Raisa told Grauer in the interview that the last time she saw Toscanini was when he visited with her at her daughter Jolly's apartment in Verona in 1956. He told Raisa that his one remaining career ambition was to conduct *Falstaff* at La Piccola Scala in Milan.

9. Wire of Federico Candida, *Musical Digest*, 10 February 1925.

10. Toscanini had been the music director of La Scala from 1899 to 1903 and again from 1907 to 1908, just before his seven-season affiliation with the New York Metropolitan Opera.

11. There is a long tradition of illustrious "pickup" companies presenting opera and ballet seasons in Paris.

12. From author's conversations with Carol Longone, 1978 – 1982.

13. Stone, *My Caravan of Years*, 199.

CHAPTER NINE

1. Raisa, Terkel interview.

2. Faith Compton Mackenzie, *Gramophone*, January 1930, 352.

3. Ibid.

4. Lanfranco Rasponi, "Con Sicurezza: Tancredi Pasero," *Opera News*, 27 January 1979, 42. Pasero thought Raisa a superb singing actress but did not find her voice "beautiful." In Sach's *Toscanini* Pasero is quoted comparing Raisa in *Turandot* to Jeritza, and he clearly preferred Raisa. Pasero entertained many quixotic opinions about the famous singers of his era.

5. Harvey Sachs, *Toscanini*, 178. Gavazzeni (b. 1909) was clearly precocious when he formed these opinions.

6. Raisa, Terkel interview.

7. Mary Jane Phillips-Matz quotes Serafin on Jeritza and Turandot in her *Rosa Ponselle: American Diva* (Boston: Northeastern University Press, 1997), 221–22.

8. Letter from Vivian Liff to author, 23 April 1979. Liff, the noted authority on recording history, was told this anecdote by the person involved at the Hayes factory.

9. *Musical America*, November 1924, interview.

10. Postcard (feathered headdress, p. 133). Translated from Yiddish by Raisa's brother-in-law, Irving Goldenberg, and later by Rudi Van den Bulck.

11. Harold Rosenthal, *Two Centuries of Opera at Covent Garden* (London: Putnam, 1958), 451.

12. Arthur Meeker, *Chicago, with Love: A Polite and Personal History* (New York: Alfred A. Knopf, 1955), 227–28.

13. There had been significant radio broadcasts of opera dating back to the teens and early twenties, but the Chicago broadcasts starting in 1927 were the most ambitious undertaken by an important opera company to date. Jim McPher-

son, "Before the Met: The Pioneer Days of Radio Opera," *Opera Quarterly* (winter & spring 2000).

14. Karlton Hackett, *Chicago Post*, 25 November 1927.

CHAPTER TEN

1. *Musical Courier*, 13 October 1928, 16. "Herbert Johnson announced that Raisa had cabled that she would be unable to fulfill her contract, having been ordered by her physician to remain in Italy."

2. It was believed that Muzio used her mother's "illness" as an excuse to absent herself from Chicago that season. Muzio reappeared at the Rome opera singing Norma on 26 December. Her mother disliked the Chicago winters.

3. Frida Leider, *Playing My Part*, trans. Charles Osborne (New York: Meredith Press, 1966), 107.

4. Ibid.

5. Elsa Alsen, the renowned Wagnerian soprano, and in the 1950s and 1960s an active attendee at the programs of New York's Vocal Record Collectors' Society, generously related to me her memories of her seasons in Chicago. When I told her that her career was not adequately covered in the musical journals, she said that was because she didn't advertise. She believed that one's coverage was in proportion to one's advertising.

6. Robert G. Breen, "Rosas Meet on a High Note," *Baltimore Sun*, 7 March 1962. In 1962, after Raisa went to New York to be interviewed on the Met's *Turandot* broadcast, she visited her friend Ponselle in the Baltimore suburbs. The *Sun* had been alerted to this reunion and sent a reporter to conduct a joint interview.

7. Roberto Caamaño, *La Historia del Teatro Colón 1908–1968*, vol. 2 (Buenos Aires: Editorial Cinetea, 1969), 179.

8. Quoted in Moore, *Forty Years of Opera in Chicago*, 126.

1. A photograph of the original stone with Raisa praying by it was published in the *Musical Courier*, 13 September 1930. The more elaborate replacement stone gives her mother's name and at the bottom states in Yiddish that this monument was erected by her daughter, Rosa Raisa, in 1930.

2. Numerous press notices announced the birth of Rosa Giulietta Frieda Rimini. Her baby album contained hundreds of congratulatory telegrams from opera celebrities and friends from all over the world. Garden, Schipa, Ponselle, Martinelli, and Gigli are a few that I remember seeing in 1983. The baby album has since been lost.

3. Unidentified Chicago periodical, August 1931.

4. Metropolitan Opera Archives. In Herbert Witherspoon's file are the preliminary plans for the 1932–1933 Chicago season, and they do not include Raisa and Rimini. Tiana Lemnitz was also on the list of new singers to debut in 1932–1933. Charles Jahant is the source of the Mária Németh information; he received it from Monte Fassnacht, who was on the staff of the Chicago Opera management.

5. From several "Mefisto's Musings" columns in *Musical America* over the period in question.

6. Associated Press, 18 December 1933. Raisa returned to the United States for the first time since February 1932; she had been living in Italy all the time she was away. She must have been financially hurting, because at the end of the article it says, "She came here, on money expressly advanced, to appear with the revived Civic Opera Company."

7. Leider, *Playing My Part*, 104.

8. Giulietta Segala, Raisa's daughter, told me this. She also indicated that Toscanini was upset that Raisa was not able to record her Alice Ford in the complete Columbia *Falstaff*.

9. Ida Cook, *We Followed Our Stars* (Toronto: Harlequin/Mills & Boon, 1950), 72.

10. Letter from Raisa to Francis Robinson, 11 June 1962. Raisa's letters to Robinson are in the Vanderbilt University Library, Nashville, Tennessee.

CHAPTER TWELVE

1. Dea Cornbleet, Raisa's secretary and friend, told me this in 1987.

2. Beniamino Gigli, *The Memoirs of Beniamino Gigli* (London: Cassell, 1957), 183. Gigli mentions this performance in passing, but the intent and context make clear that he is making a quasi-political point.

3. Robert Tuggle, *Turandot*, Met Opera Web site: www.metopera.org/history.

4. Glenn Dillard Gunn, *Chicago Examiner*, 31 December 1933.

5. The quoted fragments are taken from two sources: Hume's obituary tribute to Raisa in the *Washington Post*, 20 October 1963, and a letter he wrote to me dated 3 March 1961 in response to my inquiry for clarification of his statement in the liner notes for the RCA *Critic's Choice* compilation he selected that "Raisa's voice was the greatest I ever heard."

6. Account in *Musical America*.

7. From cast information supplied by Charles Jahant and Thomas Kaufman.

8. Letter from Raisa to Bruno Zirato, in my collection.

9. Stinson is quoted in the Eva Turner *Record Collector*, vol. 11, 35, describing Turner as "the greatest singer known to Chicago. Not one of the other vocalists at the Chicago Civic Opera is animated as she is with the sheer spirit of greatness." (At the time Stinson wrote this, in 1928, Raisa was not with the company.) On another occasion Stinson declared Austral the greatest, after a concert of hers in Chicago with orchestra. These assertions have to be read as comparison with Raisa, whom he reviewed continuously for fifteen or more years. When I interviewed Dame Eva in 1985 about her seasons at the Chicago Opera she had nothing but praise for Raisa, whom she remembered particularly in *La Juive*. She did not hear Raisa in *Norma*. In her letters to Francis Robinson (1962 and 1963), Raisa on several occasions praises Turner as a fine lady with a great voice.

10. *Il Dibuk* had its world premiere March 24, 1934, at La Scala with Augusta Oltrabella as Leah, Franco Ghione conducting. Oltrabella later recorded Leah's big scene for Voce del Padrone (HMV).

11. Louis Biancolli, "I Love It, Says Raisa of Role She'll Create, Leah in 'The Dybbuk,'" *New York World Telegram*, 2 May 1936.

12. Paul Hume, letter to the author.

13. Smith is fairly accurate with his Chicago totals, but Raisa also sang 235 times on the Chicago Opera's North American tours.

CHAPTER THIRTEEN

1. Phone conversation with Giorgio Tozzi, October 2000.

2. In 1982 I spoke with Edwin McArthur about Raisa. He first heard her in the early 1920s in his native Denver in both opera and concert. He was a good friend of Giorgio Polacco and moved in circles that valued Raisa.

3. Lanfranco Rasponi, "Con Principio: Dusolina Giannini," *Opera News*, 15 December 1979, 13. This essay was not included in his book, *The Last Prima Donnas*. Many of Rasponi's essays first appeared in *Opera News*.

4. I was unable to locate documentation of this concert, although I checked all possible listings in the *New York Times* index for 1943. As her brother-in-law, Irving Goldenberg, specifically remembers this event and the political context of the time, it is unlikely that he is confusing the 1943 concert with Raisa's April 1937 appearance at a Madison Square Garden concert sponsored by *The Morning Freiheit*, a Yiddish-language left-wing newspaper.

5. As in many interfaith homes, Jolly was given the option of religion. Jolly opted for Rimini's Catholic faith and was baptized April 26, 1940.

6. Raisa had been photographed in her dressing room several times over the

years and these pictures always show the cameo photos of her father and mother on the dressing table and a Star of David mounted on a plaque that was given to her in Buenos Aires by a Jewish organization.

7. Anecdote told to me by Olga Trevisan in 1969, New York City.

8. In the *Musical America* account of the concert, "So great was the enthusiasm of the audience that they remained in their seats to cheer the artists. Mr. Gigli sang for the police force last year. The two artists, in addition to several solos, sang popular duets from the opera. They were accompanied by Enrico Rosati."

9. Family anecdotes told by Raisa's sister Frieda and brother-in-law, Irving.

10. Jolly's wedding album contained the rare Gigli-Callas photo. I saw this photo in 1983 when I visited Jolly, but as it was in an elaborate leather-bound wedding album I did not ask at the time that it be removed in order that I might copy it. In the interim this album appears to have been lost by the family. I now regret being so thoughtful!

11. On the "early" draft of the memoir that Jolly gave to me, she has noted next to Raisa's paean to Mrs. Stone, "omit."

12. Conversations with Dea Cornbleet, October 1987.

13. Letter from Raisa to Francis Robinson, 12 March 1962. In Raisa's letters to Robinson there are gossip and news about personalities in the music world who were their mutual friends.

14. Raisa to Robinson, 11 June 1962.

15. Raisa to Robinson 23 March 1962.

16. Raisa to Robinson, 19 June 1962

17. Author's conversations with Raisa's daughter, Jolly, October 1983.

18. Raisa to Robinson, 23 November 1962.

19. Raisa to Carol Longone, 11 November 1962.

20. Raisa to Robinson, 20 August 1962. Sutherland does not remember meeting Raisa (letter from Sutherland to author, October 2000). It appears that Sutherland gave two concerts at the Hollywood Bowl in 1962 because Raisa told Robinson that the first one sold out and her family's ticket request was returned as "could not fill order," and Raisa had a previous commitment for the night of the repeat concert. The two Sutherland chronologies I have consulted do not list the second concert.

21. She returns to the subject of Sutherland in several letters and always uses the adjective "phenomenal."

22. Raisa to Robinson, 6 November 1962.

23. Raisa to Robinson, 23 April 1962.

24. Raisa to Carol Longone, 30 October 1962.

25. Raisa to Longone, 31 November 1962.

26. Carol told me that Sills sang in an operalogue of Bizet's *Pearl Fishers* in the early 1950s. Sills's teacher, Estelle Liebling, a friend of Carol's, had recommended Sills for the assignment. Lanza had obviously met Carol very early in his career, and probably sang for her; he inscribed a very early photo of his to Carol. On the verso he wrote contact information: "Room 201, 211 S. Beverly Drive, Beverly Hills, California."

27. Raisa to Longone, 26 August 1962.

28. Raisa to Robinson, 6 July 1962.

29. Raisa to Longone, 20 August 1962.

30. *New York Times,* 2 October 1963. The obituaries that came off the wire services four days after her death stated that her only survivors were her daughter and grandchildren. The *New York Times* obituary mentioned that she was also survived by her sister Frieda Goldenberg of New York City. The *Times* at that time had its own archive and integrated its information with the news from the wire services. It appears that public notification of her death was held up for four days to enable Jolly to carry out Raisa's burial wishes.

31. Raisa's granddaughter, Suzanne, remembered that instead of her Star of David, her mother placed in Raisa's coffin the miniature Torah to which Raisa had been so devoted.

32. Raisa's pupil Anne Dinkowitz later recalled that Raisa always made sure Yarzheit prayers were said for her deceased parents on the anniversaries of their deaths. Letter from Dinkowitz to Irving and Frieda Goldenberg, 20 August 1964.

33. Extensive conversations with Jolly at her home in Santa Monica, October 1983. In 1975 Jolly's husband, Dr. Segala, asked the cemetery for estimates on the cost of relocating Raisa and her maid, Ida Bosi, to Italy, but took no action.

34. After Raisa retired from the stage in 1938, she and Cassidy became close personal friends. When Cassidy started visiting Europe after World War II, she stayed at Raisa's villa outside Verona; see Claudia Cassidy, *Europe on the Aisle* (New York: Random House, 1954).

35. Marilyn Horne remembers in the early 1960s at a Los Angeles function sitting at the same table as Raisa. When one of the parties at the luncheon brought up the subject of religion and pointedly asked Raisa about her faith,

Raisa said, "I believe in God. Period!" Letter from Marilyn Horne to author, October 2000.

36. Raisa, Terkel interview, November 1959 (unedited). This compliment of Terkel's is not on the edited interview in the Marston *Rosa Raisa: The Complete Recordings* (53001-2).

37. I think Jolly realized that I would probably be the one to write Raisa's biography. She knew that I was interested in her parents primarily as opera singers, but she also knew that I had a natural curiosity about the Jewish background, and she clearly wanted me to know her version of Raisa's religious status.

38. Ruth Miller Chamlee, letter to Carol Longone, 23 October 1963.

39. Jolly and Dr. Segala attended, but left immediately after the conclusion of the services and spoke to no one. Ruth Miller to Carol Longone, 23 October 1963.

40. Ruth Miller Chamlee sent copies of the eulogies to Carol Longone.

CHAPTER FOURTEEN

1. Charles Jahant thought Raisa's voice one of the four loudest he had heard. The others: Turner, Catarina Mancini, and Suzanne Joyul.

2. Claudia Cassidy, undated "On the Aisle" column, *Chicago Tribune*.

3. There is a clear implication that on occasion everything was not just right. From an undated "On the Aisle" column.

4. When on my first of many visits I asked Carol how she would describe Raisa's voice, she blurted out, "It was a Jewish voice"; then, realizing that I might have taken that assertion the wrong way, she lovingly described its power, beauty, and Jewish melancholy.

5. On her naturalization papers Raisa gives her height as 5 feet 4 inches.

6. Paul Hume, *Washington Post*, 20 October 1963.

7. Raisa to Robinson, 16 July 1962.

8. Raisa to Robinson, 31 July 1962.

9. *Opera* magazine, November 1952, 467. Smith also incorporates in his essay speculation on what the Muzio Norma must have been like; having heard her in many roles in Chicago, he felt he could reconstruct her performance. Smith's oft-quoted review of the Callas Covent Garden debut Norma is in *Opera*, January 1953, 40.

10. Teodoro Celli, "A Song from Another Century," trans. Herbert Weinstock, in *Opera Annual* (London: John Calder, and New York: Taplinger, 1959), 26–27.

11. Cecil Smith, *Worlds of Music* (Philadelphia: J. B. Lippincott, 1952), 153.

12. In 1926, W. J. Henderson's magazine, *Singing*, featured an article titled "Chicago Still Behind New York in Balanced Critical Tradition? Slow Growth, Not Lavish Expenditure, Must Mark Musical Development," by Francis Boardman. "Is there any real reason why New York should be unreservedly accepted as the musical capital of these United States,—any reason which Chicago, with its huge resources, ambitious spirit, and strategic geographical position, could not match?"

Bibliography

Aldrich, Richard. *Concert Life in New York, 1902–1923.* New York: G. P. Putnam's Sons, 1941.

Baxter, Robert. "Of Songs and Singers." *Opera News,* 9 April 1983.

Breen, Robert G. "Rosas Meet on a High Note." *Baltimore Sun,* 7 March 1962.

Biancolli, Louis. "I Love It, Says Raisa of Role She'll Create, Leah in 'The Dybbuk.'" *New York World Telegram,* 2 May 1936.

Caamaño, Roberto. *La Historia del Teatro Colón 1908–1968.* Buenos Aires: Editorial Cinetea, 1969.

Celli, Teodoro. "A Song from Another Century," trans. Herbert Weinstock. *Opera Annual.* New York: Taplinger, 1959.

Cook, Ida. *We Followed Our Stars.* Toronto, London, Sydney: Harlequin / Mills & Boon, 1950.

Davis, Ronald. *Opera in Chicago.* New York: Appleton-Century, 1966.

Dillon, César, and Juan A. Sala. *El Teatro Musical en Buenos Aires II: Teatro Coliseo.* Buenos Aires: Ediciones de Arte Gagliamone, 1999.

Drake, James A. *Rosa Ponselle, A Centenary Biography.* Portland, Ore.: Amadeus Press, 1997.

Encyclopedia Judaica, vol. 13. Jerusalem: Keter Publishing House, 1971.

Epstein, Milton. *The New York Hippodrome: A Complete Chronology of Performances. From 1905 to 1938.* New York: Theatre Library Association, 1993.

Finck, Henry T. *My Adventures in the Golden Age of Music.* New York and London: Funk and Wagnalls, 1926.

Garden, Mary, and Louis Biancolli. *Mary Garden's Story.* New York: Simon and Schuster, 1951.

Gigli, Beniamino. *The Memoirs of Beniamino Gigli.* London: Cassell, 1957.

Jahant, Charles. "Muzio Onstage." *Saturday Review of Literature,* 28 December 1957.

Kolodin, Irving. *The Story of the Metropolitan Opera, 1883–1950: A Candid History.* New York: Alfred A. Knopf, 1953.

Laird, Ross. *Brunswick Records.* 4 vols. Westport, Conn.: Greenwood Press, 2001.

Lauri-Volpi, Giacomo. *Voci Parallele.* 1955; rept. Bologna: Edizioni Bongiovanni, 1977.

Leider, Frida. *Playing My Part.* Translated by Charles Osborne. New York: Meridith Press, 1966.

Matz, Mary Jane. "First Ladies of the Puccini Premieres: Geraldine Farrar." *Opera News*, 3 February 1962.

McPherson, Jim. "Before the Met: The Pioneer Days of Radio Opera." *Opera Quarterly*, winter–spring 2000.

Meeker, Arthur. *Chicago, with Love: A Polite and Personal History*. New York: Alfred A. Knopf, 1955.

Mojica, Fray José Francisco de Guadalupe, O.F.M. *I, a Sinner*. Chicago: Franciscan Herald Press, 1963.

Moore, Edward C. *Forty Years of Opera in Chicago*. New York: Horace Liveright, 1930.

Moreau, Mario. *Antores de Opera Portugueses*, vol. III. Amadora, Portugal: Livreiros Bertrand, 1995.

Panizza, Hector. *Medio Siglo de Vida Musical (Essayo Autobiografico)*. Buenos Aires: Ricordi Americana, 1952.

Phillips-Matz, Mary Jane. *Rosa Ponselle: American Diva*. Boston: Northeastern University Press, 1997.

Ponselle, Rosa, and James A. Drake. *Ponselle, A Singer's Life*. New York: Doubleday and Company, 1982.

Rosa Raisa, The Complete Recordings. Marston 53001-2, 1998.

Rasponi, Lanfranco. *The Last Prima Donnas*. New York: Alfred A. Knopf, 1982.

Rosenblatt, Samuel. *Yossele Rosenblatt, the Story of His Life as Told by His Son*. New York: Farrar, Straus and Young, 1954.

Rosenthal, Harold. *Two Centuries of Opera at Covent Garden*. London: Putnam, 1958.

Sachs, Harvey. *Toscanini*. Philadelphia and New York: J. B. Lippincott, 1978.

Scott, Michael. *The Record of Singing*, vol. 2. New York: Holmes and Meyer Publishers, 1979.

Sheean, Vincent. *First and Last Love*. New York: Random House, 1956.

Smith, Cecil. *Worlds of Music*. New York and Philadelphia: J. B. Lippincott, 1952.

Stone, Goldie. *My Caravan of Years, an Autobiography*. New York: Bloch Publishing Company, 1945.

Tuggle, Robert. *The Golden Age of Opera*. New York: Holt, Rinehart, and Winston, 1983.

Universal Jewish Encyclopedia. 1938 edition. New York: Funk and Wagnalls, 1938.

Index

Page numbers given in *italics* indicate illustrations.
Chicago Opera will be referred to as CO in subentries.
Spelling and capitalization of artists' names conform to their autographs.

[329]

of, 213; RR and, 97–99, 116–17; RR
compared with, 196; salary of, 161; in
Turandot, 149; vocal technique of, 214
My Caravan of Years (Stone), 24, 311–
12n. 8

Nabucco (Verdi), 165, 202
Naples, 11–12, 15–18, 148
Navarraise, La (Massenet), 212
Nave, La (Montemezzi), *67, 67*–68
NBC Orchestra, 184
Nehru, Mme. Pandit, 209
Németh, Mária, 136, 160
Nepomuceno, Alberto, *Abul,* 32, 200
Nerone (Boito), *107,* 119, 318n. 2; cast page
of, *112–13;* premiere of, 105–14; RR se-
lected to create role for, 101, 207
Nespoulous, Marthe, 149
New Boston Opera, 171–72
New York American, 55–56, 177
New York City: CO in, 49–53, 55, 93–94;
music critics, 86
New York City Opera, 184
New York Globe, 91–92
New York Sun, 51
New York Times, 51
Nilsson, Birgit, *193*
Nordica, Lillian, 99–101, 119, 137
Norma (Bellini), 91, 93, 182, 240; Callas in,
209–10; with CO, 141–45, *142,* 152; in
Italy, 164, 172; in Mexico, 66; Mocchi
on, 314n. 5; in New York, *60,* 75–78,
84–86, 167–68, 315n. 4 (ch. 6); radio
broadcast of, 153; RR's recordings of,
209; in South America, 59–62, 149–50,
314n. 1 (ch. 5)
Nozze di Figaro, Le (Mozart), 26, 141

"O patria mia" (Verdi), 17, 29, 40, 47, 52,
138, 145
Oberto, Conte di San Bonifacio (Verdi),
17
Olczewska, Maria, 141, 152
Opera Guild of Southern California,
204–5
Opera News, 86
"Ora soave" (Giordano), 43
Orchestra Hall (Chicago), 179
Orfeo magazine, 19

Otello (Verdi), 26, 38, 46, 82–84, 93, 101

Pacetti, Iva, 160, 164
Pacini, Giovanni, *Saffo,* 72, 212
Pagliacci (Leoncavallo), 26, 36, 82
Palmer, Jeanne, 279n.
Pampanini, Rosetta, 160
Pane-Gasser, John, 170
Panizza, Ettore, 105–6, 122, 134–35, 150,
167
Papi, Gennaro, 170
Paris Opéra, 26, 82, 122
Parker, Henry T., 53, 102
Parsifal (Wagner), 24, 200
Partita, Una (Zandonai), 164
Pasero, Tancredi, 134, 148, 149, 150, 166,
319n. 4
Pasta, Giuditta, 52–53
Pathé Frères Company, 45–46, 200, 231
Patti, Adelina, 12, 39, 145
Pattiera, Tino, 88
Pavia (landlady), 11–12
Pavloska, Irene, 138–39
Pederzini, Gianna, 148, 166
Pedrini, Maria, 164
Pelléas et Mélisande (Debussy), 198
Perini, Flora, 32, 119, 256n.
Pertile, Aureliano, 32, 36, 37, 106, 120,
222n. 8
Petite Messe Solennelle (Rossini), 12–13
Peyser, Herbert Francis, 85, 167–68
Piazza San Marco (Venice), 138, 164
Piccaluga, Nino, 164
Pinza, Ezio, 106
Pique Dame (Tchaikovsky), 172, 174, 180
Pittsburgh Gazette-Times, 102
Pius XI, 106
Pizzetti, Ildebrando, 43
Plaza del Toreo (Mexico City), 46, 66
Plaza Hotel (Buenos Aires), 34
Polacco, Giorgio, 63, 91, 114, 119, 126, 137,
151; as CO artistic director, 92; friend-
ship with Riminis, 46–47, 116–17, *118;*
Rimini's death and, 188
Polese, Giovanni, 23
Poli-Randaccio, Tina, 164
Ponchielli, Amilcare, *La Gioconda. See
Gioconda, La*
Ponchielli Centennial, 172, 277n.